The Boy
Who Loved
Too Much

A True Story of Pathological Friendliness

Jennifer Latson

Simon & Schuster

New York • London • Toronto • Sydney • New Delhi

Simon & Schuster
1230 Avenue of the Americas
New York, NY 10020

First Simon & Schuster hardcover edition June 2017

SIMON & SCHUSTER and colophon are registered trademarks
of Simon & Schuster, Inc.

For information about special discounts for bulk purchases,
please contact Simon & Schuster Special Sales at 1-866-506-1949
or business@simonandschuster.com.

The Simon & Schuster Speakers Bureau can bring authors to
your live event. For more information or to book an event,
contact the Simon & Schuster Speakers Bureau at 1-866-248-3049
or visit our website at www.simonspeakers.com.

Interior design by Lewelin Polanco

Manufactured in the United States of America

3 5 7 9 10 8 6 4 2

Library of Congress Cataloging-in-Publication Data

Names: Latson, Jennifer, author.
Title: The boy who loved too much : a true story of pathological friendliness /
Jennifer Latson.
Description: New York : Simon & Schuster, 2017. | Includes bibliographical references.
Identifiers: LCCN 2016043207 | ISBN 9781476774046 (hardcover) | ISBN
9781476774053 (pbk.)
Subjects: LCSH: Williams syndrome—Patients—Case studies. | Friendship in
children—Case studies. | Social interaction in children—Case studies.
Classification: LCC RJ506.W44 L37 2017 | DDC 618.92/8—dc23

LC record available at https://lccn.loc.gov/2016043207.

ISBN 978-1-4767-7404-6
ISBN 978-1-4767-7406-0 (ebook)

For my parents, Chuck and Carole,
who believe that differences are what make people cool

"We got a future. We got somebody to talk to that gives a damn about us. . . . Because I got you to look after me, and you got me to look after you, and that's why."

—John Steinbeck, *Of Mice and Men*

Contents

Author's Note

The narrative that follows is based on my immersive observation and reportage. For moments in the past, and for those I was unable to observe, I relied on extensive interviews to re-create scenes that were factually accurate. I have changed some names and identifying characteristics, including for Eli and Gayle, members of their family, and the people in their community, as well as for others with Williams syndrome and their relatives. I have not changed the names of Williams clinicians or researchers.

Preface

The first time I met Eli, in the late winter of 2011, he was waiting for me at his front door. Gayle had told him to expect a visitor: a writer who wanted to observe him "in his natural habitat," as Gayle put it. She always waited to deliver exciting news like this—a guest!—until the last possible moment, so the anticipation wouldn't overwhelm him. Still, Eli had been restlessly awaiting my arrival for the two hours since he'd gotten home from school.

At first, all I saw were pudgy fingers wrapped around the door, which was open just a crack. I heard Gayle's command: "Do *not* go out there, Eli." An eyeball appeared in the crack between the door and its frame. It bulged wide when it saw me. Then the baby-faced boy, who had just turned twelve, flung the door open. He rubbed his palms together, beaming as if he were about to open a Christmas present. Then he waved frantically, as if I might not have noticed him and might simply turn and walk away. "Hi, Kenny!" he bellowed into the snowy parking lot of his apartment complex.

Eli spoke with exclamation points: earnestly and emphatically.

His voice was deep and loud—a man's booming baritone—but cheerful and childishly nasal.

I heard Gayle's voice again, in a stage whisper: "Her name's *Jennie*." He corrected himself without pausing, without embarrassment. His smile never faded. "Hi, Jennie!"

The greeting was comically hyperbolic, yet Eli radiated sincere, earnest warmth. Meeting me truly was as exciting as opening the biggest present under the tree. I reminded myself, before my ego swelled in proportion to Eli's enthusiasm, that meeting *anyone* was this exciting for him.

———

WHEN I FIRST HEARD OF WILLIAMS syndrome, it had been described to me as a "cocktail party syndrome" that made people socially fearless, quick to greet strangers and to strike up a charming conversation laden with compliments and endearments. Fascinated, I began searching for more information about the disorder. I came across a news story that called people with Williams syndrome indiscriminately loving and "biologically incapable of distrust." Another account dubbed Williams "the anti-autism": a genetic fluke that stripped one in every 10,000 people of the inherent wariness, skepticism, and inhibition that were hardwired into the rest of us—especially introverts and New Englanders, both of which I happen to be.

Initially, I felt partly envious of this social ease and partly indignant that our conformity-loving culture saw fit to label it a disorder. *Who are* we *to tell* them *they're doing it wrong?* I thought righteously, concluding that, in another time and place, people with Williams would have been canonized as saints, not diagnosed with an illness. *If they love and trust everyone unconditionally,* I thought, *maybe they're the ones doing it right. Maybe it's the rest of us who need treatment.*

As a journalist, I felt driven to probe more deeply. I wanted to know what Williams could tell us about the genetic basis of our personalities. How could a flipped switch that shuts off about two dozen genes—a tiny twist of the 20,000 or so genes that form a DNA strand—make us inherently loving, trusting, and outgoing? And why wasn't that our default mode?

The more I came to understand Williams syndrome and to meet a wide range of people who had it, the more I saw that the social impulses that partly defined the disorder weren't so clearly a gift. Their unique combination of gregariousness and guilelessness exposed a paradox in Western culture: we say we like extroverts, but when an extreme extrovert comes barreling toward us with open arms, we shy away. It's not just warmth or openness that we value; these traits must be coupled with a more sophisticated sense of when to turn them on and off. People with Williams syndrome never turn them off. They have the social drive but not the cognitive ability to use it effectively.

With their unconditional love for humankind, people with Williams seem to come closer than any of us to what religious leaders, gurus, and self-help authors tout as an ideal. But the truth is more complicated. The response I've seen to people with Williams has ranged from warmth to amusement to pity to contempt. Reverence rarely makes an appearance. Nor do their overtures of friendship tend to meet with genuine reciprocation. The cruel irony of the disorder is that the very people who crave social connection the most aren't well adapted to get it. Their insatiable drive to connect is, in itself, what ultimately pushes people away.

If not a model of behavior, then, Williams struck me as a lens that magnified some of the fundamental challenges of being human. All of us risk being taken advantage of to some degree, but what would it be like to go through life this irremediably vulnerable, biologically unable to peel your heart from your sleeve and lock it safely inside? All parents fear for their kids' safety, but what would it mean to be the parent of a child who lacked the defenses most children come by innately? The disorder exponentially increases a parent's normal anxieties and exaggerates one of the universal perils each of us faces: the danger of opening our hearts only to be met with rejection or exploitation. Maybe that's one reason why some of us inwardly recoil when we see people with this condition. They hold up a mirror to the part of ourselves we're trying our best to conceal: that utterly defenseless, deeply tender inner part that yearns for connection and kindness—and can so easily be crushed.

In 2012, after becoming immersed in the world of Williams and establishing myself as a fixture in the lives of Gayle and Eli D'Angelo, I attended the biennial Williams Syndrome Convention in Boston, where I joined a group of first-timers—parents whose children had recently been diagnosed—at a bittersweet "welcome lunch." By then I knew enough about the disorder—which typically entails moderate intellectual disability and serious health complications along with the social symptoms—to recognize that Williams was not simply an invitation to an endless cocktail party. So did the parents, many of whom stared red-eyed at plates of lukewarm pizza. Their babies, meanwhile, cooed at everyone they saw. Toddlers tore across the mauve carpets to hug new people, while older children greeted each other exuberantly.

Karen Levine, a developmental psychologist who specializes in Williams, stood at the front of the banquet hall, working her way through a PowerPoint presentation about the disorder. Although she runs a busy private practice and teaches at Harvard Medical School, Levine gives off an easygoing, carefree energy. She smiled warmly as she delivered a speech that was part pep talk, part primer—a version of the talk she'd once given Gayle, who had brought Eli to her office for an evaluation when he was four.

Levine hoped the last slide of her presentation would offer some perspective, or at least some comic relief, to the roomful of dazed parents. In it she offered a clinical diagnosis for a little-known disorder called TROUS: The Rest of Us syndrome. Seen from the perspective of someone with Williams, this disorder includes traits such as extreme emotional distance, pathological suspicion of strangers, and a critically limited capacity for hugging.

Although I had come to accept that Williams syndrome was justifiably labeled a disability, I was gratified to hear Levine echo my initial sense that the world would be a kinder, gentler place if people with Williams formed the majority, and the rest of us were the ones with a rare clinical disorder.

"These people very rarely say 'I love you,'" Levine noted of TROUS sufferers, still channeling the Williams worldview. "They might only say it a few times a day."

———

ONCE I ENTERED THEIR APARTMENT THAT first day, Eli hugged me twice, then stepped back, catching a look from Gayle. I could see little resemblance between mother and son. He was short for his age and pudgy, his face all cheeks and dimples. His thick lips parted into a toothy smile so wide it forced his cheekbones up, squeezing his narrow eyes nearly shut. His curly brown hair was tousled, with tufts that stood on end, giving him a wild look. Gayle, on the other hand, was impeccably put together, with raven hair framing pale skin and features more refined than her son's. Her almond eyes were outlined strikingly with dark eyeliner, her lip gloss applied just so. She greeted me calmly, a model of reserve to whose example Eli was oblivious.

She offered to take my coat, which I had to pass over Eli's head, since he was anchored to the spot just in front of me. He squeezed my hand and pumped it like we had just signed a million-dollar business deal.

"Hello!" he chirped. "Nice to see you! I like your shirt!"

He was instantly enchanting, even to someone like me, who is not easily enchanted. I am certainly not much of a hugger. I can count the number of times I've hugged my own grandmother on a single hand.

Gayle ushered me over to a mint-green couch, where I sat with my notebook on my lap while Eli hovered nearby, never sitting, interrupting our conversation with bursts of chatter. He was in constant motion, a garrulous hummingbird. His conversation was a jumble of questions.

"How'd you sleep? You have a dog? Where's your dad?" He made direct eye contact, but barely paused to listen to my answers. His mind was already racing ahead to the next question, his plan apparently to prolong our interaction by rapid-fire interrogation rather than with a leisurely back-and-forth dialogue.

The thrill of entertaining a guest, coupled with Eli's natural hyperactivity and short attention span, propelled him into a whirling flurry of activity. He banged plastic food-shaped toys together atop a wooden butcher block in a corner of the living room, reenacting the role of *Iron Chef*'s Masaharu Morimoto, his second-favorite TV personality. He was half watching the TV, which played an episode of *Sesame Street* that he had rewound to the segment featuring Cookie Monster (his favorite TV personality). He tumbled a plastic hamburger patty in a plastic bowl and announced that he was making cookies. He sang as he cooked. As I later discovered, he sang constantly, all day every day. At the moment it was a hit by the Commodores.

"'She's a BRICK [pause] *HOUSE.*'"

When I seemed distracted by the hubbub, Gayle laughed.

"Oh, you're probably not used to all the background noise," she shouted. "I usually just yell over it."

Eli buzzed over to the couch, offering me an imaginary cookie. "I love her," he announced to Gayle as I pretended to eat the plastic burger-cookie.

"Oh, that's nice," she said with a good-natured smile and the practiced air of someone who was used to hearing declarations of love.

————

IT WAS EASY TO FALL IN LOVE with Eli. Once you got to know him, it was also easy to see how his endless capacity for love could put him in danger. Gayle worried about his well-being whenever he was out of her sight, which, apart from school, was hardly ever. She didn't let him outside to play in front of their apartment, to socialize with the other boys who ran wild around the common spaces. Even though Eli craved social interaction above all else, Gayle couldn't justify the risks, from bullying to the physical and sexual abuse that people with Williams are uniquely susceptible to.

"I wish I could let him, but I just can't," she told me.

While Eli's safety was Gayle's foremost concern, it wasn't her only worry. Assuming Eli made it through childhood unscathed, there was the question of what kind of adulthood he would have. Would he be able to master the skills necessary to live alone? Could he achieve some measure of independence? Would he be able to protect himself from exploitation? Could he ever overcome the endless urge to hug everyone he saw?

At twelve, Eli was on the cusp of a critical transition. When he entered adolescence, he'd be expected to establish himself as a person apart from his mother, make his own friends, and begin to forge his own way in the world. But as he baked pretend cookies in his pretend kitchen, he seemed more like a toddler than a tween, with no trace of the sophistication he'd need to navigate the typical world of teenagers—a world in which hierarchies were established, cliques were formed, and rivalries could be cutthroat.

Eli, earnest and artless, seemed destined to land at the bottom of the adolescent social order, where he'd be an easy target for those at the top. And while he gave no thought at all to climbing the social ladder, he eagerly wanted to make friends. So far, his attempts to do so had mostly fizzled. Most of the kids he knew at school were nice enough to him, but they didn't invite him over on the weekends. In his special-needs class, he had too little in common with the other students—none of whom had Williams—to establish a meaningful rapport. To make the connections he coveted, he'd need to develop some of the social tools with which most of us come pre-equipped. Whether or not he could do so would mean the difference between being an active member of the human tribe or living a life on the margins, facing an especially acute loneliness.

After this first night in Eli's company, I went on to spend three years shadowing him and Gayle, documenting their individual journeys as well as the immense bond that united them. As I watched Gayle care for her son during the most difficult years of both of their lives, she became, in my mind, the hero of a war on two fronts: one,

the battle to keep Eli safe; the other, to help him achieve his full potential. On both fronts, she fought with a ferocity born of boundless love.

———

WHEN ELI GREW TIRED OF MAKING cookies, he begged Gayle to
draw a picture of Cookie Monster. She humored him, although similar
portraits of the Muppet, done in blue crayon, were already scattered
throughout the living room. When she finished, Eli reacted with the
delight of someone who had just been given a signed Picasso.

"Oooh," he said. He took the paper from her and grasped it tightly,
crumpling the edges in his fists. Then he began to sing again, switching from the Commodores to " 'C' Is for Cookie."

He remained cheerful until it was time for me to go. He seemed
surprised to learn that I was not spending the night—that our friendship would be interrupted. His face fell.

"You're leaving?" he asked plaintively.

I told him I'd see him again. He smiled.

As soon as I had stepped across the threshold, he called out, "I
miss you!"

One

Unlocked

G ayle didn't know where to turn. She had been driving east for hours on an unfamiliar highway (I-80) in an unfamiliar state (Pennsylvania), searching with increasing desperation for a place to stop for the night. She had been checking each exit since 9 p.m. But every reputable hotel from Clarion to Punxsutawney had been booked full. Now it was past 11. She tapped her crimson fingernails anxiously on the steering wheel.

Twelve-year-old Eli was scribbling with crayons on a notepad in the backseat. His crayons were the fat kind that kindergartners used; Gayle bought them because they were easier for him to grip than the slender version. He clutched a red crayon tightly in his fist and drew furious circles, throwing his full weight into the task. Then he lifted the crayon from the page and stabbed it rapid-fire—a manic pointillist creating a fusillade of dots. A few tore through the paper. He lifted his artwork and admired it in the dome light, which Gayle had left on for him. He chirped with glee, smiling to himself. Then he selected a blue crayon, bent his head over the notepad, and began again. As he worked, he sang a selection of hits from Disney's *Lion King*. Every few minutes he asked enthusiastically, "When are we gonna get to the hotel?"

Road trips were a source of great excitement for Eli, since they meant a new cast of characters and new social opportunities he wouldn't find at home. Home was a town house in a small Connecticut apartment complex where Eli and his mother lived by themselves. Eli's father hadn't been around for years.

From his kitchen window Eli often watched other boys his age playing in the parking lot. From the French doors overlooking his back patio, he caught glimpses of them shooting basketballs through the hoop behind the subdivision's communal grass patch. But he'd never joined them. Even if he'd been invited, Gayle wouldn't have let him go.

Road trips, however, meant stopping at diners and hotels—places where you could meet new people and see unfamiliar vacuum cleaners and overhead fans, to Eli's great delight. And this had been a nice, long summer road trip: two days north to Michigan and now two days back. Eli squirmed giddily in anticipation of all the adventure still in store.

"We'll be there soon, Eli," Gayle said. Her voice was worried, slightly exasperated. She asked him to sing a little more quietly.

———

IT WAS NEARLY MIDNIGHT, AND ELI was dozing, when Gayle finally found a motel with a vacancy: a low white-brick building near an oil refinery in Clearfield, Pennsylvania. But as soon as she pulled into the parking lot, she was tempted to turn around and keep driving. The warm air drifting through her open window carried the acrid smell of diesel fuel on a cloud of cigarette smoke. The parking lot was filled with work trucks around which men stood in groups dimly lit by streetlights. Tractor-trailers lined the edges of the parking lot, bordering the motel like a menacing metal hedgerow.

Gayle considered getting back on the highway. If she drove all night, they could be home by morning. But she knew she was too tired. They were stuck here at the Clearfield Budget Inn.

Eli woke up when the car rolled to a stop. He surveyed the land-scape enthusiastically, oblivious to the seediness of the place.

"I've never been here in a long time!" he exclaimed, clapping his hands together.

Gayle stepped out of the car and into the July heat, and opened the back door to let him out. She could feel the eyes of the men on her, the only woman in their midst, and on Eli, who was now rocking back and forth on his heels with excitement. Both Gayle and Eli were rumpled from hours in the car. Gayle, a youthful forty-one-year-old, wore a purple camisole and capri-length cargo pants that revealed some of her tattoos. On her back, feathery wings spread outward from her spine. Her left shin was covered with a series of colorful images: on the back, a dragonfly; on the left, flaming dice; on the right, a serpent coiled around a sword; and on the front, a red heart with a banner that said "Eli."

Her long black hair, usually wavy, had gone limp in the muggy heat. She had pulled it up into a clip, revealing the discs that had stretched dime-size holes in her earlobes.

Eli wore a black T-shirt and the baggy denim shorts that Gayle had bought at Kohl's just before the road trip, hoping these wouldn't split at the seams like his last pair. She described her son as "husky," but it was his pear shape that made him hard to shop for. Boys' clothes weren't designed with this shape in mind.

She ran a protective hand through Eli's dark curls. His features were those of a much younger child: chubby cheeks, an upturned nose, and a smile so wide it made his eyes crinkle. They were crinkling now. His face was bright with joy, and he tugged at Gayle's arm, pulling her toward the light, the trucks, the men. She jerked him forcefully in the other direction.

In the sweltering front office, the motel's owner, an Indian man with thinning white hair, slid open a thick glass window—*Bullet-proof,* Gayle thought. He looked as tired as Gayle felt. She rummaged through her purse to find her wallet and handed him her credit card. Eli, meanwhile, bounced up from behind her, smiling broadly.

"I'm Eli! What's your name?" he said, extending a hand to the motel owner. The counter was higher than Eli's head, but he stood on his tiptoes and strained to reach. The man gave him a quizzical look. Without answering, he reached through the window and shook Eli's hand.

Turning to Gayle, the motel owner nodded toward the parking lot. "Don't worry about those guys," he said. "They're here for the summer, working construction. They just like to relax out there after work."

Only slightly reassured, Gayle took the room key.

"He likes me," Eli declared as they left the office, pointing his thumb toward his own chest.

"I'm sure he does," Gayle agreed blankly. She was already scanning the row of doors for the number on her key. She slung Eli's backpack over her shoulder, rolling her suitcase across the uneven pavement with one hand and holding Eli's hand with the other.

Eli peered at the faces of the men in the parking lot, hopeful that someone would return his gaze, but they looked away when he caught their eyes. One man lit a cigarette; another stubbed one out on the pavement. One man mumbled something too quietly for Gayle to hear. The others laughed.

Apart from the rest of the group, one man sat alone on the sidewalk, his elbows propped on bent knees, his head drooping heavily in his hands. His eyes were closed. Gayle noticed his sinewy arms, his muddy work boots. Maybe he was just tired from a long day, but Gayle's instincts told her he was more likely drunk or high. She looked for a way around him, but he was on the walkway just in front of her room. There was no other way to go.

She whispered to Eli through clenched teeth, "Do. Not. Say. Anything. To. Him."

"Why?" Eli replied in an ordinary voice. They were ten feet from the man, and closing in.

Gayle raised a finger to her lips. "Because. He's sleeping."

Eli's eyes never left the stranger. When they were less than an arm's length from the man, Eli shouted, "Are you sleeping?"

The man raised his head and gave him a dark, bleary look but didn't speak. Eli grinned at him. The man dropped his head again. Gayle pulled Eli past, fumbled to unlock the door to their room, and dragged Eli inside. She shut the door hard behind her.

The motel room was outdated—forest-green carpeting, purple-and-green-swirled curtains and a pink bedspread—but it looked clean, at least. Gayle checked the mattress ticking for bedbug shells but found none. There was still a faint smell of smoke inside, which grew stronger when she turned on the air conditioner. She could hear the men's voices outside, even over the rattling of the AC, and wondered if she'd be able to fall asleep here. Eli, meanwhile, pulled off his Velcro shoes and his shorts, dove under the polyester bedspread, and was snoring before the lights went out.

The next morning Gayle spent close to an hour looking for the room key, which she had somehow lost. She dumped out the contents of her suitcase, her purse, and Eli's backpack. Eli chattered happily while she searched, asking questions she only half answered.

"What are we going to have for breakfast, Mom?"

"I don't know. We'll see."

"We can go to a diner?"

"Maybe. I don't know what's around here."

"I think there's a diner!"

"Oh, you do?" She couldn't help but smile at his optimism. He stood at her shoulder, looking up at her expectantly. She set down the backpack she had been rifling through and gave him a hug before continuing her search.

When she knelt to search under the bed, Eli sprawled atop the shiny pink bedspread and watched her. When she moved into the bathroom, he jumped up and followed her. Gayle crouched to look behind the toilet.

"You can draw a picture of a truck?" Eli asked from the doorway, tilting his head sideways to see her face.

"Not now, Eli. But maybe later." She opened the cupboard below the sink and looked beneath the extra rolls of toilet paper. She couldn't really imagine how the key could have gotten under a roll of toilet paper, but she was out of ideas.

"But you can draw it for me?"

"Yes, OK. But later."

She squeezed past him, back into the bedroom. She pulled the dresser away from the wall in case the key had slipped behind it. It hadn't. Eli flopped back down on the bed. He cupped his chin in his hand and sighed, growing bored. Gayle rechecked every place she had already looked. The key was nowhere.

Finally she instructed Eli to wait in the room while she flagged down the motel owner. He was also apparently the motel's one-man housekeeping crew: she saw him a few doors down with a cart full of cleaning supplies. She sheepishly confessed to losing the key.

"I have it," he said. "You left it in the door last night."

Gayle's mind raced with retroactive terror. As if they weren't vulnerable enough already, she'd made it even easier for danger to creep in. She pictured a lineup of the men who must have passed their door while they slept, and the key turn that would have brought them inside. Not only had the door been unlocked, it had been advertised as such. The dangling key chain might as well have been a neon welcome sign.

Gayle shuddered. This was, after all, the central struggle of her life: trying to shelter her son from the world. Eli himself was perpetually unlocked, open, and vulnerable. He carried a welcome sign wherever he went. Gayle was the only barrier between him and everything that lurked outside the door.

She dashed back to the motel room, which she had left unlocked this time by necessity. Eli's face was pressed to the window. It lit up when he saw her and, behind her, the motel owner. He waved at both of them ecstatically, as if he were being rescued from a desert island and it had been years since he'd seen another human being.

Two

Diagnosis

On a brisk mid-March morning in 2000, Gayle hurried to her cubicle at work. She was in a rush to boot up her computer, to search the internet for a medical term she had just heard for the first time.

"Williams syndrome" meant nothing to her—nothing specific—and yet something about it filled her with dread. In the short drive from Eli's day care center to the office building where she'd worked an administrative job since she was just out of high school, the dread had risen to a level of near panic. Her hands shook as she typed the words into a search engine. She clicked on the first website she saw, an online medical dictionary, and scanned the screen quickly. She read as much as she could before her eyes filled with tears and blurred the words. Then she ducked her head over her trash can and threw up.

———

SHE KNEW SOMETHING WAS WRONG WITH her baby. She'd known that for a while. Eli cried often, as if in pain. He didn't sleep. He wasn't gaining weight.

Gayle knew this wasn't just normal baby stuff because her cousin and her best friend had both had babies around the same time she had Eli, and theirs were different. They ate more, slept more, and moved more. They were already taking their first steps and saying their first words. At thirteen months, Eli wasn't walking or speaking. He wasn't even crawling.

Eli's pediatrician, Dr. Hanover, agreed that there was cause for concern. He'd recently given Eli one of the bleakest labels in the medical book: "failure to thrive." Eli was only in the fifth percentile on growth charts. Tiny.

Eli's health problems, seemingly unrelated to each other, were piling up. Dr. Hanover had referred him to a gastroenterologist, who diagnosed Eli with reflux and prescribed him a baby dose of Pepcid. The pediatrician also diagnosed a slight heart murmur. He noted that one of Eli's pupils dilated much more than the other in light—something called Horner's syndrome. He sent Eli to an ear, nose, and throat specialist to see about his frequent ear infections and hypersensitivity to sound.

By Eli's one-year checkup, it was also obvious that his motor skills were not developing as they should. Dr. Hanover put in another call, and on March 1 two women visited Gayle's home to evaluate her son.

The pair worked for Connecticut's Birth to Three program, which provides services for children with developmental delays. They played with Eli for an hour in the living room of the family's split-level ranch while Gayle and her husband, Alan, watched nervously. During their visit, the women recorded the following assessments:

"In back lying, Eli easily brings his feet to his hands. He rolls to his tummy and returns with ease. He is not yet able to transition into sitting by himself. . . . Eli's gross motor skills appear to be at approximately an eight-month level. . . .

"Eli is an alert baby; he enjoyed interacting with the evaluators during the session. He can alternate his gaze between two objects and enjoys staring at his hands. . . . Eli looked for a ring that was partially hidden under a washcloth, indicating the emerging understanding of object permanence. Eli's skills appear to be at approximately an eight-month level in the cognitive domain."

It was in the "personal-social domain" that the evaluators felt Eli performed best. They judged his social skills to be roughly on par with his age, and wrote: "Eli was cheerful for most of the evaluation. He smiled readily at the unfamiliar evaluators and enjoyed engagement and physical handling for nearly a full hour.... Mom reports that Eli is a 'cuddly' baby who especially enjoys singing."

The evaluators left the session feeling perplexed. They agreed that the baby was engaging, alert, and attentive in a way that seemed to belie an intellectual disability.

But they also agreed that something was very wrong with him. They had no idea what it was. They deemed him eligible for state-funded early-intervention services and left it at that.

In their final report, they wrote: "Eli is a delightful young boy who is very sociable. It is difficult to suggest an explanation to account for the overall delays exhibited during this evaluation. Eli's interest in his environment is an asset that will assist him in acquiring further advances in developmental skills."

They called Gayle a few days later to tell her that a physical therapist would begin visiting Eli at his day care center to help him learn to walk. Gayle was grateful. She hoped her son just needed a little extra help to catch up. *Maybe once his reflux is under control and he puts on some weight,* she thought, *he can bring those motor skills up to speed. Then everything will be back on track.*

———

BEFORE CHRISTMAS, GAYLE HAD TAKEN a group photo of Eli and his day care classmates. She'd put a print of the beaming baby faces in each child's cubby as a gift for their parents. She thought of the photo again one morning, a week or so after the Birth to Three evaluation, when she told an aide at Eli's day care to expect visits from a physical therapist.

"She'll be coming in to help Eli with walking," Gayle said when she dropped Eli off before work. "Eli's motor skills aren't where they should be, so they hope this will help him catch up."

"Oh, good," the aide said. "Has he been having health problems?"

"Well, he has a heart murmur, but it's mild," Gayle said, unsure exactly how to answer. "He has pretty severe reflux. He also has a condition that makes one of his pupils dilate more than the other; it's called Horner's syndrome. Do you know anything about Horner's? I think it has something to do with them using forceps when he was born, but I'm not sure."

"No, I don't," the teacher said, "but you should ask Jonathan's mom. She's a pediatrician."

The teacher nodded toward a tall woman who was squeezing her son's puffy coat into his cubby. Gayle recognized Jonathan's mom from the day care center's holiday party but hadn't known she was a doctor. She was a quiet woman who didn't socialize much with the other mothers.

"Oh, you're a pediatrician?" Gayle said, and Jonathan's mother looked up from the row of wooden cubbies. Gayle smiled at her. "Do you know anything about Horner's syndrome?"

The woman deliberated for a second without returning her smile. It occurred to Gayle later that she'd been contemplating whether to reveal what she had been holding back. Then she decided to let it out.

"No," she said slowly. "But . . . have you ever seen a geneticist?"

"No," Gayle said, taken aback. "Why would I see a geneticist?"

The pediatrician responded slowly, as if choosing her words carefully.

"Well, Eli has some characteristics that could be part of a certain syndrome."

"What do you mean?" Gayle said, trying not to sound defensive. "Characteristics? Like what?"

"The heart murmur, the developmental delay, the wide smile," the woman said, lifting her hand to her face and squeezing her cheeks when she said "wide smile," although she wasn't smiling. "They're all signs of a certain syndrome."

"What syndrome?"

"It's called Williams syndrome."

The woman shifted her weight from one foot to the other, as if keeping her muscles limber for a quick retreat. From her strained tone and awkward manner, Gayle could tell that, whatever else Williams entailed, it was supremely bad news.

"Oh," Gayle said, feigning nonchalance. The dread was forming already, a hard knot deep in her stomach. "I guess I'll have to ask Eli's pediatrician about that."

"There's a doctor at Yale who specializes in Williams," Jonathan's mom offered helpfully, giving Gayle an unfamiliar name. "You might want to contact her."

Gayle nodded, hoping her face didn't betray how much she was unraveling inside. It was all she could do not to bolt from the room in search of an internet connection. She mustered all her willpower to keep herself composed.

"Well, thanks for the information," she said in just a slightly higher voice than normal, clutching her purse close. "I'll check into it."

———

ALONE IN HER CUBICLE, SHE COMPOSED herself and forced her eyes back to the screen, to the description of Williams syndrome. Caused by the deletion of twenty-six genes from one strand of chromosome 7, it manifested itself in young children as a heart murmur, sleeplessness, fussiness, sensitivity to sound, and "a highly social personality from birth." People with Williams, the website said, tend to be extremely outgoing, friendly, and affectionate—even as babies—to relatives and strangers alike.

Eli had every symptom on the list.

Gayle lingered first over the syndrome's cardiac effects. A heart murmur, she learned, could be a portent of supravalvular aortic stenosis, or SVAS, a dangerous narrowing of the main blood vessel leading away from the heart. SVAS is common in people with Williams, one side effect of a missing elastin gene, which also frequently leads to pulmonary stenosis, obstructing the flow of blood from the heart to the lungs. Because of these conditions, the risk of heart attack and sudden death are much higher among people with Williams, and even infants often undergo surgery to expand their narrow blood vessels.

Gayle consoled herself with the pediatrician's assurance that Eli's heart murmur was mild. He would have heard more than a slight murmur if Eli's arteries were blocked, wouldn't he?

She followed a link to photos documenting the unique facial characteristics of people with Williams syndrome. She hadn't noticed anything unusual about Eli's face before. *He's a baby,* she thought. *He looks like a baby.* But all the pictures of kids with Williams looked uncannily like Eli, with upturned noses, protruding ears, pointy chins, thick lips, and wide, gap-toothed smiles. *Eli's teeth have just started coming in, though. Of course he's gap-toothed.* Still, she felt rattled. The pictures of older people with Williams pushed her over the edge. The adorable elfin faces looked uncannily out of place on adults. *They don't look as cute anymore,* Gayle mused. Feeling guilty, she instantly tried to unthink the thought.

She hit the back button, returning to the list of symptoms. She noted the irony that, despite their lack of social anxiety, people with Williams often suffer from severe generalized anxiety and specific phobias. In fact, they are about five times more likely than the general population to be diagnosed with generalized anxiety disorder.

She began scrolling through the cognitive effects, but her heart snagged on the words "intellectual disability." The average IQ for someone with Williams is around 55, making most people with the syndrome mildly to moderately intellectually disabled. Eli's attentiveness to people might not have been the sign of heightened intellect that the state evaluators took it to be. It might have been another symptom of the disorder: the "highly social personality" that is the reason Williams is often called the opposite of autism.

This tendency, the hallmark of Williams syndrome, is both its silver lining and its most disabling feature. In their unstoppable urge to connect with others, those with the syndrome alienate the people they hope to befriend, and often attract people who are more eager to take advantage of their indiscriminate affection than to reciprocate it.

Gayle couldn't stand to read any more. She picked up her desk phone and punched the number for Eli's pediatrician, which she had memorized. Her breath came fast and ragged. She told the receptionist she needed to speak with Dr. Hanover immediately: it was an emergency. She waited on hold for a minute or two, which felt like an eternity. Then the doctor picked up.

"Could Eli have Williams syndrome?" she asked. The doctor paused for a moment.

"I never thought of that," he said. She heard the clicking of a keyboard over the phone, and wondered if he was looking up the same online medical dictionary she had consulted. "I suppose he could."

———

GAYLE HAD TO WAIT SEVERAL WEEKS for an appointment with the Yale geneticist Jonathan's mom mentioned: Dr. Barbara Pober. In the meantime she dropped Eli off late at day care every day to avoid running into the pediatrician. It took everything she had to get through ordinary interactions without breaking down; seeing Jonathan's mom again now would push her over the edge.

The edge felt dangerously close, all the time. She made it through each day on autopilot; inside, she felt hopeless, desperate, overwhelmed. She balked when Eli's pediatrician said, about the possibility of Williams syndrome, "You know, kids with disabilities today, it's not the end of the world." He tried to explain: the stigma was not what it once was. People with intellectual disabilities weren't shuffled off to homes and institutions anymore. Parents had access to more resources, better services. Early intervention increased the prospects of independence in adulthood . . . But Gayle had stopped listening. *It IS the end of the world,* she thought. *How can you say it's not?*

Seeing other children who were the same age as Eli but leaps and bounds ahead of him developmentally, she felt her throat tighten.

Looking at their parents, she realized: *They have this hope for the future that I don't have anymore.*

Gayle's family was supportive, but sometimes being around them only deepened her sense of loss. She grew frustrated when they pretended nothing was wrong. She didn't know which was worse: the look of pity people sometimes gave her when she told them about the possibility that Eli had Williams syndrome, or when they ignored what she'd said and acted as if it were something he'd grow out of.

Sometimes they praised Eli for being quieter and less troublesome than other kids. Gayle's cousin Marcia had a daughter, Kylie, who was the same age as Eli, and she was a restless ball of energy. At one family gathering she kept toddling off and had to be chased down again and again, while Eli never moved from his spot. Someone said to Gayle, "Look at Eli, sitting there all nice. Why can't Kylie do that?"

Because he can't crawl yet, Gayle thought but didn't say. *He's delayed. You wouldn't want Kylie to be like him. Why would you say that?*

Her emotions rubbed raw, she grew indignant when the parents of normal kids didn't appreciate how lucky they were. One day she overheard a coworker talking about his daughter, a straight-A student who had just finished her freshman year of college and gained the freshman fifteen—or maybe more like thirty. The man was telling someone over the phone, "We're going to take her to the doctor, get her some pills. We can't have this. You know how I feel about fat people." Gayle wanted to punch the man. *Can't you just be grateful that she's brilliant? You want to take her to the doctor because she's gained weight?*

She was aware that most people didn't just sit around being grateful their kids didn't have an intellectual disability. But they should, she thought. They should be thankful every day. She dwelled on this aspect of the disorder more than anything else. Without normal intelligence, Eli wouldn't be able to achieve all that she had envisioned for his life. She hadn't exactly expected him to become president or cure cancer, but anything had seemed possible. Part of her hoped he would become a musician, fulfilling a fantasy she and her husband had both entertained.

Both she and Alan considered themselves edgy, freethinking nonconformists. Their musical interests lay outside the mainstream, somewhere between punk and hard rock, from Alice Cooper to White Zombie, along with the Misfits, the Cramps, and the Ramones. And although they hadn't gone to as many rock shows since Eli was born, they still aspired to something more than their day jobs as office administrator and machinist, respectively.

They had high hopes for Eli, too: if he didn't grow up to be a rock star, then at least he would do something meaningful, something cool. They expected him to stand out somehow. And Williams syndrome—any intellectual disability—stood in the way. Gayle resented the disorder itself, the genetic anomaly that would rob her son of options in life.

She even felt irritated with Dr. Pober for making her wait so long for an appointment. At first she was told it could take months, since Dr. Pober was away on extended personal leave. Gayle refused to accept the delay. She called the office every day, bullying the doctor's staff into making an exception. Years later, after she learned that Dr. Pober's mother had reached the final stage of a terminal illness that spring, and that the doctor had taken time off to be with her, Gayle regretted her pushiness. But at the time, it didn't occur to her that anyone else's troubles could be as urgent as her own.

She counted the days to her appointment, desperate to know for sure. At the same time she dreaded the approaching date: April 10. Until that day, there was still a chance Eli didn't have Williams, and she could hold out hope for a normal life, for him and for herself. She clung to that hope even as she grieved its loss.

————

THE APPOINTMENT WAS AT 8 A.M. on a Monday morning. Gayle and Alan arrived early and made their way through the brightly painted, antiseptic-scented corridors of Yale New Haven Children's Hospital. The juxtaposition of the cheerful and the sterile unnerved Gayle. She tightened her hold on the warm, wriggling bundle in her arms. The tendons in her forearms tensed, locking around Eli like steel cables.

She had come prepared to fight against a diagnosis, to prove to the geneticist that this was all a misunderstanding. A few weeks earlier she had taken Eli to a lab for the blood test that would tell Dr. Pober conclusively whether he had the disorder. In the meantime, applying a measure of magical thinking to sway the test results, she searched for proof that he didn't. Now, in her purse, she carried a white envelope stuffed with photos of her father, her uncle, her cousins, herself. Her father had the same wide smile as Eli; she herself had had the same upturned nose as a baby. She planned to show the photos to Dr. Pober to prove that Eli's appearance was not some genetic fluke. She'd rehearsed the scene over and over in her head: Dr. Pober would look at the photos and realize that it wasn't Williams after all. Gayle would apologize profusely for wasting her time. Then she'd take her baby home.

The pediatric hospital room wasn't much different from an adult hospital room: there was an exam table lined with white paper, a blood pressure cuff hanging on the wall. But the table and the cuff were little. Kid-size. This unnerved Gayle even more. She fixed her eyes on the children's books on a side table, next to a stuffed Elmo doll, studying the titles in an effort to keep her nerves at bay. Dr. Pober didn't keep them waiting long. When she appeared, Gayle was struck by how small she was—just a little more than child-size herself. But her manner was solemn.

Although Gayle didn't appreciate it at this first appointment, Dr. Pober was the East Coast's preeminent authority on Williams syndrome. Almost everyone diagnosed with Williams in New England came to see her; she just happened to be a short drive away from Gayle—a stroke of luck for which Gayle would later be grateful. Dr. Pober had specialized in Williams since the 1980s, before the genes involved had been identified, and before it could be diagnosed by a simple blood test: the FISH test, which uses fluorescent dye to light up DNA strands so deletions become visible under a microscope. When she began her career, a Williams diagnosis could be made only by observation, like autism today, based on symptoms and facial features.

A chance assignment during her pediatrics residency in 1978 had introduced Dr. Pober to the disorder, and she immediately fell in love with the people who had it. She was struck by their warmth and their incredible empathy. They seemed able to read people's moods, picking up on cues that were invisible to everyone else. One day, when she was seeing patients in the Williams clinic, Dr. Pober was distressed about something she didn't want to share with her colleagues. She was putting up a brave front, hiding her feelings—or so she thought. A patient walked in, looked at her face, and immediately said, "What's wrong, Dr. Pober? You look sad."

Drawn to Williams despite not being particularly gregarious herself, Dr. Pober cared deeply about her patients. Parents raved about how far out of her way she went to help them, returning calls promptly and dispensing endless wisdom. None of them, however, could recall their first meeting with the geneticist happily: she had made her initial appearance in all of their lives as the bearer of terrible news.

Dr. Pober introduced herself to Gayle and Alan, her manner neither friendly nor unfriendly, just professional. She studied Eli without lifting him from Gayle's arms. She took his hand and spread his fingers, examining his nails. She seemed to have a diagnosis in mind already.

"Yep," she said, half to herself, running the tip of her finger across his tiny fingernail. "He has these wide nail beds and curved fingernails."

Like you can tell from his fingernails, Gayle thought. Dr. Pober made a note. Gayle heard the scratch of pen on paper like nails on a chalkboard, felt it like a knifepoint along her skin.

Gayle's pulse raced while Dr. Pober dug through a folder for Eli's test results. She stood motionless, paralyzed, while the doctor read the results aloud. They confirmed Gayle's suspicion and her worst fear: Eli was indeed missing the genes implicated in Williams.

Time froze. Gayle's heart dropped into her stomach, which in turn seemed to drop to the floor. She was a statue with clenched fists when Dr. Pober left the room to give the family a moment alone to digest the news.

She stared at Eli. So did Alan. He was a rugged-looking man, with frost-blue eyes and a full beard. Now his eyes glistened and his beard grew damp with tears.

Gayle did not cry. She was still in battle mode, although she'd never even had the chance to take the photos out of her purse. The fight had been over before she knew it had begun.

"What does it mean?" Gayle asked when the doctor returned. She had read enough about Williams online to answer her own question, but she wanted to hear it from an expert.

"Well, everyone's different."

"But what are some of the things it can mean?"

Dr. Pober listed the most common health effects: SVAS; acid reflux; gastrointestinal problems; high blood calcium levels; low muscle tone; joint stiffness; vision problems, including lazy eye; poor weight gain among children; obesity among adults . . .

Gayle had trouble focusing. She picked up blips here and there—words and phrases. She shifted back and forth between the real-time words of the geneticist and the script playing in her head, the list of everything she'd read about Williams and tried not to apply to her son. She thought about the lack of social inhibitions, and the endless capacity for affection, that made kids with Williams uniquely vulnerable. She began to consider a life of constant vigilance, above and beyond the constant vigilance that is every parent's lot.

She shifted her focus back to the doctor, who was now describing the intellectual abilities of people with Williams. Most had trouble with math, abstract reasoning, and visual-spatial processing, Dr. Pober said. On the other hand, she added encouragingly, people with Williams were known for their remarkable verbal abilities.

"Most adults are able to read, although there is a broad range of reading skills," she said. Once again Gayle felt as if her brain had been sucked into a tunnel where words reached it only as faint, incomprehensible echoes. She stared at the geneticist, watching her lips move and registering nothing. When Dr. Pober paused, Gayle collected herself and asked what the future would hold for Eli.

"Well, he'll likely have a job," she heard the doctor say. "Not a job like you or I have. Probably something involving repetitive tasks."

Something menial, Gayle translated. She was ready to fight again. *The audacity of this woman!* How could she take one look at an adorable baby in his fuzzy blue overalls and proclaim him capable only of repetitive tasks when he grew up? *Not a job like you or I have.* The phrase lodged in Gayle's brain like shrapnel.

She was barely paying attention when the doctor said, "He most likely won't be able to drive a car." She tuned in again when she heard her say, "Some people have intelligence in the normal range, but most do have a lower IQ than normal."

This phrase, too, stuck in her brain: *Some people have normal intelligence.* When she got home later that day, she called Dr. Pober's assistant to make sure she'd heard that right.

"You did say some people have normal intelligence, right?" she asked.

The assistant qualified the statement: "There are some folks who test normally, but there's always some deficit: poor coordination or poor visual-spatial skills. Math is almost always a challenge—"

Gayle cut her off. "But there are SOME with normal intelligence?" She was like a lawyer with a witness: all she wanted to hear was yes or no. Specifically: yes. She wanted to believe that her son would be the one to break the curve.

Years later she would look back at Dr. Pober's notes from this appointment and find that they traced the entire arc of Eli's life.

The notes read:

We spent some time discussing both short-term and long-term developmental expectations in an individual with Williams syndrome. Young children master developmental milestones, but at a slightly later than typical age. For instance, the average age of walking is two years. Most individuals with Williams syndrome develop strong language skills, but there typically is some delay in the acquisition of expressive speech. Looking ahead to the school years, most children with Williams syndrome do relatively well in the early elementary school years, often in an integrated preschool classroom and eventually in a regular class-room with extra teacher support. However, some children are in special-education classrooms from the beginning of their school experience. . . . In terms of Williams syndrome adults, most re-side with a family member or in a group home for mildly hand-icapped adults. Most individuals that we follow are employed, though typically in a supervised setting doing a repetitive job.

Something menial, Gayle would think again. *Not a job like you or I have.*

At the hospital, the words were still ricocheting in her brain as she walked back down the cold-cheerful hall, defeated. She and Alan didn't exchange words. His face was still wet with tears. Hers was blank, shocked. They retrieved Gayle's car from the valet: a two-door Chevy Cavalier, a relic of the era before Eli. Gayle leaned awkwardly through the passenger side door to strap Eli into his car seat in the back. She stared at him for a moment and thought: *Things are going to be different from this moment on.* She felt suddenly as if she didn't even know her son. For fourteen months she'd thought she understood who he was and who he would become. Now he was a stranger.

On the way home they stopped at a local diner for breakfast. They were regulars there, but everything now felt strange and foreign to Gayle. The waitress—their regular waitress, a hard-looking woman with a short, spiky hairdo and a rose tattoo on her forearm—seemed to read their distress. She frowned empathetically at Eli, who smiled at her and burbled a wordless greeting.

"Can I pick him up?" she asked. Gayle handed Eli to her without answering.

The waitress bounced Eli gently on her hip, looking intently at his parents. Alan's eyes were dry but glazed over. Both of their faces drooped listlessly. *We must look like zombies,* Gayle thought.

The waitress clearly sensed that something terrible had happened;

maybe she could tell that it had to do with Eli. Normally, Gayle would have made small talk to cover for a bad mood. She would have pretended things were fine. But today she couldn't muster the energy. She stared at the laminated tabletop, half seeing her own reflection.

She felt the waitress watching her, though, and finally lifted her head. The woman looked her in the eyes, still holding Eli, and said, "Do you know how lucky you guys are?"

Gayle was touched. She smiled weakly but couldn't speak. She knew she would cry. The waitress held her gaze.

"Do you know how special he is?" she asked.

Gayle blinked back tears. She wondered what exactly the woman had seen in Eli to make her say that: the twinkle in his eyes, or the way he held his hands out to her even before she asked to pick him up? Or was it something she saw in Gayle: the shadow of grief and loss that suggested she needed to be reminded of what she had?

The waitress had seen Eli before—they'd been there often enough with him—but she'd never paid him this much attention. Now it was as though she could see into his soul—and into Gayle's.

Her words startled Gayle out of her stupor. She got the message: *Snap out of it and love this baby.* She reached out her hands to take back her son.

Three

Putting Williams
on the Map

Every baby has roughly a one-in-10,000 chance of being born with Williams syndrome. The likelihood is the same across countries and cultures, classes and races; scientists have found no geographic or demographic variables that make people more or less susceptible to the genetic deletion that causes it. Unlike Down syndrome, for example, it's not correlated with older mothers—or, like autism, with older fathers.

The number of Americans with Williams—approximately 30,000—pales in comparison to those with Down syndrome, which affects one in seven hundred people, or about 400,000 Americans. That number is rising, despite the prevalence of prenatal testing and the fact that about 70 percent of expectant mothers who are told their child will have Down syndrome choose to terminate their pregnancies. The growing Down syndrome population, then, is partly due to a marked increase in older motherhood and partly to health care advances that have made it possible for people with Down syndrome to live longer, healthier lives than ever before. Some scientists have estimated that the number of Americans with Down syndrome will double by 2025 to 800,000.

The number of Americans on the autism spectrum, meanwhile, is estimated at about one in sixty-eight, or more than two million people. Most of us have at least met someone with Down syndrome, autism, or Asperger's. Many of us will never meet someone with Williams. But we all benefit from research on the disorder. Despite its low prevalence, Williams syndrome has led to groundbreaking advances in gene mapping and been singularly helpful in unlocking the connections between our genes and our behavior.

It's notable among genetic disorders in that it involves a small, specific group of genes—twenty to twenty-eight, by most geneticists' counts—and generates symptoms that are so distinct and observable. (People with Down syndrome, by contrast, have an extra copy of chromosome 21, giving them an additional two hundred to three hundred genes. That makes tracing symptoms back to the contributing genes exponentially more complicated, since symptoms depend as much on the interplay between genes as on the individual genes themselves.) And people with Williams are in a unique position to educate researchers, thanks to their striking verbal abilities.

The study of so-called microdeletions, like the one that causes Williams syndrome, provided geneticists with some of their earliest entry points into the human genome—the massive, dauntingly detailed blueprint for who we are as human beings. Although a road map of the genome has existed since 2001, when researchers working on the Human Genome Project published a rough draft of the three billion bases that make up a DNA strand, much of the map remains essentially undecipherable even today.

What the researchers mapped was the sequence of chemical "letters" that make up human DNA: the bases adenine, thymine, cytosine, and guanine (which geneticists abbreviate as the letters *A*, *T*, *C*, and *G*), strung like beads in varying patterns along each of twenty-three paired chromosomes. But identifying the letters didn't mean they could read the map in a meaningful way. Linking genes to the traits they code for remains a distant Holy Grail for scientists, since most traits seem to depend on multiple genes, or perhaps even hundreds.

More recently, geneticists have concluded that the non-gene portion of DNA—which they had once written off as "junk" DNA despite the fact that it constitutes roughly 98 percent of the genome—may in fact play a pivotal role in regulating genes, perhaps by switching them off or on, or by controlling how much protein results from a given gene's activity.

There was a lot to work with—too much, at least in the early days of the Human Genome Project, which began in 1990. The impetus for the project—a massive, worldwide research effort funded in part by the U.S. National Institutes of Health—was to seek out the genetic roots of common disorders, such as cancer and schizophrenia, and to use those findings to develop more effective treatments. Instead, the project revealed that disorders like these involved more genetic variables than researchers had previously imagined. Most of the im-plicated genes accounted for only relatively slight increases in the risk of developing these disorders, some of them no more significant than environmental factors.*

Meanwhile, rarer disorders with small, isolated genetic foot-prints—including Williams, as well as single-gene diseases like cystic fibrosis, sickle-cell anemia, and Huntington's disease, a degenerative brain disorder—led to clearer revelations about human biology and evolution.

Take congenital leptin deficiency, an exceedingly rare disorder that causes extreme obesity from infancy. In 1994, when scientists isolated the single-gene malfunction behind the disorder, it marked a milestone in understanding how weight is regulated by the brain. The gene (called OB, as in obese) codes for the production of leptin, a hormone that sends signals to the hypothalamus about whether the body has sufficient fat reserves. Low leptin levels set off a hormonal

---

* Promising inroads have been made, however, and even partial genetic links have led to groundbreaking advances in individualized treatment for diseases such as cancer.

alarm bell, warning the brain that the body urgently needs to stock-pile more fat, which triggers a corresponding increase in appetite. So people with a mutated OB gene can't stop eating because their brains sense, incorrectly, that they are starving. (Following this discovery, drug companies quickly began exploring whether supplemental leptin might be a magic bullet for obesity in the general population. It isn't.)

The same year that geneticists pinpointed the OB gene, they traced the most common form of dwarfism, achondroplasia, to a mutation in a gene called FGFR3, short for fibroblast growth factor receptor 3, which plays a key role in skeletal development. FGFR3 is one of a number of genes involved in bone growth, and the hallmarks of achondroplasia—shortened limbs, a normal-size trunk, and an enlarged forehead—helped scientists pinpoint exactly what types of bones it affects and at which developmental stages. The discovery of FGFR3's connection to short stature led to a flurry of identifications, some within a matter of weeks, of other bone disorders that could be traced to the same family of growth-regulating genes.

This burst of interest in rare bone disorders was a boon for the medically neglected people who had them, many of whom had struggled to find doctors who could treat or even diagnose them correctly. It also helped spur an increase in funding for research into rare diseases, which policy makers had largely ignored in favor of more prevalent disorders—with the justifiable intention of doing the most good for the most people. As researchers have pointed out, however, a single rare disease may only affect a handful of people, but, as a class, rare diseases are not so rare at all. In the U.S., a rare disease is defined as one that afflicts fewer than 200,000 people. But that definition applies to more than 7,000 disorders that collectively affect more than 25 million Americans.

New incentives soon emerged to encourage the study of these disorders. In 2009, the National Institutes of Health established its Therapeutics for Rare and Neglected Diseases program, which provides government funding to facilitate research and drug development. And in 2011, the National Human Genome Research Institute established the Centers for Mendelian Genomics, a network of researchers from around the world charged with tracing the genetic root of every Mendelian, or single-gene, disorder. Three years into that ambitious effort, researchers reported having averaged an impressive three genetic discoveries per week, successfully linking Mendelian conditions to 375 genes not previously associated with health effects.

The scope of this research is broader than treating the conditions themselves, of course. Aside from helping people who have them, studying these rare disorders has given scientists a more precise key to cracking the genetic code. It has allowed them to examine the effects of one altered gene at a time, linking it to observable symptoms with relative clarity and certainty—especially compared to the most common method of studying gene function, which is essentially the opposite approach: attempting to unravel complex genetic interactions while working backward from a trait to its corresponding gene or genes.

Using that method, known as a genome-wide association study, geneticists compare complete sets of DNA across large numbers of people. To find the genes for blond hair, for example, they'd gather a group of blonds and analyze their genetic sequences alongside those of people with other hair colors, in the hopes of finding statistically significant commonalities within the blond group. These studies are cumbersome, costly, and time-consuming, however, and on their own they are rarely conclusive.

Studying what goes awry when a gene is missing or mutated is an easier and more definitive way to determine its function. There simply aren't enough known Mendelian disorders, however, to allow geneticists to solve the genome's puzzle one gene at a time. And although the technology exists to disable single genes in the laboratory, scientists studying altered cells in a petri dish won't get very far in understanding the role a gene plays in development, or in traits like cognition or social behavior. Much of this research is conducted instead on "model organisms," such as mice, rats, and flies. But what happens in a mouse doesn't always translate exactly to what will happen in a human.

This is why Williams is so tantalizing to geneticists: it offers them the opportunity to study the curious DNA behind a dazzling array of features that no amount of lab research could illuminate. Mice missing the Williams genes could never demonstrate the unique language abilities or musical skills common to the disorder, for example. Only people can do that. People with Williams, furthermore, are some of the most valuable research subjects on the planet when it comes to one of the trickiest realms in genetics: personality.

———

WILLIAMS IS RARE ENOUGH THAT IT isn't one of the standard conditions included in prenatal screenings for pregnant women. And although it can be diagnosed with a simple blood test once an infant is born, many doctors just don't know to test for it. Its constellation of strange, seemingly unrelated symptoms are often mistakenly attributed to various more common disorders, including autism.

One boy was diagnosed as a baby with fetal alcohol syndrome. Only when he was nineteen did a new doctor check for Williams. Suddenly the dichotomy between the boy's math skills (abysmal) and his verbal abilities (nearly normal), and between his spatial skills (so bad he couldn't draw a simple stick figure) and musical talents (which included perfect pitch and the ability to play some instruments by ear), made sense. Williams explained them all.

A woman who recently celebrated her ninetieth birthday had been known throughout her life for her love of music, her radiant warmth, and her ability to bond instantly with people she'd just met. But she wasn't diagnosed with Williams until she was eighty-three. And one high-functioning woman with Williams wasn't diagnosed until she had a baby—who also had Williams. The DNA deletion that causes Williams is random, but once it has happened, it can be passed down. Having one parent with Williams gives a child a 50 percent chance of inheriting the syndrome. With two Williams parents, there's a 50 percent chance of Williams, a 25 percent chance that the child's DNA will remain fully intact, and a 25 percent chance that both copies of chromosome 7 will have the Williams deletion, in which case the pregnancy isn't expected to be viable.

Given the odds of running into someone who recognized Williams syndrome just by looking at him, Eli's diagnosis in infancy was a fluke. Babies with Williams tend to be diagnosed primarily when their doctors notice signs of SVAS, the narrowing of the aorta that Eli was lucky to have in its mildest form. It's such a rare condition, except among people with Williams syndrome, that it tends to be a giveaway for cardiologists. In fact, it was a cardiologist, John C. P. Williams, who first identified the syndrome in 1961, when he noticed that four children being treated for SVAS at his New Zealand hospital also shared similar facial features and intellectual disabilities. Dr. Williams published a paper on the similarities, suggesting that they might constitute a syndrome. A year later the German physician Alois J. Beuren arrived independently at the same conclusion, noting that three of his patients with heart defects both looked and behaved similarly. He wrote, "All have the same kind of friendly nature—they love everyone, are loved by everyone, and are very charming."

For a time, the disorder's unique facial features became its defining trait. After Williams published his 1961 paper, it became known as "elfin face syndrome" (or "elfin facies syndrome"), but "Williams syndrome" eventually caught on instead—although "Williams-Beuren syndrome" is more common in Europe.

Dr. Williams, however, was not interested in pursuing his namesake syndrome further. He returned to his regular cardiology studies, never to publish anything more on the subject. The following year he left New Zealand for a job at the Mayo Clinic, where none of his colleagues were aware of his research into the disorder or later recalled him ever mentioning it, according to the biologist Howard Lenhoff. In 1966, Dr. Williams moved to England, where he worked with Nobel Prize–winning physiologist Andrew Fielding Huxley at University College London. And in the early 1970s he simply vanished, leaving his colleagues, friends, and family to search for him in vain. It was a mysterious end for a mysterious man, whom colleagues described as "private" and "odd," according to Lenhoff.

In a biography of the New Zealand writer Janet Frame (a close friend of Williams) the historian Michael King describes Williams as an awkward, standoffish man, who once proposed to Frame by saying "Why don't we formalize our relationship?" She declined. That was a year or so before his disappearance; Frame never heard from him again. Williams's sister enlisted Interpol's help to search for him, but they could find no trace of the wayward cardiologist. In 1988 the High Court of New Zealand declared him missing and presumed dead, although King claimed that Williams contacted him "indirectly" in 2000 and asked not to be mentioned in Frame's biography. According to Frame, who died in 2004, Williams's work at the Mayo Clinic had involved classified research for NASA into the effects of weightlessness on blood pressure and heart function, and the top secret assignment had led some of his friends to postulate conspiracy theories about his disappearance. If he were alive today, he would be in his nineties.

John Williams may have had more in common with autistics than with those who had the disorder that came to bear his name. He certainly didn't invest much time in getting to know them. Perhaps a man whose marriage proposal sounded more like a legal document than a declaration of love was uncomfortable around people who might declare their love for anyone at any time.

Four

Milestones

For the rest of the year after that first genetics appointment, while Gayle contemplated Eli's diagnosis, he remained in a kind of developmental limbo: not talking, not walking, barely crawling. Then, on Christmas Eve, two months before his second birthday, he was playing on the floor by the Christmas tree, festively attired in red footie pajamas. Gayle noticed a red blur out of the corner of her eye and turned to see Eli up on his feet, bobbling toward the tree. Despite her religious skepticism, she couldn't help but consider this a Christmas miracle. Unwilling to believe that Eli's life would turn out the way Dr. Pober had predicted, she'd clung to the dim but real hope that he would be an exception to the Williams syndrome rules. Now she felt that hope flare up again as she watched Eli take his first unsteady steps across the carpet. Maybe the developmental delay was behind them, and he was back on track—a little behind the curve, but catching up.

Gayle started a scrapbook to commemorate the stages of their life together as a family. She bought heavy art paper and fancy pens. She made elaborate borders for Eli's baby pictures, capturing the classics:

Eli in his high chair, making a mess of spaghetti, and at bath time, swaddled in a towel. She wrote captions in careful block letters.

But months passed, then years, as stages came and went in the lives of Eli's peers. He didn't catch up.

At day care, while other kids babbled and chattered, Eli gestured wordlessly, pointing at what he wanted (pinwheels and the propellers of toy planes, primarily) and crying or flailing if he didn't get it. He didn't even produce nonsense syllables, apart from the repeated sound "dee." "Deedeedeedeedee," he'd say, but his inflection was flat, whereas even the youngest children in his day care could modulate their voices to mimic the inflections of conversation.

For years, Eli's communication was limited to eye contact and touch. These he used to great effect, at least with adults, whom he drew in by smiling at them and holding his hands out for a hug. If this didn't work, he'd simply toddle over and wrap himself around the person's legs. Seated people were often surprised to find him crawling onto their laps. It didn't matter who they were: he'd hug a stranger as eagerly as he'd hug his grandmother. He catapulted himself into the arms of a schoolmate's mother one day and climbed into the lap of a burly man at a shoe store the next.

Gayle waited impatiently for Eli to start talking, willing him to reach this next developmental stage before everyone else his age shot too far ahead. Meanwhile, strangers marveled at Eli everywhere he went, complimenting Gayle on how cute he was. "Not shy at all!" they'd proclaim. Sometimes they'd call him precocious. Gayle bit her tongue, knowing that, because of his small size and babyish features, they thought he was two or three when he was actually four or five.

She tried to introduce him to the life she had imagined for her child. She took him to the playground, where other kids flew down the slides, rocketed across the monkey bars, and launched themselves high on the swings. She already knew that Eli's low muscle tone and poor dexterity—symptoms of Williams syndrome—meant he couldn't do these things. She could have lifted him to the top of the slide and let him go, but he would have coasted down limply and probably landed face-first in the sand. Still, she wanted him to be there with the other kids, to share in this fundamental childhood experience.

Eli didn't seem to feel that he was missing out on the playground equipment; he was more interested in the people. By five, he had mastered the word "Hi," and he felt compelled to greet everyone at the park, chasing them down, shouting "Hi! Hi! Hi!" But his single-minded focus, and the poor spatial perception that is another peculiarity of Williams, often put him in harm's way. Invariably he'd stand too close to the swing set, oblivious to the danger, and Gayle would have to race to grab him before he was knocked to the ground.

When he shouted "Hi," the other kids tended to stop in their tracks and stare at him. Gayle could see that other five-year-olds found his behavior puzzling. They seemed unsure how to respond. Often they turned and ran from him. Even before reaching school age, they'd already acquired a sense of what was socially appropriate—and knew that this was not. Whether their awareness was innate or conditioned, they all reacted to the outsider in their midst the same way: by avoiding him.

Gayle stopped bringing him to the playground.

———

FOR SEVERAL YEARS AFTER ELI'S FIRST appointment with Dr. Pober, Gayle couldn't talk about Williams syndrome without breaking down in tears. Some mornings she would wake up to a fresh wave of sadness, as though she were learning the diagnosis for the first time. She would open her eyes and feel a vague heaviness, a generalized dread. It felt as heartbreaking after a year as after a day. She started taking antidepressants.

She couldn't curb the nagging question: *Why me? Why did I have a child with Williams?* She started taking antianxiety medication. For a while she and Eli both took the same prescription. His, in lower doses, treated his hyperactivity and repetitive behaviors: rocking back and forth, kicking his legs, picking the skin around his fingers. Hers treated her endless worry for Eli's safety, and for his future.

After learning that their son had a genetic disorder, both she and Alan worried that they had caused it somehow. Alan blamed the various drugs he had experimented with in the past. Gayle wracked her brain for any bad karma she'd accrued, or—more practically—any family history of intellectual disability. But none of it could have given Eli Williams syndrome, as they later understood. This was some consolation, but it still left the question unanswered: why them?

Gayle and Alan separated when Eli was eight. And although some studies have reported astronomical divorce rates among parents of disabled children, Gayle didn't blame Williams syndrome for the split. She didn't like to talk in detail about the divorce, which left her as Eli's sole provider, with full legal and physical custody. But she believed she and Alan just became different people over time, and probably would have grown apart regardless of the challenges of raising a son with special needs. While he was in the picture, Alan was loving and patient with his son's developmental delays.

After the divorce, Alan's presence in Gayle and Eli's life was largely limited to the pages of the scrapbook Gayle had begun when Eli was a baby—a book that had since been relegated to a box in the garage, behind the Christmas ornaments. The early pages show a young couple embracing the joys of parenthood: cradling Eli at his first Christmas, picking pumpkins with him as a toddler, posing with him next to Big Bird at Sesame Place theme park.

In later pages, their smiles look plastered on—more noticeably so in contrast to the thousand-watt grin of their chipmunk-cheeked child. A page from the year before their divorce shows Gayle with Alan at a hard-core hip-hop festival. Alan, by this time, was a die-hard devotee of the genre; Gayle was not, but tried to be supportive. In the photo she smiles thinly, her face puffy (a side effect of antidepressants) and her eyes red (a side effect of, well, depression).

The scrapbook ends here. In fact, it can't accurately be described as a book. It remains a loose collection of laminated pages, never bound together. Gayle gave up on the project, which lost its charm after her marriage dissolved and the family shrank to two. In any case, she was too busy taking care of Eli to bother with bedazzling its block letters.

———

BY THE TIME GAYLE BECAME a single mother, she had a good job with a large insurance company, evaluating policies and calculating risk. Without a college degree, she'd worked her way up from a clerical position on the strength of her work ethic and sharp intelligence.

Highly conscious of the image she projected to the world, despite her nonconformist tendencies, she recognized the value of fitting in. She chose her outfits carefully and always woke up early to devote ample time to her hair and makeup regimens. For work, she skipped over the concert T-shirts in her wardrobe to pick twinsets instead. She covered her tattoos. Her hair hid the discs in her earlobes.

She was no longer quite the "bigmouthed bitch" she'd been called—and called herself—in her youth. Her reputation was so deeply rooted, however, that when a cousin of hers was feuding with some of the other moms in her daughters' dance program, and felt nervous about facing them when she picked the girls up after class, her husband said, "Bring Gayle with you. She'll take care of it." Gayle had to remind them that she hadn't been in a fight since high school, and most of those weren't very physical. She could usually get out of a scrape with a few well-chosen insults and intimidations.

But her family and her oldest friends still saw her as the teenager who teased her hair high and slathered on thick eyeliner and purple lipstick. They pictured the girl in the Catholic school uniform who snarled, "What are you lookin' at?" whenever someone gave her a sidelong glance. They thought of her as the girl the nuns busted for smoking, the one who routinely got detention for pushing her knee socks down to her ankles. They remembered the girl who got kicked off a city bus for fighting.

Gayle had resisted authority especially, refusing to blindly obey rules she didn't agree with. And although she had already mellowed and matured by the time Eli was born, the irony wasn't lost on her that his disability forced her to work with the authorities, on whom she depended for his services. Diplomacy and tact became well-honed strengths. But that didn't mean the bigmouthed bitch was no longer within her. That part of Gayle lived alongside the responsible part, the professional who knew how to play by the rules. In battling bureaucracy on Eli's behalf, whenever diplomacy failed, the bitch was back.

Although she was raised Catholic and educated at parochial school, Gayle had never been devout. After Eli was baptized, she never stepped foot in church again. Still, she believed in an order to the universe, a reason things happened. Looking back at her initial dismay that Eli's disability would cramp her rock-and-roll lifestyle—that her son might not grow up to be *cool*—Gayle cringed at her own shallowness. Who, God or otherwise, would have entrusted that tough-talking young woman with the care of this uniquely vulnerable little boy?

She sometimes thought of her sweet, cheerful son and almost couldn't imagine how their paths had crossed. It seemed like a cosmic clerical error.

———

AT SEVEN, ELI SUDDENLY BEGAN SPEAKING in sentences. One day he was barely verbal; then, almost overnight, he seemed to have grasped the English language in its entirety—vocabulary, grammar, inflection. By this time, however, Gayle no longer took it as a sign that he would beat the developmental odds. She couldn't identify the exact moment when that hope slipped away. Every time Eli mastered a new skill, belated as it was, Gayle had been thrilled. Some part of her still hadn't stopped collecting evidence against his diagnosis, long after she'd carried the envelope full of photographs to her first appointment with Dr. Pober.

But, every time, she butted up against the truth: the pace of Eli's development almost perfectly matched Dr. Pober's projection. He wasn't catching up. He was following the standard Williams track with almost textbook precision. Gayle never stopped celebrating the milestones, but she stopped seeing them as proof that Eli was on a path to a normal life. Too many things weren't normal. They became more obvious as he grew.

Most people with Williams are slow to start talking, partly because of their developmental delays and partly because of their weak muscles and poor motor skills. Their tongue and larynx muscles take longer than normal to gain strength and dexterity, so their ability to speak is even further delayed than it otherwise would be. In fact, some linguists believe those muscles may be less at fault for speech delays than the muscles in their hands, since rhythmic hand banging is a precursor to babbling in typical infants. Tellingly, delays in rhythmic hand banging correspond to the speech delays of children with Williams.

Once they start talking, though, usually about two years later than normal, they don't stop. Eli quickly became a fluent conversationalist, which expanded his social repertoire considerably. Still, he struggled with basic spatial and motor skills. At five, he took an IQ test that put his skills in block design and puzzle completion in the bottom tenth of a percentile for his age. His evaluator noted, "He seemed to enjoy playing with the test materials, but was not able to follow directions for how to use them." Nonetheless, Eli "smiled and laughed and seemed delighted to come to the testing session." At eight, he took the test again, with the same dismal results in spatial perception and reasoning. But now his verbal abilities were a relative strength. The evaluator noted that he was "curious, cooperative, and friendly," adding, "He smiled and talked about what he was doing as well as what he saw in the assessment room."

In these tests he harnessed his verbal abilities, imperfect as they might be, to impress his evaluators and win them over. The evaluators, who were employed by the school district and had no experience with Williams, seemed surprised by Eli's linguistic strengths and his bubbly personality, given his overall IQ in the "extremely low" range. But Gayle was well aware that a tendency to be skilled with language, despite deficiencies in spatial reasoning, math, and logic, was a signature trait of Williams. She'd come across a 1991 article in *Discover* magazine that called people with Williams "smart and mentally retarded, gifted and inept at the same time." She chafed when she read the description, but she couldn't argue with it—other than the use of the term "mentally retarded," which had since fallen out of favor.

She sometimes wondered if it might be easier to have a child whose disability was consistent across the board, even if that meant his language skills were as bad as his spatial skills. At least that way your heart wouldn't jump at the glimmers of brilliance. You would always know what to expect. And it would be easier to accept that the disorder was real, the prognosis correct. You could stop hoping the gifts would make up for the deficits.

———

EVEN WITHIN THE WILLIAMS COMMUNITY, different parents react to their child's diagnosis in vastly different ways. Some downplay its effects, insisting that their kids are "not like the other Williams kids"—that they play sports, earn As in school, and don't hug strangers. And while there are some very high-functioning people with Williams who test in the normal range of intelligence and who observe the standard rules of social engagement, descriptions like these often turn out to be exaggerations. In some cases, kids earned As because their class goals were adapted to their abilities. If they joined a sports team, they often spent most of their time on the bench, because their poor visual-spatial skills made them a liability. Some kids learned to refrain from hugging, but often they still stood too close to people or touched them too often. An exceptionally capable woman in her twenties with Williams said she still had to constantly remind herself to stand an arm's length away from the person she was talking to. Otherwise she would inevitably drift too close.

One family sent their son—the same age as Eli, with similar intellectual abilities and behavioral tendencies—to a summer sleepaway camp organized by their church. They did not inform the camp's organizers that he had Williams syndrome. In fact, they never used the word "Williams" at school or in social settings. The boy's father said it was because he didn't want his son to be labeled.

"It creates too many preconceptions," he explained. "People think that's all he is. They expect less."

So the parents told the camp counselors their son "needed a little extra help" and left it at that. At the end of the week, they picked him up and discovered that he had spent the whole week either in the infirmary, where he landed with Williams-related gastrointestinal trouble, exacerbated by greasy camp cuisine, or in the chaplain's office, where he sought refuge after being ostracized by his peers. The camp's director said he was sorry the boy had suffered, but chastised the parents for not being up-front about his condition.

"You should have told us," the director said. "We're really not equipped to handle special needs."

On the opposite end of the spectrum, some parents become so overwhelmed by their kids' limitations that they overlook their strengths. A woman named Gloria, whose daughter has Williams syndrome, was floored to discover when her daughter was just five that another girl in their small New England town also had Williams. The two girls were even the same age. Gloria was so thrilled to find a ready-made friend for her daughter that she contacted the other girl's mother and arranged a play date at the local McDonald's.

While the kids cavorted on the bright plastic playscape, the women chatted. Gloria asked about the other mother's plans for her daughter's education. Would she insist on inclusion, meaning the girl would take all or most classes in a regular classroom with her typical peers? Was she already working with an occupational therapist? What about a speech therapist? The other woman shrugged. She hadn't thought much about the future, it seemed. Her gaze drifted to the ball pit, where the girls squealed with delight while they played.

"She's retarded," the woman said nonchalantly. "There's nothing I can do to fix that."

Gloria, horrified, never set up another play date. She didn't see the woman again until a chance encounter in the grocery store a few years later. There the woman's daughter was running wild in the dairy section, licking the lids of the yogurt containers. The woman did nothing to stop her or to discipline her, as if she simply expected this kind of behavior. Gloria's own daughter watched with wide eyes, bewildered by the scene. She knew these antics weren't acceptable; she'd be in trouble if she tried anything like it. In comparison to the other girl, she was a model of decorum.

The other mother was apparently oblivious to the immense capacity people with Williams have for personal growth. While some forms of intellectual disability cause people to plateau relatively early, people with Williams keep learning all their lives. The rate of learning tends to be much slower than normal, of course. And it doesn't come easily; it needs to be nurtured and encouraged. Gloria was painfully aware that nothing in her daughter's life would be easy, but she also lived with hope for the future. So did her daughter—and she achieved many of the goals she set for herself. In middle school she was in a typical classroom with nondisabled peers, where she was challenged but stimulated. She auditioned for parts in school plays, and got them. She made friends.

———

ONE SUNDAY AFTERNOON, MORE THAN A decade after Eli's diagnosis, Gayle sorted through a plastic bin filled with Eli's medical records and school evaluations. Her weekends, like the rest of her free time these days, centered on Eli and on shuttling him to the special-needs sports leagues and Williams syndrome events that eclipsed her former social life. In the downtime from these activities, she tried to catch up on her rest—and to maintain some semblance of order in her home, where she was perpetually organizing and de-cluttering from the chaos of raising a kid. She was forever selling outgrown clothes on eBay and furtively removing Eli's old toys: the ones he never touched anymore but would insist he couldn't part with. Today she was tackling the documents she'd been shoving into a bin for years, which she meant to file neatly away. But she couldn't help reading through each one first, reliving the trajectory of Eli's life so far.

While Gayle sat at the dining table, leafing through the files, Eli, now twelve, perched at the edge of a blue recliner across the open living and dining room, facing a collapsible TV tray that held Gayle's laptop. He stabbed at the keys. He was a proficient typist, and could spell most words phonetically, letting autocorrect do the rest. This came in handy when he searched the internet for floor-scrubbing videos, as he did compulsively. At the moment he was on YouTube, looking for videos of his school's custodian, whom he called Mr. Dave. He either didn't realize that someone would have had to record a video for it to appear online, or he was sure that someone had seen fit to memorialize Mr. Dave as he scrubbed the school floor. Eli, for one, idolized him for his Tennant 5400 automatic scrubber: the top of the line, according to Eli.

Eli's obsession with floor scrubbers—and with his other favorite YouTube subject, vacuum cleaners—had evolved from an aversion earlier in his life. Because of his acute sense of hearing, the sound of vacuums in particular had made him plug his ears and cry as a toddler. Over time, his sensitivity lessened and he became intensely drawn to what he'd once feared. Now he craved the drone of the vacuum and the whir of the floor scrubber.

This craving for certain sounds is common in Williams, and goes hand in hand with a tendency to be highly musical. Like Eli, many people with Williams sing constantly, and they tend to be good at it. The late neurologist and author Oliver Sacks, in his book *Musicophilia: Tales of Music and the Brain*, called people with Williams "a hypermusical species." A number of them have been labeled musical savants, with innate gifts that include perfect pitch and an ability to play instruments by ear. One woman with Williams, now in her sixties, is an opera singer who has memorized more than two thousand pieces in twenty-eight languages. She also taught herself to play the accordion.

And while researchers haven't conclusively determined whether musical talent is more common in Williams (one study reported that three in ten people with Williams had perfect pitch, compared to one in a thousand among the rest of us, while another study found that people with Williams were in fact less likely than the general population to have perfect pitch or rhythm), there is a wealth of evidence that people with Williams have a much stronger emotional response to music than the average person does. Even young children with Williams who can't talk yet suddenly start crying when they hear a sad song. Older children often beg their parents not to play ballads about heartache, which they find too devastating. On the other hand, upbeat songs will get most people with Williams on their feet and dancing.

But everyone has their preferences: one girl with Williams, a little younger than Eli, had a visceral reaction to classical music; she'd scream if her mother happened to turn on the classical radio station. At a school assembly, when the band began playing a classical melody, she clapped her hands over her ears and bellowed, "SON OF A BITCH!!!"

Eli, who once participated in a study on musical ability in Williams conducted by Vanderbilt University researchers, didn't quite have perfect pitch, but he was a strong singer and a natural drummer, with what the researchers called an "innate musical orientation."

Unlike the girl who hated classical music, Eli enjoyed nearly every musical genre—everything from punk rock to opera, especially as performed by Luciano Pavarotti, who was another frequent subject of his YouTube searches. He could listen to the tenor sing the same song over and over, long after Gayle wanted to stuff her ears with cotton. Of course, there were certain high-pitched sounds that Eli couldn't stand. A crying baby was torture to him. But he couldn't get enough of floor scrubbers.

"Mom, how do you spell 'custodian'?" he called out.

Gayle spelled the word without lifting her head from the records. She had just come across a fat envelope from her congresswoman, to whom she had written when an old boss hassled her about all the time she was missing for Eli's doctors' appointments. The envelope contained a stack of materials on the Family and Medical Leave Act that outlined Gayle's legal entitlement to care for a special-needs son. She skimmed the documents and scowled, remembering the arguments she'd had with her inflexible supervisor, who seemed to think that carting Eli to specialists every other week was an extravagance Gayle could easily dispense with. At one point he finally conceded, "Look, I don't know what it's like to have a kid with special needs. And, honestly, I hope I never do."

"I hope you never do, either," Gayle said. She meant it. She took no comfort in knowing that, after she left the company, the man's son was diagnosed with special needs of his own.

Across the room, Eli pecked at the keyboard: "mr dave custodian scrubbing mashene." He craned his neck, bringing his face inches from the screen as he examined each video that popped up.

Gayle now worked for a different company, which allowed her to work from home one or two days a week and to rearrange her hours when she had to take Eli to appointments. She was grateful for the flexibility and grateful to have her mother, whom Eli called Mimi, and a constellation of aunts, uncles, and cousins close by. She relied on Mimi to watch Eli while she worked. Often it was Mimi who met Eli at the bus stop, got him a snack, and supervised him for the afternoon while Gayle sat at her desk in a corner of the living room, scrolling through spreadsheets and ignoring the sounds of floor-scrubbing videos and Eli's endless singing from the other side of the room.

———

ELI GAVE UP ON HIS SEARCH for Mr. Dave the custodian and his scrubbing machine, which had yielded no relevant results. He typed "Tennant 5400" into the search bar instead. He knew this search would be fruitful. He'd done it many times before.

Soon the familiar teal housing, emblazoned with "5400" in white block numbers, appeared on the screen. It glided across a warehouse floor like a giant mechanized snail, leaving a glistening trail in its wake. Eli shrieked with joy, as if it were a novel sight. The camera panned to the back of the scrubber, to the corrugated black hoses Eli adored so much that he often asked Gayle to draw them. With its twenty-one-gallon cleaning solution tank, four-sided breakaway squeegee, adjustable brush pressure, and the horsepower to clean up to 30,000 square feet an hour, the Tennant 5400 was, to Eli's mind, the Cadillac of floor scrubbers. Best of all was the gurgling whoosh it made and the crinkly texture of its ridged plastic hoses—like bendy straws through which it slurped soapy water up from the floor.

"See, Tennant 5400!" Eli shouted to no one in particular. "I can't wait to use it someday. When I am a janitor."

He found an image of the floor scrubber's console and zoomed in on the dials and knobs. He pressed his index finger to the computer screen, pretending to flip the "on" switch. His finger left an oily print on the screen.

"Beep!" he said, pushing a button.

"Beep!" he said again, pretending to turn a dial.

Gayle looked up from her pile of papers and watched him beeping cheerfully at the screen. When Dr. Pober first told her Eli would most likely do an unskilled, repetitive job as an adult, Gayle couldn't imagine him working as a checkout clerk, a fast-food cook, or a custodian. She had been sure there was something better in store for him. Now, watching Eli dream of a career as a janitor, she realized she would be thrilled to see him cleaning floors for a living if it made him happy. Her disdain for menial labor had been replaced by a new fear: that even this job might be beyond his abilities. He didn't really want to *clean* a floor, she thought. He just wanted to admire the floor scrubber. And he didn't have the coordination to push it down a hallway in even lanes, or the self-discipline to keep going until every square inch was clean. He'd abandon his post in an instant if he saw someone he wanted to talk to.

If not janitorial work, though, then what? There were sheltered workshops for people with intellectual disabilities, where he could stuff envelopes or roll napkins around silverware for less than minimum wage. But even if he had the self-control to stay seated and on task, would he find any fulfillment in it?

Gayle reassured herself that he was still a child, that there was time for him to mature and grow. Maybe in a few years he'd have the sustained attention and impulse control he would need to do something more meaningful. She shuffled through psychological evaluations that listed his distractibility and short attention span as "areas of concern" and school reports documenting the meltdowns he still had when he wasn't allowed to play with a pinwheel or spin the propeller of a toy helicopter. She stuffed these into manila folders and shoved them in a file box, as though putting them away with enough force would lock them securely in the past.

"Mom, can I have a snack?" Eli bleated from across the room.

"Do you have your pants on?" she asked, again without looking up from the stack of papers. She heard a heavy sigh.

"I will get them on."

"Oh, thanks so much," she said, smoothing out one of the creased pages.

Eli's tendency to forgo pants at home didn't really faze Gayle. He found the khakis he typically wore to school constricting, so he usually changed into fleece pants at home. Sometimes he just pulled the school pants off and left it at that. Gayle would have humored him if she hadn't been afraid he might get so used to going without pants that he'd take them off in the school bathroom one day, forget to put them back on, and stroll the halls in his underwear. So she tried to reinforce the habit. His seminudity was inoffensive now, but a day would come when it would be more unseemly.

"I can have a little cereal now?" Eli said. "I put my pants on!" Gayle, distracted by an old bill from Eli's cardiologist, didn't answer right away.

"I did it, Mom! I did this for you!" Eli insisted, standing and pointing to his pants proudly. "Mom!"

"Eli, I'm in the middle of something," Gayle said, finally looking up.

"She's not being nice to me!" he said in an outraged voice, referring to his mother in the third person, as he tended to do when he had harsh words for her. He thrust his head forward, head-butting the air to emphasize his frustration.

"Oh, you need a pill, don't you?" she asked rhetorically, looking at the clock. It was time for another Ritalin. He took three doses a day to help curb his distractibility. Gayle gave the pill to Eli with a glass of water. Then she poured him a bowl of Chex and set it at the edge of the dining table, where the milk wouldn't slosh onto her records.

Apart from the pile of papers on the table and a galaxy of brightly colored plastic Bristle Blocks that Eli had spread across the floor, their condo was clean and cozy. Eli's tastes dominated the décor: his vast collection of toys, and the many drawings of Cookie Monster, overshadowed any trace of Gayle's own personal style. There were no concert posters to remind her of her hard-rock days, although their legacy lingered in small ways. (She'd named her Wi-Fi network Alice Cooper.) Gayle had once scoffed at parents whose lives were entirely subsumed by their kids—but that was before she had a child with special needs.

When it came to his passions, Eli was strong-willed and demanding. A home without multiple vacuum cleaners seemed to him a barren wasteland. And Gayle didn't have the heart to deprive him. A row of cast-off vacuums from his relatives, and a Dustbuster that had been a gift from his school bus driver, lined the kitchen wall. Eli's favorite was Gayle's actual, working vacuum: an Oreck that he treated like a household pet.

"Where's that little Oreck? Oh, there you are!" he would coo, and smile lovingly at the vacuum. He'd push it back and forth on the kitchen's linoleum floor—turned off, since the sound of it turned on was still too much for him in close range. He furnished the vrooming noise himself.

He also developed passing fixations that changed focus every few months. Right now he was obsessed with tiki heads, the Polynesian totems popular at luaus, and in particular with flaming tiki heads, whose oversize gaping mouths doubled as fire pits. The position of honor on the living room wall was currently occupied by a cardboard cutout of a tiki that Gayle had made at Eli's request. On the floor were several plastic milk jugs she had carved into jack-o'-lantern faces. Inside, she had placed slips of red and yellow construction paper cut into the wavy outlines of flames that fanned up from the base—*voilà*, flaming tiki heads. Eli treasured these, although they would eventually fall out of favor. Only the vacuums and spinners would endure.

The doorway between the kitchen and living room was hung with paper spirals that swirled languidly when anyone walked through: "my twirlies," Eli called them. Some Gayle had cut out from paper plates and decorated; others came precut and glitter-covered from a store that sold party supplies. Both varieties were beloved. A few lay mangled on a side table, having been handled until the spirals flattened and the paper tore, but that only meant they were favorites. Eli couldn't help but touch the things he loved, and he lacked the finesse to be gentle with them. His appreciation was literally heavy-handed; the object of his affection was often destroyed.

Best loved of all was the floor scrubber Gayle had made him out of an oversize cardboard box to which she had attached spiraling cords and the tubes from her uncle's old CPAP breathing machine, in imitation of the wires and hoses of the Tennant 5400. On top of the box, to model the buttons and dials, she affixed a kitchen timer and made labels: "start/stop," "wet/dry/squeegee," and "speed: high/medium/ low." On the front, she glued a red flashing bike light. Eli entertained himself for hours by pushing the scrubber around the apartment, making a whirring sound as he went, bumping into furniture and occasionally into his mother, whom he sweetly asked to move.

"I'm scrubbing, Mom!" he would say. She usually obliged him and stepped aside.

The way Eli lit up when she made something for him was one of the greatest pleasures of her life. His elation pushed the boundaries of the human capacity for happiness. Although he told Gayle he loved her at least a dozen times a day no matter what she did, she couldn't resist making the extra effort to see him beam with delight.

Part of her, too, felt that she owed it to him—or that the universe owed it to him—to make his life as joyful as possible. Because what if this was all there was? What if the future didn't hold the endless floor-cleaning fun he expected? She could barely admit this motive to herself, even while she scoured the towering shelves at Home Depot for wheels to make his cardboard floor scrubber complete. Deep down, though, she felt compelled to make him as happy as possible here and now, just in case this was the best his life was going to get.

Five

A Genetic Street Lamp

I n the decades after John Williams published a paper on his elfin-faced patients, researchers paid the syndrome relatively little at-tention. Two breakthroughs launched it from obscurity into the scientific spotlight.

The first came in 1985, when Ursula Bellugi, a linguist and neuro-scientist at the Salk Institute for·Biological Studies, met a girl with Wil-liams syndrome who had been referred by Bellugi's colleague, Noam Chomsky. Bellugi was floored by the fourteen-year-old's language skills, despite her dismal spatial abilities and overall IQ of 49. When asked to draw an elephant, the girl scratched a few unrecognizable squiggles on paper. But when asked to describe an elephant, she gave a detailed, el-oquent response: "It has long gray ears, fan ears, ears that can blow in the wind. It has a long trunk that can pick up grass, or pick up hay . . . If the elephant gets mad it could stomp. It could charge, like a bull can charge. They have long big tusks. They can damage a car—it could be dangerous." Bellugi was so fascinated by the disconnect between the girl's verbal abilities and spatial weaknesses that she spent the next de-cade building a lab dedicated to studying this cognitive conundrum.

Bellugi's startling findings spawned a wave of interest in the little-known disorder. Most provocatively, she concluded that the highs and lows of intellectual ability in Williams were strong evidence in support of a theory of multiple intelligences first proposed by Harvard psychologist Howard Gardner in 1983. Gardner's theory was a radically unorthodox way of conceiving how the brain was wired: not as a unified intellectual force, with overlying intelligence guiding interconnected cognitive functions, but as a hodgepodge of distinct, segregated abilities. If correct, his theory would have revolutionized the way students were taught and intelligence was measured, since standardized tests had been designed to gauge intelligence with a single number—a meaningless assessment, in Gardner's view.

His theory struck Bellugi as the perfect model to explain the dramatic variability of Williams cognition. Rather than exist on a level plain, Gardner believed, and Williams syndrome seemed to demonstrate, that each independent type of intelligence—mathematical, linguistic, spatial, musical, even interpersonal—formed its own separate peak or valley, meaning that aptitude in one area didn't necessarily correlate with aptitude in another.

This theory, and the support that Williams syndrome provided, sparked a controversy among intelligence experts, most of whom had long believed in a "general intelligence factor" that meant tests of cognitive strength in almost any area could predict overall intelligence. This school of thought held that researchers could even extrapolate from the general factor to predict someone's future quality of life—everything from success in school and work to the chances of divorcing or having illegitimate children.

Bellugi and other researchers believed Williams might provide the evidence that would turn this theory on its head. Despite having roughly the same average IQ as people with Down syndrome, who showed consistent impairment across cognitive areas, many people with Williams performed significantly better on certain tests, such as those that measured concrete vocabulary. When asked to name ten animals, people with Down syndrome tended to choose generic nouns: cat, dog, "horsie," etc. People with Williams syndrome were apt to offer more specific, exotic names: weasel, salamander, Chihuahua, ibex, yak.

People with Williams also proved to be remarkably creative, expressive storytellers. They were intrinsically gifted performers, modulating their vocal pitch, volume, and stress (for example: "OH, my POOOOOOR little wabbit") to heighten the drama of their stories. Asked to tell a story on the spot, a teenage girl with Williams invented a fairy tale about a chocolate princess in a chocolate world that was in danger of melting, but who saved her kingdom by changing the color of the sun. (The same girl, at fourteen, composed her own music but had the visual-spatial skills of a five-year-old and couldn't make change for a dollar.)

One linguist asked kids with either Williams or Down syndrome the question, "What if you were a bird?" Typical answers from kids with Down syndrome were "Fly in the air" and "I not a bird, you have wing." Kids with Williams were able to offer up more elaborate scenarios, such as "I would fly and if I liked a boy, I would land on his head and start chirping" and "I would fly where my parents could never find me. Birds want to be independent."

Bellugi and her colleagues were justifiably impressed. But over time they began to realize that people with Williams were not the linguistic savants they had appeared to be. Their gifts turned out to be limited to certain aspects of language, including the relatively sophisticated ability to grasp metaphors and hypothetical statements, while other elements of language eluded them. They struggled in particular with what is called relational vocabulary and includes concepts such as "under," "over," "behind," and "above," which parallel the spatial relationships that typically stymie people with Williams. Shown a picture of an apple in a bowl, people with Williams offered a variety of descriptions, including "The bowl is in the apple" and "The apple is around the bowl"—nearly every possible description but the correct one. This discovery posed a direct challenge to the assumption that the brain's language center was largely insulated from other regions, including the area that processes spatial relationships.

However, people with Williams also struggled with nonspatial parts of speech, including conjunctions such as "and" and "or," and disjunctions such as "neither . . . nor." They had trouble with pronouns. And, despite their chattering, fluent conversational style, they often failed to correctly answer a pointed question, particularly one of the *wh-* questions: who, what, where, when, and why. One school-age boy, asked when Columbus sailed to America, answered "*Niña, Pinta, Santa Maria.*" Despite an evident familiarity with the facts of the voyage, he was baffled by a sentence structure most of us have mastered by the age of three. Linguists take failures like these, in contrast to striking abilities with other parts of speech, as a sign that however the Williams brain processes language, it's very different from the way a normal brain does—and that people with Williams are more impaired than they appear to be in casual conversation.

In the decades that have passed since Bellugi first encountered a child with Williams, both she and the scientific community at large have come to discount Gardner's theory of multiple intelligences in the face of compelling counterevidence. Study after study has shown that strength in one area of intelligence does, in fact, predict strength in the others, even in people with Williams. The evidence is unequivocal enough that intelligence researcher Linda Gottfredson could proclaim with confidence, in a 1998 article for *Scientific American*, "Despite some popular assertions, a single factor for intelligence, called g, can be measured with IQ tests and does predict success in life."

Bellugi, now in her eighties, acknowledges that the general intelligence theory appears to have been right all along. The revolution in education and assessment never materialized: old-school teaching and testing styles may be imperfect, but not because of the fundamental assumptions they make about intelligence, as Bellugi now agrees. Contemplating her error in retrospect, she has come to believe that she was so won over by her Williams subjects that she initially overestimated their abilities.

"It's my fault. I'm the guilty party," she confessed cheerfully in an interview. "But in an interesting way. I'm not embarrassed about it. When I started out, a hundred years ago, I was just so impressed with the Williams kids."

She's not the only one to have been sidetracked by the charisma of her research subjects. Just as Eli charmed his evaluators into overestimating his cognitive abilities, people with Williams routinely, if inadvertently, sabotage studies by ignoring the task at hand and focusing all their attention on the researcher instead. A deaf scientist once noted that the people with Williams who came through her lab. persisted in talking to her even after she signaled that she couldn't hear or speak. "They seem to be fascinated, continuing to smile and talk to me, all the time looking right into my face while they try to imitate my signs," she wrote.

In one study, people with Williams consistently turned the tables on their interviewer and began asking her questions such as "Do you have a dog?" "What's your favorite singer?" and "Where were you born?" When asked to describe a significant moment in their lives, several of the interviewees said, "Being here is the best thing that ever happened to me."

These studies often reveal less about the nature of Williams than they do about the effects of charm and flattery on a supposedly objective investigator, turning tests of cognition into sociological case studies that demonstrate how easily a warm smile and a kind word can divert our attention and blind us to faults. And they prove that, despite not being perfect speakers, most people with Williams are smooth talkers, abundantly capable of harnessing their strengths to distract from their weaknesses.

––––

THE SECOND BREAKTHROUGH that catapulted Williams out of scientific obscurity was the discovery, in 1993—three years after the official launch of the Human Genome Project—that everyone with the disorder was missing one copy of the elastin gene. Called ELN for short, this gene regulates the body's production of elastin, the pliable protein that makes skin bounce back to its original position when you pinch it. It's especially vital in blood vessels, where it provides for stretch and helps facilitate blood flow.

After pinpointing the elastin gene deletion, scientists raced to study the surrounding DNA. They soon found that people with Williams were missing twenty-six to twenty-eight neighboring genes on one of their two copies of chromosome 7. The missing genes represent a tiny gap in the chain of more than a thousand genes on one half of this chromosome alone. And given that chromosome 7 is just one of the twenty-three paired chromosomes that contain the roughly 20,000 genes that make us human, the gap narrows to what is essentially a paper cut in the human genome, which is why geneticists call it a microdeletion. But its effects are astronomical by contrast.

A tiny number of people with Williams have "atypical deletions," meaning they're missing some but not all of the Williams genes. This subset is so rare that it doesn't account for the spectrum of abilities among people with Williams that has long perplexed researchers— why some people with Williams have an IQ of 35 and others an IQ of 95, for example, given that all, or mostly all, are missing the same twenty-six genes. Geneticists agree that at least part of the answer has to do with environment and upbringing, and part has to do with the strength of the extant copy of those genes. People with atypical deletions are in high demand as research subjects, though, since they help geneticists zoom in even further on the correlation between missing genes and their effects.

What makes Williams especially popular with geneticists is that the findings from this rare disorder have far-reaching repercussions for the rest of us. Williams research has so far helped identify genes that play a role in hypertension, low bone density, and high blood sugar, in addition to shedding light on the complicated interplay between gene structure and social behavior.

"Williams syndrome is a street lamp," says Dr. Pober, the geneticist who diagnosed Eli and is one of the leaders in Williams research. "It shows us that these characteristics and behaviors are linked to these twenty-six genes. Then the problem is matching up genotype and phenotype: which gene deletion leads to anxiety and phobias, which one leads to musicality. Of course, it's not always a one-to-one match."

As yet, the elastin gene is the only one of the bunch whose function is incontrovertibly accepted by geneticists. Other relationships are still disputed or require further testing. But each of the unique symptoms of the disorder—everything from heart problems and an elevated calcium level to hypersensitive ears and a tendency to develop debilitating anxiety, as well as deficiencies in depth perception, impulse control, planning, and problem solving—could potentially be traced back, at least in part, to the genes that aren't there. Even the extraordinary abilities that come with Williams, especially in language and music, can paradoxically be traced to those missing genes: people who have an extra copy of the same genes, instead of a missing set, have strong visual-spatial skills but severely delayed speech and expressive language, and they tend to suffer from social phobia. A number of people with a duplicate of the Williams genes, in fact, meet the criteria for autism.

And while the possible causes of autism are hotly debated, there is compelling evidence of at least some genetic basis. The onetime theory, devastating to many parents, that it was the result of childhood neglect—specifically from uncaring "refrigerator mothers"—has been widely discounted in favor of biological explanations. Research shows that autism is one of the most heritable of all neurological disorders. A study of identical twins found that when one was diagnosed with autism, the other was diagnosed roughly nine times out of ten. Because twins overlap in both nature and nurture, another study examined fraternal twins, who share less DNA than identical twins but, presumably, the same environment. When one fraternal twin had autism, the study found, the other had it between two and three times out of ten. It seemed likely, then, that shared genes more than shared upbringing explained the coincidence. Non-twin siblings, parents, and even distant relatives of people with autism are also more likely to have autism than the general population. So researchers are actively searching for the genes that might play a role, particularly in the region deleted in Williams. But while geneticists have tentatively identified many genes that could be implicated in autism, scientists have yet to agree that any of these plays a definitive role.

One of the Williams genes is among those correlated, to some degree, with autism. This finding was no great surprise to Williams experts, since people with Williams often demonstrate symptoms more commonly associated with autism: repetitive movements such as rocking, hand flapping, or picking at skin; perseveration, or repeating a word, phrase, or gesture over and over; echolalia, or repeating words that others say (or lines from songs, or fragments of movie dialogue); and a fascination with things that spin—as well as with mechanical objects such as vacuum cleaners. Researchers examining the overlap between the two disorders have concluded that some people with Williams also meet the criteria for autism spectrum disorders, although the proportions have varied widely from study to study, from as few as 5 percent to as many as 50 percent of people with Williams.

Eli is among the many people with Williams who display some of the classic signs of autism. Even before he could talk, he was so preoccupied with vacuums, floor scrubbers, and spinning things (one of his first words was "twirly") that he threw volcanic tantrums whenever he encountered one of these beloved objects and was not allowed to stare at it, touch it, or hold it. But he's never been diagnosed with autism. Dr. Pober considers a double diagnosis both futile and somewhat absurd. Many ailments share symptoms, she argues. Both mononucleosis and depression sap people's energy, but that doesn't mean someone suffering from one is also suffering from the other. Likewise, Williams is its own distinct disorder, even if it has some of the attributes of autism. The two disorders even differ anatomically: autopsies have shown that the brains of people with Williams are smaller than normal, while the brains of people with autism are larger than normal.

A number of genetic disorders, in fact, have symptoms in common with autism. Rett syndrome, which impairs motor function and affects girls exclusively, includes some autistic features, as does fragile X syndrome, which causes intellectual disability. But autistic traits are just part of the larger constellation of symptoms that make each of these syndromes unique. Similarly, a Williams diagnosis trumps an autism diagnosis, Pober says, since—in addition to some shared behavioral issues—Williams also entails health problems that autism doesn't, which require careful oversight. But she doesn't argue with the idea that studying the areas where the two disorders intersect, and where they diverge, might hold the keys to a better understanding of both.

In a 2006 case study of a six-year-old girl who met some of the criteria for autism and some for Williams, DNA testing revealed that she was missing a handful of the Williams genes as well as fourteen other genes "downstream" from those usually deleted in Williams. She was overly friendly with strangers, but she didn't have the elfin facial features common to Williams. She also lacked the medical problems that usually accompany Williams, and her verbal skills were strikingly worse than usual for Williams. Although affectionate, she had little interest in or aptitude for conversation. Researchers concluded that one or more of her missing genes might have made her susceptible to autism, or exacerbated her autistic symptoms, during the early stages of her development.

One gene in particular has long been linked to autism, albeit inconclusively: the gene that codes for the protein involved in transporting the neurotransmitter serotonin, which is active in the nerve pathways involved in emotions, sleep, and anxiety, among other things. People with autism commonly have unusually high levels of serotonin in their blood, which has led some researchers to suspect that a variant of this gene might be related to the development of autism (and to a number of psychiatric disorders, including depression, although these links remain controversial). In 2013, geneticists studying the DNA of people with severe autism came across two boys diagnosed with autism who turned out to have the classic Williams syndrome deletion—a surprising discovery, since neither showed any trace of the Williams personality and both were incapable of speech. However, both boys had elevated blood serotonin levels, as well as the same variant of the serotonin transporter gene commonly found in people with autism. The researchers concluded it was possible that this gene variant could have overridden the effects of the missing Williams genes, producing autism symptoms instead.

In terms of social behavior and language aptitude, of course, people with Williams and people with autism are about as opposite as they could possibly be: hypersocial versus antisocial, loquacious versus laconic. Eye-tracking studies confirm that they look at the world very differently. When shown scenes of people interacting, people with autism spend less time than average watching the faces of the people involved; they pay more attention to inanimate objects. People with Williams, on the other hand, are fixated on the faces of the people in the scenes, which they watch for much longer than normal.

Studies of language processing in the two groups have revealed dissimilarities that match their social differences. A 2011 study looked at how both groups reacted to sentences ending with a word that fit semantically but was contextually unexpected: for example, "I take my coffee with cream and paper." Most people, when hooked up to devices that measure electrical waveforms in the brain, show a spike in brain activity when they hear the word "paper," demonstrating surprise. The researchers expected people with Williams to show a similar pattern, given their language abilities, while they believed people with autism would react less noticeably. They were half-right. People with autism were less surprised than normal, but people with Williams were much *more* surprised than the control subjects. The experiment showed that both groups process language in unusual ways, but very differently from each other.

While people with Williams tend to be more proficient speakers, the neuroscientist Carolyn Mervis argues that they have just as much trouble engaging in "successful conversation" as people with autism. In Williams, conversational barriers include overfamiliarity and the persistent repetition of questions or phrases. When they themselves are asked questions, people with Williams have trouble coming up with responses that continue the conversation. Like people with Asperger's syndrome, people with Williams can't always tell the difference between relevant and irrelevant information to bring up in conversation. Neither are very good at choosing conversational topics that might interest someone else.

For all their charms, people with Williams syndrome have as much trouble as people with autism in making meaningful social connections. They just arrive at this trouble from different directions. And, as Gayle learned in the case study she never signed up for, they get there fast.

Six

Eli Turns Twelve

Eli turned twelve in February 2011, but because he wanted an outdoor, pirate-themed party—with a fire in the fire pit—his birthday party was postponed until Memorial Day weekend. Mimi hosted it at the modest ranch house she shared with five other relatives, a twenty-minute drive from Gayle and Eli's apartment. Two more relatives, Eli's great-aunt and great-uncle, lived just across the street. Their hilltop cul-de-sac was so quiet that the only sounds before Gayle and Eli's arrival were the tinkling of wind chimes and the occasional yapping of a neighbor's Pomeranian. It was safe to assume that when Eli bolted from the car bellowing "WE'RE HERE!" the whole neighborhood heard. It was also likely that they weren't surprised, since this was how Eli announced himself whenever he came over.

Eli yanked open the screen door to the house and let it slam behind him. He ran into his aunt Jean—really his eighty-year-old great-great-aunt—on the half flight of stairs to the living room.

"Where's my present?" he asked. His tone wasn't demanding, just intensely curious. He'd been asking about presents for weeks now. Ever since he could talk, in fact, he had asked endless frantic questions about the topics that preoccupied him. This birthday party was one; he'd been looking forward to it with great enthusiasm, but even joyful anticipation sent him into an anxious tailspin. Dr. Pober called it anticipatory anxiety, and it was one of the more debilitating behavioral symptoms of Williams. The endless questions could be annoying, especially to Gayle, who often fielded the same inquiry dozens of times a day, but for Eli it was merely an attempt to alleviate his anxiety. To keep his fixations from swirling endlessly in his head, he phrased them as questions and sent them out into the world. That just seemed to externalize the feedback loop, however. Gayle did her best to redirect his attention, but it was usually a lost cause.

Jean, who knew the routine, let the rude greeting slide.

"Hello, my Eli," she said, bending to hug him.

His dark hair was curlier than usual on this humid, unseasonably warm May afternoon. Jean plucked at the curls, which sprang back into place while he scanned the living room over her shoulder. On the hunt for presents, he barged on, charging past Jean, then past Mimi, who was whipping cream in the kitchen for the chocolate cake she made Eli every year for his birthday. He burst out the door to the back deck, where other relatives were setting out food and plastic utensils.

A breeze ruffled the leaves of an old oak tree that shaded the deck, making the eighty-degree day comfortable. Feathery seedpods drifted onto a blue awning that sheltered a bowl of chips and taco dip on the picnic table. Eli darted around the deck, peeking under the table just in case any presents were hidden beneath the folds of the red tablecloth.

After greeting her mother and Jean, Gayle followed Eli outside, where she began hanging a stack of brightly colored metallic curlicues he had picked out as party decorations. She taped them to the edge of the awning, where they twisted in the breeze, creating cascading spirals that momentarily diverted Eli from the search for presents.

"Mom, can I twirl these?" he asked, pointing to what was left of the stack, but with his head turned to see those already spinning above him, out of reach.

"Of course you can," she said, hanging another. Eli selected a glittering green one and dangled it from his hand, blowing on it when the wind died down.

"I hope it's not raining," he said soberly, putting his fear for the future into present tense.

"What do you think will happen if it rains?" asked Aunt Jean, who had joined the group on the back deck. Accustomed to Eli's favorite discussion topics—fans and floor scrubbers, vacuums and spinners—his relatives often tried to broaden his conversational horizons, even if only tangentially.

"Those twirlies will get wet," he said with a frown.

Gayle's uncle Chris appeared from the kitchen, bearing a plate of hot dogs, and fired up the gas grill. Chris, in his late fifties, was a former Coast Guard officer who now worked at the post office. While he waited for the hot dogs to cook, he helped himself to the taco dip and sat on the bench next to where Eli stood, still focused on the twirling spirals.

"I'm getting dizzy with all these twirlies around," Chris said.

"I know!" Eli agreed, his eyes squinting almost closed from the width of his smile. "I love it!"

———

WITHOUT MIMI AND THE REST OF her tight-knit family, Gayle didn't know how she would have made it through the early years of single motherhood. This house was where she'd found refuge after her divorce: she and Eli had moved into the den and slept on a pullout couch for almost a year until she could get back on her feet. It had made a full house even more crowded—Gayle's late grandmother was still living here then, along with Jean and Mimi, Chris and his wife Suzanne, plus their two kids, Jake and Emily—but Gayle had always felt comfortable and supported here. Eli loved seeing so many friendly faces together under one roof. He'd have traded the space and privacy of their own home to move back here in a heartbeat.

He still saw Mimi almost daily, either here or at his house. A few years earlier, she had retired from a thirty-year career at the phone company to care for her ailing mother. But her mother died a short time after, and since then she'd spent her free time watching Eli after school and in the summer while Gayle worked.

In addition to their strong physical resemblance, down to the dark hair that Mimi wore in a shoulder-length bob, Gayle and Mimi also had a degree of cautiousness in common. Mimi could be even more guarded than Gayle, and she was especially careful when it came to Eli's safety. Motivated by the fear that he'd draw the wrong kind of attention, she was quicker to correct his behavior. And although she spoiled him as much as any grandmother would, cooking him his favorite foods and giving him the toys he couldn't convince Gayle to buy, she could sometimes be stern. Eli had learned to read her face, and when her eyes stopped smiling behind her gold-rimmed glasses, he stopped smiling, too.

It had taken Mimi longer than Gayle to come to terms with the extent of Eli's disability. In truth, more than a decade after his diagnosis, Mimi still hadn't fully come to terms with it. Working their way slowly through the stages of grief, Gayle remained in a protracted depression—not as overwhelming as it once was, but still a constant nagging presence. Mimi was entrenched somewhere near denial.

"It's harder for me, you know," Mimi once told Gayle. "I have to grieve for my grandson's troubles *and* my daughter's."

"Oh, I know—you have it so much rougher than me," Gayle said, half joking. "You have it twice as hard."

"That's not what I meant," Mimi said.

Gayle knew what she was trying to say: Mimi wanted to take care of them both. But her impulse to take care took the form of wanting to fix Eli, to normalize him, something Gayle already knew was impossible.

Although Mimi loved Eli deeply, she struggled to accept the ways in which he was different, or the fact that he always would be. Even as a twelve-year-old, Eli was so childlike that Mimi could believe his behavior was part of a phase he'd eventually outgrow. It was jarring for her to encounter adults with Williams, on the rare occasions that she did, and see in them Eli's boundless exuberance and uninhibited friendliness.

On one of these occasions, Mimi had accompanied Gayle to an event hosted by the Williams Syndrome Association and been shocked to see two people with Williams, both in their thirties, ordering drinks at the bar.

"Do they let them drink?" Mimi whispered to Gayle.

"Does *who* let them drink?" Gayle answered. "They're adults. They can drink if they want to."

Mimi told Gayle about a woman with Williams she had met at the gathering, who was about Gayle's age and wore a wedding ring.

"See, I wondered if they had sex," Mimi explained. "But then I met that woman, and she said she was married. I said, 'For how long?' And she said, 'Seven *blissful* years.' So I guess they must, right?"

"Why would you wonder that?" Gayle said. "Like, even if they were in a relationship, you thought they wouldn't have sex? Why not?"

"I guess I didn't think they knew how," Mimi said, turning her palms up noncommittally.

"Oh, I think they can figure it out," Gayle said.

"I wonder if they ever get pregnant?" Mimi asked.

"Sure they can," Gayle said. "Of course they can. They really shouldn't, but it's certainly possible."

Mimi shrugged. Unlike Gayle, she hadn't researched the disorder endlessly, attended all the events, and joined the Facebook groups. She'd become aware of the symptoms as Eli expressed them or Gayle explained them, but she'd never probed as deeply into how the syndrome developed over time. She hadn't spent the hours Gayle had mulling over what it would mean as Eli grew up. She knew he was unlikely to ever be truly independent, but she hadn't thought much about the rites of adulthood that he might or might not achieve: a job, a relationship, even a drink at a bar.

———

THE DOORBELL RANG AND ELI GASPED, flapping his hands excitedly like an overwrought penguin. Aunt Jean patted his shoulder.

"Relax," she said.

"But I want to see my presents!" he said breathlessly.

Eli's cousin Kylie emerged on the deck, sun-drenched and freckled, her wet hair slicked back into a ponytail. She had just come from a friend's pool party, as she announced to her grandparents, who were already there; they were the ones who lived across the street. Marcia, following on her daughter's heels, said wearily that she was surprised Kylie hadn't blown off the family party entirely.

"She's always ditching us for something better," Marcia said.

It was hard not to be struck by the difference between the two twelve-year-olds. The gap between them had only widened as Marcia's daughters—Kylie and her seven-year-old sister, Morgan—grew up on the standard track, hitting all the developmental milestones on cue, while Eli followed a different path.

Kylie was a precocious twelve, with near-perfect report cards and a robust social life. While Eli was still invited to her birthday parties (and pool parties, and dance recitals), they were far different affairs from his own quiet, peerless celebrations. At hers, he was surrounded by her throng of friends, who were polite but tended to ignore him.

He seemed unaware of their rejection, content with whatever attention he happened to get. Kylie herself went out of her way to acknowledge him. It was Gayle whose feelings were hurt. The older Eli got, the more apparent it was that he was tolerated, but not quite included, by other kids his age.

His exclusion wasn't motivated by cruelty as much as by the natural tendency behind friend selection—gravitating toward others like us—that the preteen population hones to a razor-sharp precision. Eli was not like the other kids. He wasn't like his cousin. Despite having a family in common, they were about as far from each other on the social spectrum as two kids could be.

Eli was so thrilled by Kylie's arrival that he stopped blowing on his twirly and flashed her a wide smile. She wore an expression of practiced nonchalance and a hot-pink, glitter-monogrammed Abercrombie & Fitch T-shirt—a recent purchase from a trip to the mall with her friends.

"Kylie, look!" he said, holding up the curling strip of paper that now dangled limply from his hand. "My twirly!"

She walked over and hugged him, then eyed the decoration quizzically.

"What's this?" she asked.

"It's my twirly," he repeated.

"But it's not twirling," she said tentatively, clearly on unfamiliar conversational ground.

Eli, looking crestfallen, contemplated this observation without responding.

———

AFTER THE MEAL, GAYLE'S COUSINS Jake and Emily—Chris's kids, both in their early twenties—arrived after working late on the holiday. Like Gayle, Emily had an edgy aesthetic, with dark hair streaked electric blue and thick eyeliner applied in a cat-eye swoop. As soon as she opened the front door, Eli barreled toward her with open arms. She caught him and squeezed him tightly.

"Where's my present?" he asked, gasping from the force of the hug. Emily said she wasn't ready to give it to him yet.

"What is it? Is it a Dustbuster?" he asked.

"What are you wishing for?" she asked.

"I'm wishing for a Dustbuster," he confirmed. "And a Hoover Platinum cordless stick vac."

Jake, as shy and quiet as Eli was outgoing and loud, played guitar in a local band. He invited Eli to every gig he played; Eli was his biggest fan. And the feeling was mutual. Jake and Emily had grown up around Eli and treated him like a little brother. They had driven long distances to accompany Gayle and Eli on Williams syndrome awareness walks and attend fund-raising events.

Now they helped Chris gather kindling, acquiescing to Eli's repeated entreaties for a "crackling fire," although the evening was so warm that no one besides the birthday boy wanted one. Once the flames were lit, Eli stood at the deck rail, staring into the fire pit. He rocked back and forth on his heels, transfixed by the flames. "Is it crackling?" he called down.

Even when the logs were fully engulfed, Eli stood apart, silently watching the fire flicker. The crackling was still not enough to satisfy his aural cravings. He begged Chris to add new logs.

"You want to make it a bonfire," Chris said.

"Yeah!"

"We're going to be out here until midnight," Chris sighed good-naturedly as he put another log on the pile.

Chris was perhaps the strongest male figure in Eli's life, dominated as it was by women. He humored Eli's unusual requests without judgment, other than raising practical arguments against, say, building a fire on a very warm night—and then overriding his own objections. Very little that Eli did ever fazed him, from the tantrums to the wardrobe malfunctions that plagued the awkwardly sized preteen.

One night, while Gayle and Eli were over for dinner, Eli accidentally split the seam of his pants from the crotch all the way down one leg. Chris never batted an eye. Neither did Eli. While Gayle hunted for safety pins, Eli strolled through the house with the loose swath of khaki flapping behind him like an obscene superhero cape, unmindful of the fact that he was exposing his camo-print boxer briefs to the world.

"Good thing those are camouflaged, so we can't see anything," Chris quipped. Gayle appreciated her uncle's dry wit and the soothing influence he had on Eli.

But being around her family could be taxing, too. Her relatives approached Eli's condition with varying degrees of avoidance. They tended not to talk openly about it, presumably driven by a polite desire not to probe too deeply or remind Gayle of her suffering. She would have preferred that they probe. It bothered her when they didn't know the specifics of the disorder—especially if they didn't seem to want to learn more. They rarely asked what she was going through or what challenges lay ahead for Eli. Gayle sometimes wondered if these questions hadn't occurred to them or if they just thought it would be rude to bring them up.

For a disorder whose hallmark was nonstop socializing, Williams had had the contradictory effect of isolating Gayle from the outside world, from former friends, and even from her family. Many of her old friends still got together even after becoming parents, but Gayle, who would never let a sitter watch her son and who didn't feel comfortable letting Eli roam unsupervised with other kids while the grown-ups talked, had drifted out of touch.

These days it was hard to remember who she was apart from Eli, or who she'd once been. She could see a reflection of her former self in her friend Marilyn, who still attended the rock shows and horror movie conventions Gayle had once frequented. While Gayle shuttled Eli to and from the pediatric cardiologist's office or his special-needs soccer practice, Marilyn was more likely packing for her next adventure.

Gayle felt a sort of nostalgia for this life, but not envy. She didn't feel like she was missing out; there was simply no room in her world for this part of herself. Eli took up most of the space she had once devoted to her own interests. Her social circle, meanwhile, had shrunk to include only members of her family and the few friends she trusted most. But even among this select group, she sometimes felt like an outsider. If her friends and relatives didn't quite get Eli, in some ways they understood her even less. When she talked to the people she once felt closest to, it seemed like they were speaking different languages.

The only people who truly spoke her language were other parents of kids with Williams. Gayle was so motivated to seek their company that she traveled across the country to attend conventions hosted by the Williams Syndrome Association. She drove hours—to Boston one weekend, to New York another—just to have lunch with fellow Williams moms. She spent hours on the WSA Facebook page responding to other parents' postings and sharing her own questions, struggles, and successes.

The Facebook group was a font of information: the combined wisdom of hundreds of families who had already been through what Gayle was going through at any moment. It was here, not in the cardiologist's office, that Gayle got her best education on the progression of SVAS, the dangerous heart condition nearly universal to Williams. She had worried when Eli's mild stenosis was downgraded to moderate, so she crowdsourced the group to find out whether that meant he was on a path that would inevitably lead to surgery. A few other mothers offered hope: their children had been diagnosed with moderate stenosis that improved without surgery. Luckily, the same thing happened to Eli. But Gayle also heard from parents whose stories didn't end happily, so she knew that the condition could worsen at any time and that it sometimes proved fatal.

As vital as the answers they supplied was the emotional support Gayle found in the Williams community. She once bragged to them about a doctor's appointment at which Eli hadn't hugged a single person in the waiting room. They immediately understood what a colossal victory it was. Another time, she joined in a venting session about people who bullied and mocked kids with special needs. Gayle shared an anecdote about a former coworker who had made offensive comments during a phone call she overheard one day.

"I'm not eavesdropping, but a few key words jump out at me, like 'the retards,' 're-re bus,' and 'loser cruiser,' accompanied by some snickering," Gayle explained. "I wasn't completely clear of the context, and it was a 'private' phone conversation he was having, so I didn't know what to do. I knew I would be mad at myself if I didn't speak up, so I did. I said, 'I'm not sure if you are aware that I have a son with special needs, and I was very surprised to hear what I heard.' Basically he tried to say his kids had been in some special classes for ADD and they called the bus that themselves, or some bullshit like that. In any event, he said, 'I will keep your sensitivity in mind.' What?? My 'sensitivity'? Seriously—GRRR. But sometimes I end up feeling worse when I confront someone, mostly because I am not satisfied with their response. Anyone been in this situation?"

A number of other mothers commiserated, sharing similar stories. This was a topic that cropped up frequently in the Facebook group. There seemed to be no shortage of available anecdotes about the casual cruelty shown to people with Williams, or to anyone with an intellectual disability, and no end to the anger and hurt it evoked in their parents. One Williams mom complained about a woman who made a snide comment to her four-year-old when the child acted up on a shopping trip.

"I asked her if that made her feel better, being so mean to a child with special needs," the mom said. "Her response: 'Yes.' I was depressed for weeks. I still think about it."

Of course, any mother would have reacted viscerally to this kind of affront. It wasn't the mother's response in the moment that was unique to the Williams community but the extra baggage that came with it, making the hurt linger. The mother of a typical child who has a run-in with a nasty stranger can shake it off as one of those things that just happens every now and then, and might even prove to be a valuable teachable moment, offering a lesson in how to react to rudeness.

Parents of kids with Williams can't brush these encounters off so easily. Each incident adds to the mounting evidence that the world is an unwelcoming place for their kids. The value of a teachable moment disintegrates with the knowledge that the lesson won't stick in the mind of someone predisposed to see people—all people—as worthy of love and trust. No amount of teachable moments will thicken their skin or strengthen their defenses. What the woman didn't say in her Facebook post, but Gayle understood implicitly, was that this one unpleasant exchange had brought forward the fears that constantly lurked in the back of her mind. It was a stark reminder that people could be cruel, that her child was vulnerable, and that even her efforts to shame a single person into shaping up had proven utterly futile.

Gayle hadn't yet been able to reach this level of unspoken understanding with her friends or family. They tried to be helpful but couldn't quite put themselves in her shoes. They didn't understand the anxieties underlying her complaint about a rude coworker because they didn't share them. They couldn't relate to her enormous sense of triumph when Eli walked through a doctor's office without hugging everyone because they didn't see what was remarkable about it. Sharing thoughts and stories like these outside the Williams community, Gayle often drew the same uncomprehending stares Eli did when he talked about twirlies.

She could identify with another woman who complained to the Williams group after an unsatisfying attempt to unburden herself to a close friend. The woman had been talking about her grief over the milestones she was unlikely to witness in her daughter's lifetime—like watching her walk down the aisle on her wedding day. The friend replied, "Don't be silly; of course you'll see her walk down the aisle!" It was meant to be reassuring, but it came across as so flippant and dismissive, it only riled her. Of course it was possible for someone with Williams to get married, but it was a much more complicated prospect than the fairy-tale wedding she had dreamed of for her daughter. And the comment revealed that her friend was miles away from understanding her plight. As she told the Williams group, "My friends really don't get it at all. They see my daughter as just sweet and loving and joyful. They truly have no idea what we go through on a daily basis."

Gayle knew the feeling.

———

LATER IN THE EVENING, AFTER ELI had eaten cake and opened presents—a *Pirates of the Caribbean* DVD and action figures, plus an assortment of twirlies—he invited Morgan and Kylie to watch his new DVD with him in the den. It was a rare moment of connection, occupying a narrow strip of the Venn diagram on which Eli's interests and those of his cousins overlapped. The quality time was short-lived, though. He soon irritated the girls by insisting that they watch the DVD in Spanish. Kylie and Morgan wanted to see the movie, but they also wanted to understand it. Eli, on the other hand, usually watched movies in a halting, nonlinear way. He'd replay a favorite scene over and over, sometimes in English, sometimes in other languages— whatever the DVD settings might include: French, Spanish, German, Dutch . . . Then he'd mimic some of the foreign words and phrases, not always comprehending them, but simply enjoying the sounds. It wasn't an uncommon habit among people with Williams, who tended to have a knack for foreign languages. But it didn't go over well with his cousins.

On the deck, where Gayle sat with the rest of the adults, strains of the negotiations wafted through the screen door: the girls' high-pitched requests for English, followed by Eli's booming, insistent refusals. Gayle was tempted to run in and referee. She even contemplated overruling Eli's language selection so he didn't miss out on a fleeting chance to bond with his cousins. But she forced herself to stay put. As far as teachable moments went, this one offered a helpful lesson for Eli in the way his eccentricities might alienate others. *And anyway,* Gayle thought, *it's the kid's birthday party. If he wants to watch a movie in Spanish, well, let him.*

Uncle Chris chuckled at the snippets of dialogue from the den.

"Change it back!" Morgan pleaded.

"*La Perla Negro es un barco real,*" Johnny Depp insisted.

"*La Perla Negro es un barco real!*" Eli repeated.

"I wonder why he wants to watch it in Spanish?" Mimi asked. "I guess he likes to hear the different sounds."

"Yup, I think so," Gayle said.

Eli is obsessed with sounds—you know that, she thought. Even seemingly innocuous comments like this sometimes piqued her. She'd felt the same way on another occasion when Chris, watching Eli destroy a beloved craft project Gayle had made for him, asked with exasperation, "Why is he so destructive?"

He just IS, Gayle thought then. *He's always been this way.*

She knew they were only commiserating with her, not looking for an explanation. So although the comments sometimes added to her frustration at the moment, she shrugged them off because they were well-intentioned.

The only way someone could truly offend her was to use the R-word in front of her. She expected to come across this word occasionally; she knew that "retarded" was simply part of the American vernacular. But she didn't expect to hear it from her friends, relatives, or coworkers—not when they knew she had a kid with an intellectual disability. Still, it slipped out from time to time, even among people who knew her well enough to know better. At another family gathering, Uncle Jim uttered it without thinking when Morgan acted up, running circles around the picnic table and pulling her sister's hair.

The scene was almost exactly the same then as it was at Eli's birthday party: everyone out on the back deck, eating hot dogs on a summer afternoon. And so everyone heard when he said, "Morgan, you're acting like a retard." It was a record-scratch moment: conversations broke off abruptly and all eyes turned to Gayle. Her face paled but she said nothing. Eli, oblivious, reached for another spoonful of sauerkraut.

"Mmm, this is good!" he said cheerfully. Gayle swallowed her hurt and chalked it up to a momentary lapse of judgment on her uncle's part. She was thankful Eli didn't know the word, or at least didn't register the way it could apply to him. The handful of people who'd used the word around her in the past had always insisted, if confronted, that it didn't apply.

"I didn't mean it that way," they'd say. "I don't think of him like that."

Eventually, Eli's cousins tired of the battle for English-speaking pirates. Morgan retreated to the deck and crawled into her grandmother's lap; Kylie appeared in the doorway and gave her mother a pointed look. A few minutes later they were saying their good-byes. On their way out, the girls stopped to give Eli a hug good-bye, but he was focused on the TV screen.

Gayle and the remaining adults cleaned up the party's aftermath. Eli was left alone in the den while Captain Jack Sparrow swaggered on the screen, trilling his *r*'s.

Seven

Elves on Earth

For years, a framed illustration of a scene from *A Midsummer Night's Dream* hung above Gayle's desk, where she could see it every day. Drawn in wispy lines and muted watercolors by the Victorian artist Arthur Rackham, it showed Puck whispering to a fairy among gnarled tree roots in an enchanted forest, smiling and tilting his head jauntily. Gayle had been struck by how closely the elfin prankster resembled Eli, with his high cheekbones and narrow chin, jutting ears and upturned nose. Even Puck's curly hair, disheveled by the breeze, was a ringer for Eli's. Gayle sometimes joked that on days when Eli's hair was curlier than normal, she knew he would be more rambunctious than usual—extra Puckish.

She was not the first to note the resemblance. Some folklorists believe that, centuries ago, real people with Williams syndrome might have been the models for fairy-tale elves. Before the advent of modern medicine, they say, Williams syndrome would have been more easily explained by magic than by science. People with Williams must have seemed like supernatural creatures—like the elves of Germanic folktales or the merry sprite in a Shakespearean play.

Apart from the physical similarity, elves are portrayed in folklore with undeniably Williams-like personalities. They're cute and child-like, bubbly and benevolent. They're often depicted as musicians and storytellers. And, unlike ogres, trolls, giants, and the like, elves love humans and are beloved by them. In the fables collected by the Grimm brothers in the 1800s, elves routinely come to the aid of people in need. In one story they make shoes for an elderly cobbler who is too tired to work; in another they free a servant girl from her masters.

A real person with Williams syndrome likely also inspired one of Charles Dickens's characters, according to University of Chicago pediatricians Darren Eblovi and Christopher Clardy. In 1841, 120 years before John Williams published his observations of the syndrome's features, Dickens ascribed those features to the titular character of his novel *Barnaby Rudge*. Barnaby, in his late twenties, is "elfin-like in face," cheerful and outgoing, known and loved by everyone in his London suburb. His indiscriminate trust is a catalyst for the novel's action: ultimately he is conned into helping incite a violent riot by people he believes to be his friends.

Barnaby resembles Eli in his affectionate nature as much as Puck does physically. When greeting his mother, Barnaby puts his arms around her neck and kisses her "a hundred times." Like Eli, he fixates on future events and asks about them endlessly. Even the events he obsesses over—including his birthday and the associated presents—are eerily identical. In a conversation that Gayle and Eli might just as easily have had, Barnaby asks his mother, "Is today my birthday?"

"Today!" she exclaims. "Don't you recollect it was but a week or so ago, and that summer, autumn, and winter have to pass before it comes again?"

Barnaby's mother could likewise be modeled on Gayle. She treasures her relationship with her son even as she fears for his future. She rues his condition but notes that, because of it, "perhaps the comfort springs that he is ever a relying, loving child to me—never growing old or cold at heart, but needing my care and duty in his manly strength as in his cradle-time."

Dickens's account of Williams syndrome is so incisive that Eblovi and Clardy offer it as evidence that medical insights aren't strictly the purview of physicians. Because Dickens wrote the book a quarter century before Gregor Mendel's experiments with pea plants laid the foundation for modern genetics, "he could not have proposed any molecular basis for Barnaby's characteristics," they write in an article for *Pediatric Annals*. But, they add, "this example of fiction providing a description of a disorder more detailed than that of medical journals more than a century later should encourage physicians to look to sources beyond traditional scientific articles for valuable clinical information."

Williams syndrome in particular may be better suited to stories than scholarly works. Even modern scientists are sometimes struck by its seeming otherworldliness.

"I find myself not wanting to say 'people with Williams syndrome'—I want to say 'Williams people,'" Oliver Sacks once observed. "They do seem to be a people with an identity of their own, which is different . . . I don't think you can just divide them into sort of heightened and diminished powers—to say that there are the high musical and social powers and diminished intellectual and conceptual and visual powers. This may be so, but it's not enough. These are a different sort of people."

Apart from inspiring folktales, people with Williams syndrome and other intellectual disabilities are believed to have played a prominent role in the courts of medieval and Renaissance Europe, as court jesters or "fools." Their musicality and good humor, their way with words, and their eagerness to please would have made them popular as entertainers. Although these roles were exploitative, the historian Suzannah Lipscomb points out that they were also a place of privilege that gave people with intellectual disabilities a much more visible role than they occupy in contemporary society. Throughout history, many have seen "natural fools" as exceptionally holy, closer to God in their simplicity and essential goodness. And while they might have been mocked, they were also well cared for in the royal court. Historians believe that Henry VIII's beloved court jester Will Somers was intellectually disabled because records show that Henry paid a caretaker to look after him. Somers, a consummate punner and a gifted storyteller whose witticisms were recorded in popular books of the time, was known for a verbal dexterity that is one of the hallmarks of Williams syndrome, although of course it wouldn't have been identified as such in the sixteenth century.

Historically speaking, it was only relatively recently that scientists offered a biological explanation for the seeming magic of these jester-like personalities and elfin facial features. Today, many people with Williams embrace their presumed heritage as court entertainers. In 2011, a British theater troupe made up of actors with special needs, including a young woman with Williams, re-created a historical jester performance in Hampton Court Palace, where Henry VIII lived. In 2014, a seventeen-year-old South African with Williams realized his dream of performing in the country's annual minstrel carnival, donning bright purple and gold clothing and face paint to dance and sing with the members of his favorite troupe. He was one of the only white performers at the carnival, a two-hundred-year-old tradition begun by slaves to celebrate a day off every January 2. Oblivious to the festival's freighted history, he just loved the music.

Gayle even knew a young man with Williams who attended clown school and regularly performed in costume and makeup at parties. He saw clowning as his calling in life. Gayle was not sure whether Eli could, or should, follow suit. At twelve, he was often funny, and loved to be the center of attention. But Gayle wasn't sure if he'd ever have the focus or self-discipline he'd need to be a performer. And she cringed at the fear that people might laugh *at* him, not *with* him.

After all, Williams syndrome has been the subject of less ambiguous derision over the years. The gap-toothed, grinning *Mad* magazine mascot, Alfred E. Neuman, first appeared on the humor magazine's cover in 1955 with an exaggerated version of the elfin features common to Williams. Even his catchphrase, "What, me worry?" captures the apparently carefree nature of people with the disorder. A similar caricature exists in different versions on advertisements, in comics, and on postcards stretching back to the late nineteenth century, often with the same catchphrase, and sometimes captioned "the idiot kid."

The humor of this look evidently hasn't worn off. Someone once sent Gayle a "Redneck Christmas" card that pictured a cartoon redneck decorating his Christmas tree with empty beer cans. His face hit a nerve, though: he had the same big gap teeth and jug ears as the *Mad* mascot. Before Eli was born, Gayle might not have minded getting a card like this. She might even have chuckled. But now it hit too close to home. *Why would anyone send me this?* Gayle thought. *Are we all just supposed to laugh at funny-looking people?* Caricatures like this no longer struck her as harmless. They dehumanized people with special needs—people like Eli.

As tickled as Gayle was by the connection between Williams syndrome and fairy-tale elves, she couldn't think too hard about it before it, too, became troubling. Elves may be charming and lovable, but there's one thing they aren't: human. Read enough fairy tales, and you will find a layer of tension between elves and humans, even in this enchanted world. Elves can be fickle. Like Puck, they are prone to mischief if it strikes them as more amusing than being kind. When wronged, they are apt to seek revenge. These elfin attributes reflect our own collective fears better than they do the tendencies of the people who inspired them, of course. Real people with Williams are the least likely among us to even contemplate vengeance—or cruelty of any kind.

There are even more sinister tales, one of which is recorded by the Grimms, of elves stealing healthy human babies and leaving deformed or disabled changelings in their place. While versions of this story could have been a way of explaining how elfin babies—or real-life children with Williams—appeared in the human realm, they also indicate a level of wariness toward these otherwise benevolent beings. Elves may be warmhearted, for the most part, but they are still outsiders. They aren't like the rest of us. They can't entirely be trusted.

The problem with the suspicion shown to the elves of folktales is that it, too, has a real-world corollary. Gayle has seen people approach Eli with similar wariness. They don't understand why he is the way he is, and this triggers the innate caution the rest of us feel when we encounter someone different. We are hesitant, skeptical. His openness closes a door in us.

Eight

School

Middle school brought Eli's differences into sharp relief. To everyone but Eli himself, his odds of achieving social acceptance looked staggeringly slim. Although he considered virtually everyone whose name he knew to be a friend, none of his schoolmates truly fit the definition. Eli himself seemed to prefer the company of adults, who tended to be more tolerant of his quirks and more willing to listen politely to a one-way conversation about floor scrubbers and vacuum cleaners.

In sixth grade, Eli's closest acquaintance was a boy on his school bus with autism so severe that he was essentially incapable of speech. Eli loved sitting next to his mute companion, whom he regaled with anecdotes about his favorite things. It didn't faze Eli that the boy never answered Eli's questions or chimed in with his own thoughts. At home Eli talked about him often, sometimes imitating the sounds he uttered instead of language, apparently in an affectionate homage. But Eli saw him only on the bus.

As a toddler, Eli had gone on occasional play dates. Now that he still behaved like a toddler among twelve-year-olds, no one invited him over. The last time he went to a classmate's house, a few years earlier, he had interacted more with the boy's mother than with the boy. He spent most of the afternoon playing by himself with the other kid's toys.

But on the whole his classmates were kind to him, even if they rarely interacted with him outside of school. They'd known him since kindergarten, and some had grown so protective of him that they told their parents—who told Gayle—whenever someone mistreated him. The incidents had so far been minor, although devastating enough as far as Gayle was concerned. At lunch one day, a group of boys tried to persuade Eli to swear. Eli, as uncomfortable with harsh language as he was with physical violence, refused. Eventually he broke down crying, and the boys laughed at him. An eyewitness account from a classmate made its way to Gayle; she called the school to ask why Eli's aide, who worked one-on-one with him, wasn't there to put a stop to it. She was told that the aide tried not to hover in the lunchroom, since Eli would never make friends with an adult stuck to his side.

"Tell her to hover," Gayle said. "He's not making friends anyway."

She spoke hastily, half in anger. But her words were the product of hours spent thinking through this dilemma: Should she allow Eli time with his peers, unsupervised, in an effort to give him access to normal social opportunities—but also run the risk of having him mocked, bullied, or exploited? Or should she shelter him, keeping him safe but depriving him of those opportunities? She leaned toward the latter, reasoning that he didn't seem able to navigate the middle school social world successfully in any case. But she still wanted him to be included in the regular student body, albeit in a limited, supervised way. She still hoped he would learn from and model the behavior of the typical students, as long as that behavior didn't consist entirely of teasing and ostracizing him.

Eli, meanwhile, seemed oblivious to the daily rejections. Classmates often slid farther down the cafeteria bench when he sat near them. He slid down after them. They sometimes pretended not to hear him when he asked a question. He repeated his question, louder.

A teacher once told Gayle it was agonizing to watch Eli at lunch, because he spent the whole period looking around for someone to talk to. But it wasn't agony for Eli. He looked forward to lunch every day, walking to the cafeteria with a bounce in his step and a smile on his face. He high-fived everyone he saw, including the boys who'd recently reduced him to tears, whose taunts he quickly forgave, or forgot. When asked, he'd call them his friends, regardless of whatever they might have called him instead.

———

ELI SPENT MOST OF HIS SCHOOL DAY in a special-education classroom, where he took part in a life skills program for students with intellectual disabilities. His own IQ was difficult to gauge precisely. Although one test put it at 45, in the bottom tenth of a percentile for his age group, his teachers believed the true number was higher. They blamed his distractibility for undermining his performance. But while Eli consistently bungled the standardized tests he took, he always did so with panache. The previous year, he had taken the Wechsler Intelligence Scale for Children and scored in the "extremely low" range on every section. He couldn't reproduce simple designs with blocks. He was flummoxed by *wh-* questions. When asked, "Why do people brush their teeth?" he mimed tooth brushing and said, "Use toothpaste." Asked, "What is a cow?" he answered, "Moo."

But the test administrator noted that his comparatively sophisticated rhetorical moves belied the starkness of his score. When he didn't know an answer, he tapped his forehead with his finger and said, "Let me think." Asked for a definition of a word he didn't know, he said, "It is a word." It was hard to argue with that.

While his classmates in the life skills program displayed varying degrees of intellectual and social disability, they were all vastly different from Eli. He was the only one with Williams; in fact, none of his teachers had ever encountered someone with Williams before. No precedent existed for his unique combination of skills and deficits. And, like many kids with Williams, he didn't quite fit in anywhere in the school system. In many ways he was the highest-functioning student in the life skills class, but he couldn't manage the coursework or social niceties of a regular class.

Few teachers, even those well trained in special education, know much about Williams syndrome; it simply isn't common enough. As a result, they often misunderstand the quirks inherent to this disorder but to no other. Because they're more likely to come across students with Down syndrome, which shares some attributes with Williams (distinctive facial features, a tendency to be overly affectionate, and a similar overall IQ, on average), this is the standard to which kids with Williams are sometimes compared. But the contrast makes students with Williams seem willfully disobedient, since their impulse control tends to be so much weaker. Eli's teacher had much more success in curbing the overfriendliness of students with Down syndrome. Eli, on the other hand, knew he wasn't supposed to hug everyone but couldn't stop. One day he'd be the model of obedience, and the next day he'd go on a hugging bender.

Compared to kids with Down syndrome, he also had a lower tolerance for frustration or boredom. Even though he could entertain himself for hours simply by flicking the sheets of paper he pretended were flames, any attempt to get him to do something less entertaining, like math, made him restless and uncooperative. One of his greatest challenges in school, as his teacher once concluded in a progress report, was that he could stay on task for at most fifteen minutes at a time.

He was more focused, or perhaps more motivated, in the regular classes he attended outside the life skills program. These were electives—gym, art, and tech ed—as well as social studies and science. His aide accompanied him to these classes, partly to help him with note-taking and the modified versions of tests he was given, and partly to monitor his behavior. If he grew too antsy, she'd escort him back to the life skills classroom. She did the same if he was too friendly or too chatty, disrupting the rest of the class. Just as he hounded his family about the things he was looking forward to, like cake and presents on his birthday, he often hounded his teachers and classmates about his favorite parts of the day: lunch and recess.

One May afternoon, in his social studies class, Eli sat through a twenty-minute movie without interruption, although he kicked his legs impatiently under the desk throughout. As soon as the movie ended, he called out, "Are we going to recess?"

"Yes, but not just yet," his teacher said. She gave the class a hand-out to read. Since Eli read at a second-grade level, his aide helped him with some of the words. Finally, the teacher told everyone to get ready for recess. Eli burst into song, bouncing happily in his seat. Although a few students giggled, most chatted among themselves, ignoring him. They'd heard him sing many times before.

Back in the life skills class, he was praised for his attentiveness during most of social studies but gently reminded not to interrupt class to ask about recess—or to sing about it. The life skills curriculum was roughly equal parts academics and social training, with an empha-sis on breaking down the barriers that kept Eli from integrating with his peers. His teachers used a token system to reward him for inter-actions that didn't involve hugging, for example, or for conversations that didn't center on floor-cleaning implements. Today he earned a token for sitting quietly throughout the movie and for respecting his classmates' personal space. If he earned enough tokens, he could trade them in for a reward: time spent drawing floor tiles on paper, for in-stance, which he would then pretend to scrub, or watching YouTube videos of floor scrubbers on the classroom computer.

Another technique his teachers used in school, and that Gayle used at home, was an adaptation of what are called "social stories," first developed by an autism specialist. Each story was a sort of script for a situation that might provoke inappropriate behavior; for Eli, these included lunchtime and gym class. The teacher would outline what was likely to happen in that situation and what a socially acceptable response might be. For lunch period, the story might go something like "There will be a lot of other students in line. You'll say hi to the people around you, but you won't hug them. You'll get your food and carry it to your table, and then stay in your seat, talking only to the people sitting near you." Eli might be given a prompt and asked to brainstorm some actions that would be appropriate in that context. He could usually name these in the abstract. But social stories and tokens had only made marginal differences in his behavior. The fact, obvious to everyone but him, that his overfriendliness was pushing away the very people he hoped to befriend had done nothing to change his approach. And as off-putting as it was to his typical peers, it could be just as abrasive, or even more so, in his life skills class and in extracurricular activities with other students with special needs.

In a special-needs sports league called Buddy Baseball, Eli had tried to befriend a boy named Josh, a tiny kid who resembled a bobblehead doll in his oversize batting helmet. Josh was on an opposing team, but the teams played each other frequently and Eli had taken a shine to him despite the fact that Josh, who had autism, seemed to find Eli's friendly overtures an acute form of torture. At one springtime game Eli was playing second base when Josh hit a double, which Eli believed presented the perfect opportunity for them to catch up.

"Hi, Josh!" Eli shouted, welcoming him to the base. In reply, Josh held his arms out stiffly, as if pushing Eli's words away, and screamed. This didn't strike Eli as antisocial; he continued his side of the conversation in the same pleasant tone.

"How you doing, Josh?" he asked.

"AAAAAAAGH!" Josh shrieked, his face scrunching in fury.

"It's nice to see you!"

"AAAAAAAGH!"

"How was your vacation?"

"AAAAAAAGH!"

Finally, the next batter hit a line drive and Josh bolted to third, then made a dash for home. Eli applauded gleefully.

"Josh, you're doing it!" he called out as his opponent rounded home plate.

The irony was not lost on Gayle that Buddy Baseball, despite its intended purpose, seemed an unlikely place for Eli to actually find a buddy. But, to Eli, Josh *was* a buddy. It would have been impossible to convince him otherwise, since his definition of friendship was nothing like his mother's, or the dictionary's. It didn't depend on shared interests or mutual affection. A friend was simply someone he'd interacted joyfully with—a definition that encompassed nearly everyone.

————

THE LIKE-SEEKING-LIKE PRINCIPLE OF CHILDHOOD (and adult) friendships is what sociologists call homophily, and it's what some believe undermines many of the goals of inclusive education. In itself, it's not an inherently evil tendency. We're all drawn to others who resemble us. So are animals. A 2013 meta-analysis of mating habits in 254 different animal species found that members of each species tended to mate with partners that were similar in size, color, and other outward traits. In human societies, peer groups typically form around shared interests, abilities, and appearances. It can be hard to join a group unless you look, talk, and act like the others in the group. If you're different from everyone else, you may find yourself excluded everywhere.

So while efforts to promote tolerance and inclusion of people with special needs have made great strides over the years, it has been an uphill battle. The disability rights movement of the 1960s succeeded in bringing intellectually disabled students out of separate facilities and into the same public schools as nondisabled students. And the passage of the Education for All Handicapped Children Act, a 1975 law requiring special-needs children to be educated in the "least restrictive environment," gave them greater access to the academic and extracurricular opportunities available to typical schoolchildren. The inclusion movement went even further, pushing for disabled students to be taught in the same classrooms as their typical peers, with an aide and modified assignments if necessary, rather than spending much of their day in a special-education classroom. While educational benefits were the movement's first priority, emphasis has shifted over the years to social goals. Parents expect inclusion to help their kids learn social skills and, ideally, make friends.

But acquiring social skills—and making friends—doesn't necessarily follow simply from sharing the same environment. In 2007, special-education researchers Per Frostad and Sip Jan Pijl studied schoolchildren in Norway, which has one of the world's most inclusive policies toward special-needs students. By asking seventh graders to name up to five of their friends and comparing the overlap between lists, they found that students with special needs had roughly half as many friends as their typical peers, on average, and that a quarter of them had no friends at all. "The data presented here give no grounds to be very optimistic about the social position of these pupils," they wrote.

They also found that seventh graders with special needs scored worse on tests of social skills than did fourth graders with special needs. Their abilities seemed to be eroding as they became more socially isolated over time, the researchers concluded. And while undergoing special training in social skills yielded short-term gains, it made little difference in the long term. Friendships still failed to blossom, and the newly learned skills faded over the course of a few months.

"This is not because they do not master the skills, but because the peer group does not change its attitude and behavior. Their image of the trained pupils does not change," Frostad and Pijl wrote. "The trained pupils do not have many possibilities to practice their new skills, the training does not pay off for them, and after some time the new skills seem of little use and are dropped."

Some studies have found that inclusion can actually backfire as a way to foster friendship, since classroom interactions highlight the differences between people with special needs and their typical peers, and can lead to rejected social overtures that leave students with special needs feeling embarrassed, hurt, and lonely.

Others have come to more optimistic conclusions. A 2014 study assessed young people with autism spectrum disorders who had undergone an intensive three-month social skills training program between one and five years earlier. The teens and young adults had mostly maintained—and even improved upon—the skills they'd been taught and, more importantly, reported having closer friendships and more friends overall.

Still, adults with social disorders like Williams and autism often name adolescence as the hardest time of their lives. Researchers say that's partly because social rules are more complex and inscrutable among teens than among children or adults. It's also because teenagers, including teenagers with Williams and autism, are consumed by the drive to establish their identities. And the easiest way to establish identity is to be part of a group. Without friends, they feel not just lonely but adrift, unsure of who they are or where they fit in the world.

Eli didn't seem to be facing this existential crisis, or at least not yet. But others his age, and some even younger, were already struggling with it. One eight-year-old girl with Williams came home and broke down crying after her classmates shunned her at school. "I know I'm different," she sobbed to her mother. "Why am I different?"

Another girl with Williams—Chelsea, who was the same age as Eli—performed so well academically that she took the same classes as typical students, although her assignments were modified. But this didn't mean she was any better integrated with her peers. While she easily charmed adults with her warm, gregarious personality, she, too, often came home in tears after being rebuffed by her classmates.

It's not uncommon for people with mild disabilities to suffer more social angst than people with severe disabilities. According to one study, those on the high-functioning end of the autism spectrum were abused by their peers more often than those with profound autism, partly because they were placed in less protective settings where social expectations were higher. Compared to people with severe autism, those with fewer autism symptoms and a higher IQ were also more likely to suffer from depression and anxiety, partly because of their heightened self-awareness.

Likewise, Chelsea's intelligence and sensitivity both helped and hurt her. Among other talents, she was a gifted storyteller, inventing elaborate tales at the dinner table to entertain her family. Her parents wrote many of them down. One day, for a sort of open-mic event in her middle school, she chose a few of her best stories to perform for her class. But before the event, her teacher called to talk to her father.

"She told me it would be good for me to be there with Chelsea, so the other kids could see that her father is . . . a man. Like their fathers," he later recalled. Intensely shy himself, he was sure she could perform better on her own than with his assistance. But he took the teacher's words to mean that her classmates saw her as so different from the rest of them that she might as well be the offspring of aliens.

He came to the open-mic event. While Chelsea told stories, he accompanied her on guitar. Her classmates applauded politely when they finished. No one taunted her, but no one approached her after the event, either.

Her father understood, from a developmental perspective, why Chelsea's classmates distanced themselves from her. He didn't see it as deliberate cruelty and tried not to take it personally.

"So much of it is tied into their own identity," he said. "At this age, they're trying to navigate these social systems for themselves, to find their place. And as soon as they recognize something in her that doesn't fit in, they want to dissociate before it becomes part of them."

Knowing that, and keeping it from breaking his heart, were two different things.

————

GAYLE'S HEARTBREAK FOR ELI WAS NOT quite the same. Eli never came home crying. He never complained about being different. He either didn't realize or didn't mind that he was unlike his classmates. He walked off the school bus singing every afternoon, whether or not he'd been teased.

Gayle wasn't sure whether Eli's imperviousness to social slights meant that he was more intellectually disabled than some of his Williams peers or simply more happy-go-lucky. Either way, she wondered if he'd grow to become more self-aware—and whether she'd want him to. She knew that adults with Williams often struggled with anxiety and depression. Some researchers have theorized that this could be the result of accumulated social failures: years of opening their hearts to repeated rejection. The developmental psychologist and neuroscientist Helen Tager-Flusberg concluded, after interviewing countless children and adults with Williams, that a "more mature conception of self" often triggered the angst of adulthood.

"With age, many of the individuals with Williams syndrome come to view their syndrome as socially disabling, or limiting their prospects and hopes for social integration, an attitude rarely seen in younger children," she wrote.

While Eli's teachers, and Gayle herself, were pushing to help him gain a "more mature conception of self," it gave Gayle pause that the insights she hoped he'd gain might also cost him the unburdened joy of his youth. He'd probably be happier if he stayed a child forever. Then again, she thought, wouldn't anyone? Adolescence might be the most challenging stage of a life with Williams, but it's also a challenge for every human being. Growing up is never easy. The reward isn't necessarily happiness; it's independence. But what Gayle wanted for Eli—what parents everywhere want for their children—was both.

Nine

Missing Genes, More Personality

The paradox of a genetic deletion that can make people gifted storytellers and accomplished musicians with warm, charming natures once prompted Jonas Salk, the polio vaccine developer who founded the Salk Institute, to say of Williams syndrome, "I never knew talent was a birth defect."

The Salk Institute, one of the nation's leading centers for genetics and neuroscience, has become a hotbed of Williams research. Here, Ursula Bellugi and the geneticist Julie Korenberg have spearheaded efforts to understand how twenty-six missing genes account for the Williams phenotype—the disorder's observable features—and what brain abnormalities underlie its behavioral quirks.

Years after researchers identified the elastin gene, the Salk team pinpointed two other genes on chromosome 7 that together play a role in the perception of spatial relationships. Their absence helps explain the trouble people with Williams typically have in drawing a simple picture, re-creating basic patterns with blocks, or finding their way through a maze. Korenberg, who has called Williams syndrome "a geneticist's dream," also led the way in tracing the characteristic elfin facial features of people with Williams to a cluster of adjoining genes.

But Korenberg and her colleagues were even more determined to understand the genetic basis of the Williams personality: that combination of empathy, gregariousness, and trust that makes people with the disorder both so lovable and so vulnerable.

Attempts to trace the biological roots of personality have been controversial ever since the Victorian psychologist (and eugenicist) Sir Francis Galton described the dichotomy between nature and nurture in 1869. The controversy has flared up again in recent years, especially since the Human Genome Project failed to fulfill hopes of pinpointing the genes responsible for traits such as intelligence and empathy, as well as for illnesses like cancer and autism. After researchers spent years—and billions of dollars—hunting unsuccessfully for those genes, some people called the quest a wild-goose chase. And some have argued that it would be reductionist in any case to view the stunning diversity of human personalities merely as differences in protein production dictated by our DNA. Detractors see the attempt to frame personality in genetic terms as a discredit to humankind, and one that underestimates our ability to shape our own lives.

But it's tough to argue with the premise that personality traits have a genetic basis: farmers and dog breeders have known it for centuries. Behavioral traits like intelligence, obedience, and gentleness can be transmitted genetically—and have been, through the selective breeding of livestock and dogs, since long before anyone understood the laws of genetics. Of course, scientists have established the heritability of behavioral traits in humans as well, largely through studies of twins, but the principle can be demonstrated easily enough by considering why Labrador retrievers make great pets, while wolves do not.

Identifying the genes responsible for these traits, however, has proved much harder than breeding them in animals. One of the main failings of early research efforts was the presumption that there was a gene for any given trait. As geneticists have come to realize, the mechanisms behind heritability are much more complicated than that: whole systems, depending on entire networks of genes, are likely implicated in any one trait. That's why the psychologist Eric Turkheimer has argued that all human traits are heritable—personality included—even as he added, in a 2014 article, that "the search for genetic mechanisms of human personality . . . will never bear fruit."

Korenberg and her colleagues believed that behavioral genetics could be fruitful if they turned the search on its head. Instead of tracking downward from, say, the social deficits of autism to genetic roots that could be anywhere in the vast wilderness of the human genome, they wanted to start with known genetic roots and work their way up. Williams syndrome offered the exhilarating opportunity to do just that. Limiting their search to the syndrome's twenty-six missing genes dramatically narrowed the field on which to chase the wild goose of sociability. That still didn't make it easy.

The Salk team's big break came in 2009, when they stumbled upon a nine-year-old girl whose genetic makeup was unusual even among the Williams population. She had the classic Williams facial features, its telltale heart defect, and the hallmark inability to process spatial relationships. However, her behavior was uncharacteristically reserved: she didn't run up to strangers, lock eyes with them, or try to hug them. And although she was less outgoing, she was capable of more sophisticated social interactions than most people with Williams. In fact, to the researchers' amazement, she easily formed meaningful connections with other kids her age. Korenberg and her colleagues wanted to know what made the girl so different.

Using the same diagnostic test once given to Eli (the FISH test, which highlights DNA in fluorescent dye), combined with two even more sensitive procedures—a high-resolution imaging test that compared her DNA to her father's, along with a technique called polymerase chain reaction, which can amplify a section of DNA by several orders of magnitude and is popular among forensic analysts—the team discovered that the girl was missing every Williams gene but one: the inelegantly named general transcription factor IIi (GTF2I) gene.

It was a discovery with monumental implications for understanding human behavior, since GTF2I's singular impact defied researchers' predictions that a wide range of genes underlay the hypersocial behavior found in Williams. "It's not simple," Korenberg said, "but it may be much simpler than we thought."

The Salk team needed to do more work to determine whether the correlation was more than a fluke, however. "It's tempting to say that the gene she kept was related to that particular phenotype. But you have to be very careful, because it's a single case, and how specific is the phenotype? Sort of specific, but not as specific as we might like," Korenberg explained.

While Korenberg and her colleagues could replicate the gene deletion in lab experiments by "knocking out" the GTF2I gene in normal DNA, they couldn't test its effects on human subjects for obvious ethical reasons. Instead, they picked one of our primate relatives, the macaque monkey—a popular species among researchers because its brain structure and elaborate social systems resemble humans' in key ways. The Salk researchers injected lab-modified DNA into a macaque embryo and raised a monkey that was missing the gene that seemed to have made such a difference in the girl they'd studied.

The results confirmed their suspicion that GTF2I helped regulate the production of oxytocin, a hormone that plays a role in social activities from parent-child bonding to romantic encounters as well as trust, attachment, and friendship. It's been called both the "love hormone" and the "trust hormone." One of its neurological effects is to relax the amygdala, a power player in regulating our emotional responses. Oxytocin essentially allows this part of the brain to let down its guard so we can develop the feeling of closeness that is essential to attachment. It also stimulates the brain's reward system, producing the feeling of pleasure in seeing a loved one's face.

Ordinarily, oxytocin is released by the pituitary gland in controlled, strategically timed doses. In monkeys without the GTF2I gene, however, the flow of oxytocin became a flood that went to all the wrong places. The same was true for vasopressin, a partner hormone to oxytocin that plays its own role in social behavior (and is involved in regulating blood pressure). Vasopressin, sometimes called the "fidelity hormone," acts on part of the forebrain to create a sense of well-being that has been known to cement the feeling of closeness oxytocin helps facilitate.

Watching these hormones course wildly through a macaque brain—which they did, again with the help of fluorescent dye—gave the Salk team a clue they hoped would help decipher some of the paradoxes of Williams.

"People with Williams are overfriendly but anxious," Korenberg said. "Oversocial, but without social judgment. They initiate and seek interaction, but have difficulty making friends. They can't sustain a conversation. They're engaging and gregarious, but they have a very limited, repetitive social repertoire. They're often insensitive and inappropriate. We can trace this to very particular [neural] pathways in Williams syndrome that are abnormal."

Other geneticists have replicated some of the findings from Korenberg's monkeys by manipulating the DNA of mice, whose genes correspond to more than 90 percent of those found in humans, including the region implicated in Williams. By removing a gene named Williams syndrome transcription factor (WSTF) from mouse DNA, scientists produced mice with tiny upturned noses and prominent ears: elfin-faced mice. Removing the mouse equivalent of GTF2I, they raised uninhibited mice that would wander brazenly through mazes. Instead of scurrying into corners, as mice normally do to escape detection by predators, these mice sauntered out into the open as if looking for a party. When a new mouse was introduced into their cage, they were much more interested in the stranger than were mice with unmodified DNA.

To explore the role that unregulated oxytocin and vasopressin played in Williams, Korenberg teamed up with the behavioral neurobiologist Sue Carter, whose decades of research into social behavior have led to breakthroughs in understanding the hormone pair.

Although scientists had long known that oxytocin played a part in maternal behavior—it induces labor contractions and aids in the release of milk after a baby is born—it was Carter who identified its far-reaching effects in the brain. She made the discovery by studying prairie voles, mouselike rodents that are anomalous for their highly social behavior and because they mate for life, raising their offspring as partners, while most mice and rats are promiscuous. What made prairie voles different from their polyamorous cousins, Carter found, was that their brains had a higher concentration of oxytocin receptors. So she conducted experiments with oxytocin and found that injecting it into rat brains made the rats more social. More of the hormone made them friendlier and less fearful toward other rats.

Vasopressin, she found, played a crucial supporting role. When injected into the brains of a promiscuous breed of voles, it was found to promote pair bonding, and the male voles reformed from playboys to committed monogamists.

So Carter, Korenberg, and other researchers were not astonished to discover that oxytocin and vasopressin ran rampant in the brains of people with Williams, although they were surprised by the degree. People with Williams, they discovered, have up to three times more baseline oxytocin than normal. And their studies demonstrated that higher levels of oxytocin correlate not only with increased social behavior but also with impaired visual-spatial skills and with increased imagination and creativity, including the abilities to pretend and to tell vivid stories.

Higher oxytocin and vasopressin also seem to be tied to the extreme music appreciation that is nearly universal among people with Williams. Scientists have already found that their minds are, on a deeper level, wired for music appreciation. On average, the brains of people with Williams are 15 to 20 percent smaller than normal. But most of that lost mass comes from the occipital and parietal lobes— partly responsible for visual-spatial abilities—while the temporal lobes, which deal with language and music, are usually normally sized or even larger than normal. A brain imaging study led by Bellugi and her colleagues found that people with Williams process music much differently than other people and use much more of their brain to do so, including parts of the cerebellum, brain stem, and amygdala—more primal neural regions, sometimes called the "emotional brain"—that lie dormant when the rest of us listen to music.

In one test, Korenberg and her team measured the amounts of oxytocin and vasopressin in the bloodstream of people with and without Williams while they listened to music. While the baseline levels for both hormones were higher in people with Williams, they jumped even more dramatically when music was played. So while music, considered a universal emotional stimulus, triggered an increase in oxytocin even in the control group, the torrent of hormones it elicited in the brains of people with Williams seemed to correspond with their exaggerated emotional response. Notably, a surplus of the two hormones also corresponded with a higher likelihood that they would approach strangers, and with the likelihood that their interactions would be considered overfamiliar and intrusive.

"You had a person who might be running up to people and, once they get there, they're not saying the right things," Korenberg said. She speculated that too much oxytocin might increase our social drive but also cloud our judgment. Among other things, it might make us prone to displays of excessive and unreciprocated affection, alienating others instead of drawing them to us.

By flooding the brains of people with Williams syndrome, this hormone—normally released only in the most intimate of moments, such as when mothers nurse their newborn children—creates a sense of closeness with everyone, turning strangers into trusted friends and instantly forging connections that most of us take months or years to build.

———

THE IMPLICATIONS OF THESE DISCOVERIES COULD be huge: by identifying the roots of these maladaptive behaviors, the Salk team opened the door to a search for possible treatments. And that could lead to effective therapy for other, more common social disorders, including autism and post-traumatic stress disorder. If too much oxytocin is partly to blame for the overly social behavior of Williams, then too little could play a role in social anxiety and withdrawal, and correcting the chemical imbalance could help with both.

In fact, a 1998 study established that people with autism had lower-than-normal levels of oxytocin in their blood. Around the same time that Korenberg was studying oxytocin in Williams, other researchers were designing experiments to test the therapeutic potential of oxytocin, given intravenously or via nasal spray, for improving the social skills of people on the autism spectrum. Two separate studies found that supplemental oxytocin helped people with autism and Asperger's use nonverbal cues to successfully assess other people's emotional states. (One asked them to identify emotions based on tone of voice, the other based on facial expressions.) And a study published in 2010 found that inhaling oxytocin gave high-functioning people with autism and Asperger's an enhanced feeling of trust and connection with others, and helped them behave more appropriately in social settings. While oxytocin isn't yet a mainstream treatment for autism's social deficits, these researchers believe it could one day become a valuable therapeutic tool.

Identifying oxytocin's role in the brain could even lead to a greater understanding of social behavior in general, influencing everything from governing styles to financial policies. For example, in one neuroeconomics study, researchers gave people ten dollars to split with a stranger. They found that those given a spritz of oxytocin nasal spray were 80 percent more generous than those given a placebo spray. Oxytocin levels in the blood of those on the receiving end of the shared money also rose in proportion to the generosity of the giver, with higher levels corresponding to a feeling of warmth and trust toward the charitable stranger.

Korenberg's next goal is to trace the brain circuits and genes responsible for the anxiety common to people with Williams. If researchers can identify those systems, it could lead to treatments for anxiety in the general population.

———

GAYLE WAS DELIGHTED THAT WILLIAMS RESEARCH might benefit the world at large. But like all parents of Williams kids, she was even more eager for advances that would improve the lives of people with the disorder, and soon enough to benefit her son. A treatment to address the social symptoms of Williams—an oxytocin eraser, perhaps—was near the top of her wish list. She dreamed of a day when her son's irrepressible overfamiliarity would subside and when, like the nine-year-old girl in Korenberg's case study, he'd be capable of forging a true, meaningful connection with someone other than his mother. Her dream come true would be his dream come true: he would finally make a friend.

Ten

People Like Eli

At twelve, Eli didn't quite grasp the meaning of Williams syndrome. Because he really only heard the term when he and Gayle attended gatherings sponsored by the Williams Syndrome Association, he associated it with holiday parties and summer picnics, awareness walks and fund-raising raffles and auctions.

So when Gayle tried asking him, "What is Williams syndrome?" Eli cocked his head thoughtfully.

"It's . . ." he began, then broke into a wide smile. "It's like a party!"

Gayle wasn't sure whether to laugh or cry at his answer. He wasn't entirely wrong. Few people were better at making cocktail party conversation, or quicker to rush onto the dance floor, than people with Williams. But it wasn't exactly the way *she'd* describe it.

Still, Gayle suspected that Eli understood more about Williams than he let on, if not quite consciously. She and Eli had recently been in line at Panera Bread when a woman ahead of them ordered a lemonade. Overhearing the woman's effusive banter with the restaurant staff, Gayle guessed that she had Williams without seeing her face.

"I love you guys!" the woman said when she got her drink, her voice as husky and earnest as Eli's. When she turned, Gayle could tell from the woman's features that she did indeed have Williams. And so could Eli.

"She's like me, Mom!" he said, pointing to the woman, who was in her forties. Gayle was stunned.

"What do you mean, she's like you?" she asked. Eli couldn't elaborate. He just shook his head and repeated himself. But by recognizing a kindred soul, he revealed more self-awareness than Gayle had thought him capable of. It meant that on some level he knew he was different from most people. It meant he could identify some of those differences when he saw them mirrored in another person: maybe the distinct facial features, maybe the warm, outgoing personality, or maybe both. To Gayle it meant that he would appreciate what it was like to be among a crowd of people like him, suddenly in the majority.

She knew that the Williams Syndrome Association hosted a yearly music therapy camp in Michigan exclusively for kids with Williams. The "therapy" aspect capitalized on the campers' love of music to teach lessons about safety and appropriate social behavior. But apart from that, it was like any summer camp, where kids sang songs around a campfire, wove friendship bracelets, and forged deep bonds with their bunkmates. It would be, Gayle thought, a unique opportunity for Eli. For once in his life he would be surrounded by peers who were *actually* his peers—not kids his age who were vastly more mature, and uninterested in talking about twirlies, or the kids in his special-education class who weren't quite on his intellectual level, and who behaved inappropriately in ways that weren't compatible with his own. He had fallen into a lonely gap between the two groups, unable to find his niche. Going to camp, Gayle thought, could open the door to friendship and belonging.

What held her back from signing Eli up was the question of money: she didn't have much. In fact, she was in the process of filing for bankruptcy. Her credit had been ruined after she moved out of the home she'd shared with Alan, who then defaulted on their mortgage. The house went into foreclosure, and she hadn't even been able to get a credit card since. Her car loan, luckily, had been approved just weeks before the foreclosure showed up on her financial record.

She was still paying off stacks of Eli's old medical bills through a payment plan with the Yale New Haven Hospital system. The new medical bills just got added to the tab. They were unglamorous expenses, such as routine visits to the gastroenterologist and occasional colonoscopies. Eli's low intestinal motility, a symptom of Williams, led to chronic constipation punctuated by accidents at the worst times: in school, where the nurse kept a stock of spare pants on hand for the inevitable calamity; at soccer practice for his special-needs sports league; and once at a pool party where a messy, mortifying moment was skirted by mere seconds when Gayle whisked Eli into a bathroom. Now these mishaps were kept at bay with Miralax and a drug called Amitiza. But the drugs were expensive.

Everything was expensive. The co-pays for Eli's anxiety and attention-deficit/hyperactivity disorder medications were a monthly burden, which, along with the specialist co-pays for the gastroenterologist, the geneticist, the cardiologist, and the psychiatrist, could mean hundreds of dollars in medical costs on a good month. And there were always unexpected extras, new devices or procedures that required hours on the phone, haggling with the insurance company. The latest on a long list was the bath chair Eli's occupational therapist had recommended so he could learn to shower by himself.

Gayle still helped bathe him. In their small, shared bathroom, she kneeled outside the tub and washed the spots he missed. He didn't have the coordination to soap himself very well. Using a washcloth, he'd scrub some skin until it was red and raw but overlook other patches entirely. And he really didn't like soap. It was a sensitivity that plagued people with Williams, many of whom couldn't tolerate certain textures and tactile sensations—another issue they had in common with people with autism. When Eli was younger, he found the feel of soapy lather so repulsive, he'd sometimes throw up in the shower. Now he could put up with it, although without Gayle's supervision he'd forgo the soap and just rinse with water. The water itself would be either scalding or freezing, since his poor motor skills made it hard for him to adjust the shower knob. He turned it in quick jerks to the left or right, overcompensating in each direction. And with his limited depth perception, he struggled to step in and out of the tub.

Eli's therapist suggested that a bath chair might make the process easier by taking the stepping and standing out of the equation. Gayle was willing to give it a shot. She didn't want Eli to depend on her to clean him forever.

So she set out to buy the chair. She had Eli's doctor write a prescription for it, so the insurance company would have proof that it was medically necessary. Then she waited in line at a medical equipment store after work one evening, clutching the prescription. The chair was a no-frills gray plastic-and-metal contraption with a sticker price of $160. Gayle wondered what the co-pay would be. The line at the store, predominantly elderly customers, was long and slow-moving, so she had plenty of time to wonder. Finally she reached the front, only to be told by a testy sales clerk that insurance never covered bath items. The woman refused to even look at her prescription. She seemed annoyed at Gayle for wasting her time.

Gayle's hackles rose. *Like I have nothing better to do,* she fumed inwardly. *Like I'm so happy to be here buying a chair for my twelve-year-old son who can't take a bath by himself.* She stormed out of the store and drove straight to another one across town, where a friendlier clerk accepted her prescription and entered it into the computer. She needed a code for Eli's condition.

"It's called Williams syndrome," Gayle told her.

"Yeah, but what is it? A neurological disorder? Brain damage?"

Gayle started to explain: "Well, it's a genetic disorder. Really it's a neurodevelopmental disability. It's sort of like autism but kind of the opposite . . ." She trailed off when she saw that the woman's eyes had glazed over.

"I'll put 'neurological disorder,'" the woman said. Her fingernails clacked on the keys and she announced that the total came to $4.50. Insurance, she said, would cover the rest. Gayle wrote a check and walked out of the store so pleased with her purchase that the devastating absurdity of her victory—successfully acquiring the kind of bath chair favored by the over-eighty set for her preteen son—didn't strike her at the moment.

It struck a week or so later, after the chair was delivered and installed, and after she'd written a sharply worded letter to the first medical equipment store complaining indignantly about its rude and incompetent sales staff. It hit her when a different sales clerk from the second store called to collect the rest of the $160.

"My insurance covered it," Gayle said.

"Insurance never covers bath items," said the clerk.

———

THERE WAS NO MONEY LEFT OVER for music therapy camp. But Gayle couldn't stop thinking about how great it would be for Eli. When she mentioned the prospect of a summer camp for kids with Williams, Eli seemed excited, although he later asked, "What's 'camp'?"

Gayle e-mailed the head of the Williams Syndrome Association to ask if she could get financial assistance. To her surprise, she did. That left transportation. Flying was out of the question financially, but driving was doable. She'd be staying with Eli at camp anyway: in the session for children aged six to twelve, parents bunked with their kids.

So at dawn one July morning in 2011, she and Eli embarked on a road trip to Michigan. The backseat was loaded with Eli's favorite things: crayons and thick card stock that wouldn't tear when he jabbed too hard, a plastic truck with bright green wheels for spinning, plastic sushi to chop, and a portable DVD player on which to watch his movie selections for the trip (*The Lion King* and a film called *Fireside Reflections*, essentially identical to the burning Yule log that airs on TV around Christmas). Before they left, Gayle positioned the DVD player on the back of the passenger seat and turned on *Fireside Reflections*.

"What do you want, roaring or flickering?" she asked, clicking through the DVD menu.

"Let's hear . . . flickering!" Eli said. The flickering flames occupied his attention all the way through Connecticut, across the New York border, and into Pennsylvania. Then the questions began. He was particularly interested in the prospect of arts and crafts at camp. He'd asked Gayle many times already whether he could do craft projects there. The answer was always yes, which was what he wanted to hear. But now he asked again, looking up from the card stock on which he was scribbling furiously.

"Oh," he said casually, as if this was occurring to him for the first time, "I am gonna do crafts?"

Gayle glanced in the rearview, where he caught her eye. "What do you think?" she asked.

"Yeah!" he said, nodding enthusiastically. He scribbled again for a minute or two.

"I'm going to do painting?" he asked suddenly, looking up with a worried expression.

"I don't know about that," Gayle said. "You'll have to see what they have planned for you."

Eli considered his crayon. "What time am I going to do crafts?" he asked.

"Well, there's going to be a system. Do you know what a system is?" Gayle said.

"Instruments?" he asked. He knew there was a musical component to the camp, so it was a logical guess.

"It means there's going to be an order to things, a schedule," Gayle said.

"Oh!" he exclaimed, nodding. "When am I going to paint?"

Even if Gayle could have answered with a specific time—basket weaving at 2 p.m., painting at 2:30—she knew he'd still ask again and again. The answers themselves weren't important. Many times he already knew them and could fill them in himself if she turned the questions around on him. But it made for a long car ride.

He had asked, "Where's Michigan?" for the first time in eastern Pennsylvania. By western Pennsylvania, he'd asked it about a hundred times. Gayle's first response was "A long way away," but that only intensified the questions. Among the rolling hills of central Pennsylvania, she tried to divert his attention back to the present.

"It's farther on," she said, "but for now we get to enjoy a fun road trip and look at all this beautiful scenery."

"What's scenery?" Eli asked suspiciously.

"It's out there," Gayle said, gesturing through the windshield. "It's those trees, and that valley."

"But where's Michigan?" he asked.

"It's west," Gayle said, her tone verging on exasperation.

"What's west?"

"To the left of east."

"What's east?"

"We're east. Connecticut is east." Her tone was now fully exasperated.

So was Eli's. "But where is Michigan?" he whined. "Can you tell me?"

"Eli," Gayle said, sighing, "you need to learn to live in the now."

"I do?" he asked, genuinely perplexed. "Why?"

"Because you need to relax," she said, softening her voice. She smiled at him in the rearview mirror. "Enjoy the moment!"

He mulled this over. Then he asked imploringly, "But where's Michigan?"

––––

THE ROAD TRIP WAS A STUDY in the varied responses Eli evoked from the general public. At a McDonald's in Port Jervis, New York, an old railroad town on the Pennsylvania border, a woman washing her hands in the women's restroom gave Gayle a sour look when she brought Eli in with her. Her look soured further when Gayle and Eli both entered the handicapped stall. The woman shook her head and stormed out of the bathroom, muttering something unintelligible, as though she were stalking off to complain to the management.

Gayle had gotten these looks before, but she couldn't let Eli go to the bathroom alone. Apart from the possibility of encountering unsavory characters, there was the question of hygiene. She considered herself and Eli lucky that his digestive troubles were no longer so severe that he had to wear a diaper into his teens, as some kids with Williams did. But he was uncoordinated enough not to do a great job of wiping or of getting himself dressed again. When he tried to do it himself, he usually hiked his underwear halfway up to his chest and tucked his shirt into it. Gayle could never understand how he didn't feel what must have been a colossal wedgie, but he was oblivious. Someday, in her quest to make Eli more independent, she knew she'd have to let him go by himself and just do the best he could. *He'd come back with his underwear around his neck, but he could do it,* she thought. But not just yet—not in a McDonald's bathroom on the interstate.

———

GAYLE HAD PLANNED TO DRIVE UNTIL she got too tired, then stop at a roadside hotel. By the time she found a room in Toledo, Ohio, at around 11 p.m., Eli was rocking frenetically, wired from overtiredness and ADHD. His last dose of Ritalin had worn off hours earlier.

They waited at the front desk of the Red Roof Inn while a clerk began the slow process of booking their room. Eli rocked forward on the balls of his feet, his head bent so that he resembled a charging bull. Over and over he thrust his forehead toward the high marble countertop with enough force that Gayle feared he would crack his skull open. She pulled him back a foot or two. He continued to rock with the same velocity, but from a safer distance.

Another family walked into the lobby: a mother and father with two skinny teenage girls. By now Eli had begun to punctuate his rocking with small yipping noises.

"Eli, stop. Be still," Gayle said.

"I think I'm ready," he proclaimed loudly. He twirled his fingers, flexing his hands into claws. "What room number is it?"

The clerk apologized sheepishly. "I'm going as fast as I can," she said, directing her words to Gayle, not Eli. "The system's a little slow."

Eli rocked harder. Behind him, one of the girls whispered something to their mother. The girls burst into giggles and then turned away, stifling their laughter. The mother smiled uneasily at Gayle and hushed the girls. Gayle stiffened. Eli turned with a half smile, hoping to be let in on the joke.

"Look forward," Gayle said, nudging his shoulder with hers and pulling him in front of her. She trailed her arms across his chest protectively. He shifted in her embrace and snuck another look at the girls.

"Look forward," Gayle repeated. Her voice was quiet but sharp-edged.

Gayle couldn't be sure the girls were laughing at Eli, but a wave of indignation pulled her spine taut nonetheless. Eli continued to rock, a hopeful expression on his face. He kept turning to look at the giggling family. He smiled eagerly at them every time, waiting for someone to deliver the punch line. They averted their eyes from his, but he didn't stop staring or smiling until Gayle shepherded him out of the lobby.

———

WHILE ENCOUNTERS LIKE THESE LEFT GAYLE reeling, Eli never seemed to mind or even to notice. He considered every social interaction worthwhile, regardless of the outcome. And his track record showed that he was far more likely to win over strangers than to invoke mockery or disdain. When he was a toddler, hardly anyone turned away from his outstretched arms: most people hugged him back and appeared flattered by the affection. Now that Gayle was trying to wean him from hugging strangers, he still found ways to connect. Instead of hugs, he often sought small favors. At restaurants he'd invariably ask for something extra: more chips, more rolls, extra crayons for the children's menu, extra children's menus to color on. The thing itself seemed to matter less than the special attention being paid to him. It never occurred to him that he was overstepping his bounds or inconveniencing the waiter. In a world where everybody was already friends, there could be no bounds to overstep. Friends were always happy to help each other out.

Most people were, in fact, more than willing to accommodate

Eli's requests. At a diner where Gayle and Eli stopped along the road, Eli was enchanted by the spiral shape of the curly straw in his soda, and asked the waitress for another one. She brought him six. He was so thrilled that he summarily flattened them, one by one, against the table. Then he asked for a second round. This time Gayle waved the waitress away. She didn't like Eli's habit of seeking favors. She didn't want him to be a beggar or to feel entitled to special treatment. She often thought of Eli's kindergarten teacher, who had once warned her that this apparent perk wouldn't work in Eli's favor in the long term, because it let him get away with behavior that wouldn't be tolerated as he aged. It would hardly be tolerated from most kindergartners. "He's lucky he's so cute," the teacher said. Implied in her warning was the fact that, as for all children, Eli's cuteness had an expiration date. His just had a longer shelf life, thanks to his pixieish looks and childlike personality.

On the last leg of their trip, Gayle stopped for lunch at a Cracker Barrel. She reminded Eli before they had even left the car that he would be expected not to hug anyone inside. He wouldn't ask the waitstaff for favors. He wouldn't beg to turn the ceiling fans on or off. He wouldn't bother the waiter, or anyone sitting nearby, with inappropriate questions. He wouldn't erupt into song.

"OK, Mom!" Eli shouted from the backseat. Once inside, he gave the waitress a vigorous handshake but not a hug. He asked about the ceiling fans, but only once. He sang portions of the *Lion King* soundtrack, but quietly. So, to reward him for his good behavior, Gayle let him pick out a small toy from the Cracker Barrel store. He chose a pinwheel in the shape of a flower.

They were on their way to the register when Eli noticed a game called Sharky's Diner, the object of which was to fish plastic food out of a plastic shark's mouth before its "CHOMPING ACTION JAWS!" snapped shut. Eli asked for this, too, but the game was $19.99. Gayle said no and got in line.

"But, Mom, I want *Sharky Dinner!*" he whined, his voice rising frantically. "Just one? PLEASE?"

He tugged on Gayle's shirt, stomping emphatically. She stared straight ahead, ignoring him.

A boy about Eli's age stood quietly in line with his father just in front of them. He turned his head and gave Eli an astonished look. Gayle registered how the scene must have appeared through his eyes: a twelve-year-old boy holding a flower-petal pinwheel, stomping his feet, and crying over "Sharky Dinner." Gayle's face flushed. She grabbed Eli's arm and looked him in the eye.

"You're not going to get anything if you keep acting like this," she said.

A saleswoman materialized from nowhere and asked Eli, in the soft tones usually reserved for toddlers, "You like the shark, huh?"

"Yeah! You can buy it for me?" he asked, smiling through his tears.

"Oh, I don't think so," the woman said, her eyes widening in surprise. "But that's a nice pinwheel, too."

"I want the shark," Eli moaned imploringly.

By now everyone in the store had looked up from the scented candles and saltwater taffy. All eyes were on Eli as he cried and scuffed his sneakers on the rug. Gayle was mortified. In a single fluid movement she steered Eli out of line, dropped the pinwheel back in its stand, and pulled her son out the door. It happened so quickly that Eli was buckled into the backseat before he realized he hadn't gotten the shark *or* the pinwheel.

Gayle pulled out of the parking lot, and Cracker Barrel disappeared behind the trees. Eli wailed and kicked the passenger seat wildly. His face was red and flushed with tears. He sat surrounded by a pile of toys, all once as appealing to him as the shark. A few fell to the floor from the force of his kicking. But eventually he stopped flailing and wiped away the tears. He seemed to recover all at once, as if he'd simply flipped the off switch on his tantrum.

"I'm sorry, Mom," he said with genuine remorse.

Gayle wondered whether he understood the correlation between his tantrum and its consequences. Now that he had cooled down, she asked him why he didn't get the pinwheel. He couldn't answer.

"Were you being loud in the store?" she prompted.

"Yeah," he said, hanging his head.

"Were you listening to what I told you?"

"No, Mom! I wasn't listening."

"And did you ask that woman to buy you something?"

"Yeah!" His head popped back up and he smiled again, displaying gleaming rows of braces. "Sharky Dinner!"

"Why did you ask her that?" Gayle asked. She had begun to think that no punishment would ever correct Eli's behavior, since even when he replayed scenes like this in his mind he couldn't see where he'd gone wrong. Apart from his toddler-like tendency to respond to frustration with tantrums, the more worrisome problem was that he couldn't see a reason not to ask for, or accept, a gift from someone he'd never met. "Do you know her? Do we ask strangers to buy us things?"

"No," Eli said, sensing that this was the correct answer. But he had forgotten the lesson an hour later when Gayle came up with a role-playing exercise to pass the time on the road. She told Eli to pretend she was a stranger he met in a store. She gave the word "stranger" an ominous inflection, dark and dangerous.

"What would you say if you met me for the first time? If you didn't know me?" she asked.

"Hi, stranger!" Eli said. In his lilting voice, the word carried no weight at all.

"Hi, little boy," she said, her voice lower than usual and just slightly sinister. "What's your name?"

"Eli! Can we go to the store?"

"Oh!" Gayle's expression registered a flicker of surprise. Either Eli didn't understand that they were role-playing or this was exactly what he'd say to a sinister stranger. She suspected it was the latter.

"I don't go to the store with *strangers*," she tried. Again the word hung heavy with implied warning.

"*I* do!" he said. He smiled earnestly, enjoying the game.

Eleven

Eli Goes to Camp

On the rural fringe of Grand Rapids, Michigan, Gayle followed a handwritten sign for Whispering Trails camp. It led her down a gravel road, through dense woods, and finally to a clearing surrounded by cabins.

For most of the summer the campground was home to sessions for children and adults with a variety of disabilities, including spina bifida, cerebral palsy, Down syndrome, and autism. The bathrooms and shower stalls were all wheelchair-accessible, and a shed housed shiny red tricycles, some of them big enough for adults. This week's camp, however, was just for kids with Williams.

It was a muggy afternoon. The air in the campground was thick and sweet with the smell of cut grass and bug spray. Gayle parked in a dirt lot and, with Eli in tow, followed a path to a low, modern building overlooking a pond and a wooden dock lined with canoes. Inside they found the camp's cafeteria and a performance space where a group of camp counselors played guitars and bongos among mismatched couches and beanbag chairs. It was chaotic and loud—not so much from the acoustic musical performance as from the delighted squeals of a handful of children dancing rapturously while their parents, exhausted by travel, looked on.

Eli walked up to the nearest guitar player.

"Hi, I'm Eli!" he announced, waving his hand in the man's face. The man, in his twenties with long brown hair tied into a low ponytail, smiled and nodded but kept strumming the guitar.

Eli pointed at him, trying to get his attention.

"Oh, what time are you going to light the campfire?" Eli asked.

Without pausing his playing, the man looked over his shoulder at the other guitarists. "Can we sing a song about campfires?" he asked. "Eli likes campfires."

The man was a music therapist named Louie Morand, whose main gig was working with juvenile offenders in an urban detention center. The hardest part of his day job was getting street-tough kids to open up and let themselves be vulnerable. "It's a different environment," Louie later explained, comparing the Williams camp to juvenile detention. "Kind of the exact opposite environment."

The campers formed a bouncing circle around Louie and the other musicians. A tall, lanky girl with Coke-bottle glasses twirled in dizzying spirals. A tiny peanut of a boy banged a tambourine against his palm. Eli grabbed a shaker from a pile of instruments and waved it wildly, flailing his body along with it. His face grew beet red and his smile ecstatic; the chattering of his shaker nearly drowned out the acoustic guitars. Louie chanted, "Go, Eli! Go, Eli!" The tall girl and the tiny boy joined in the chant.

Gayle was encouraged to see how easily and instantly Eli had been included. For the first time in a long time she relaxed the muscle that was normally tensed and ready to pull him out of an awkward encounter. It was clear from the start that in this environment he'd be unlikely to elicit the disdain, mockery, or bewildered stares she usually tried to fend off. For once his behavior was no different from anyone else's.

Gayle had always hoped his musicality would build bridges at his regular school as well. Eli loved chorus, and it had seemed at first like his best chance at finding his niche. His booming voice carried every song; it was always on pitch, always the loudest of the group. But the school's music director didn't seem to appreciate Eli's boisterous singing style.

The previous year, just before the school's holiday concert, Gayle got a call from Eli's special-education teacher, who asked whether Eli was afraid to go onstage.

"Would he be too embarrassed?" the teacher asked.

"Are you kidding?" Gayle said. "He loves being onstage. He's not embarrassed by anything."

"Hmm," the teacher said. "That's what I thought." She told Gayle she had just heard from the music director that Eli didn't want to perform in the concert. It didn't sound like Eli to her, so she wanted to call to double-check. She hung up the phone, met with the director, and called Gayle back, explaining that now he was saying Eli didn't know the material they'd be performing.

Gayle was infuriated. Eli had been practicing the Christmas songs every night for weeks. Gayle thought he sounded great. And no matter how he sounded or how well he had memorized the songs, she thought, he had every right to be onstage with the rest of his class.

She gave the teacher some choice words to share with the music director. The teacher paraphrased, but ultimately the director relented. Eli was in the show.

In the concert, his voice was loud and rich with vibrato. He raised his right hand as he sang, cupping the air and lifting it toward the ceiling the way he'd seen Pavarotti do it in YouTube videos. *He does get a little overexcited,* Gayle thought, watching her son steal the spotlight. *Maybe that's what the music director didn't want—for him to overshadow the other kids.*

But no one else seemed to mind. After the show, other parents told Gayle how much they had enjoyed Eli's performance.

"He's got flair," one said.

Later, Eli's teacher tried to smooth things over with Gayle, who was still fuming over the episode.

"Not everyone's trained in inclusion," the teacher said, using the special-ed buzzword to explain the music director's mistake.

Gayle did not find this explanation satisfactory. *In the twenty-first century, you don't know that you should try to include everyone?* she thought. *That's not special training. That's being human.*

———

ELI AND GAYLE MADE THEIR WAY to the Algonquin Cabin, where they'd be spending the next five days along with three other boys and their mothers. When they walked in, one of the boys, a ten-year-old named Eric, was performing energetic karate chops in the middle of the room, leaping into the air and then landing heavily, slicing the air with a guttural "Yah!"

Eric's mother called him over to where she stood tucking sheets around a plasticized mattress. In reply, he chopped the air defiantly. His mother shook her head.

"It's like he has no self-control," she lamented.

"I know the feeling," said Gayle. Eli, meanwhile, noticed the overhead ceiling fan and shrieked with glee.

"I love this cabin!" he shouted, bolting past Eric to the center of the room, where he gawked at the ceiling. "It's so beautiful!"

The cabin was lined with wooden bunks in facing rows separated by windows with red gingham curtains. The three other pairs of mothers and sons had arrived earlier and piled their luggage on the bunks they'd claimed. Gayle set her bags down on the beds opposite those taken by Eric and his mother. Eric had marked his bed with the blue stuffed monster he carried wherever he went—unless he was karate chopping. One bed over, a woman who introduced herself as Amy sorted through a pile of clothes to find a change of shirt for her son, eleven-year-old Duncan.

On the far end of Eli and Gayle's row were eleven-year-old Mark and his mother, Kathleen, both Whispering Trails veterans. Kathleen crossed the cabin to introduce herself to Gayle and then to Eli, who said a quick hello without looking away from the fan.

"Oh, he has the typical interests," Kathleen observed. "Fans, vacuums, spinners?"

Gayle nodded.

"The first year we were here, we tried to hide the vacuums," Kathleen said. "All the campers were obsessed. They'd run off and we'd find them in the cabins, vacuuming."

While they talked, Eli sang a bar of the *Lion King* song "Hakuna Matata."

"*When I was a young warthog,*" he bellowed, still staring at the ceiling fan.

"*When I was a young wartHOG!*" Mark bellowed back. Eli finally lowered his chin and looked at his bunkmate. Without pausing to introduce themselves, they fell instantly into the easy rapport of a lounge act.

"*It's my problem-free . . .*" Eli sang, and pointed to Mark.

"*. . . philosophy,*" Mark went on. "*Hakuna Matata!*" The boys both doubled over with laughter.

Their unfettered exuberance warmed Gayle's heart and reassured her that coming here had been the right choice. Eli was free to be himself without adjusting to fit someone else's standards. Gayle was free from the burden of explaining his actions. If he ran off to vacuum, no one would ask why. And he wouldn't be alone. This feeling of freedom was exactly what she had wished for when she signed him up for camp.

It was only an hour or two later that Gayle remembered the adage about being careful what you wish for. She was making Eli's bed when Eli wandered out the cabin door, following Mark and Eric up the hill toward the cafeteria. She looked up to find him gone.

"Where did Eli go?" she asked with a hint of panic.

"They're walking up to dinner," Kathleen answered breezily. Seeing Gayle's face go white, she added, "They're pretty safe around here."

"Oh, I know," Gayle said quickly, but it didn't stop her from dropping the sheets onto the bed and reaching for her purse. Eli had almost never been out of her sight; now he was roaming the Michigan wilderness with kids he'd just met. Her heart raced and she moved toward the door, trying not to run. But before she could escape, Kathleen launched into an explanation of camp procedure, the daily schedule, how the kids would be sorted into groups by age.

"There are five or six kids in each group, labeled by color. I think Eli's in the red group with Mark. What does it say on your schedule?"

Gayle didn't answer. Her eyes remained fixed on the window, where she spotted Eli disappearing up the path to the main lodge. She edged toward the door while Kathleen spoke.

"I'm just going to head up," she said, pointing out the window with an apologetic look. Kathleen's eyebrows rose. Gayle was suddenly self-conscious of how overprotective she appeared to be.

Kathleen seemed to read her mind. "Everyone's a little uptight their first time here," she said soothingly.

"Tomorrow I'll be better," Gayle promised. She smiled sheepishly.

"Yeah, maybe," Kathleen said, nodding.

"I'm a single parent," Gayle added. "It's always just us. I guess I keep him on a short leash."

"Sure, of course," Kathleen said. "It's all right."

By now Gayle was at the cabin door; she opened it and speed walked toward the cafeteria. She rejoined Eli just as he swooped in for a hug from a young, curvaceous woman, one of the camp counselors. Gayle's real-world instincts kicked in again, and she pried him away from the woman.

———

WHILE THE OTHER MOTHERS ALLOWED THEIR children to tear through the cabins like hyperactive tornadoes, hugging whomever they wanted, Gayle kept pulling Eli to her side, admonishing him to quiet down, to keep his hands to himself, to stop harassing the counselors. She was astonished by the laxity of the other mothers. They, in turn, were surprised by her vigilance.

One of Gayle's bunkmates—Duncan's mother, Amy—urged Gayle to think of camp as a break from the real world, a vacation from the constant supervision that Williams normally required. During the day, she told Gayle, most parents left their kids with the counselors and went into town.

"From 8:30 to lunchtime, you can do whatever you want," Amy said. "We go to Starbucks or go shopping."

"Wow, three hours of free time?" Gayle said. "I haven't had that in . . . twelve years." She smiled, but somehow the prospect didn't strike her as a relief. It took all her willpower to leave Eli behind and head to Starbucks the next morning. She ordered a latte, then stopped at Meijer for more bug spray and some snacks for Eli.

But when the checkout line moved slowly, she grew restless. She leafed through *Us Weekly* without looking at it. She told herself it was the caffeine making her jittery, but still she raced back to camp, returning well before lunchtime.

Watching other mothers relax, giving their children relatively free rein, Gayle wondered whether she was being too uptight—or whether Eli was more of a handful than the rest of the kids.

Each day the campers went through a circuit of different sessions. They sang, danced, and drummed, in turn; they played xylophones and recorders; and, of course, they made crafts. The campers earned a plastic bead for completing a session successfully, which meant keeping their hands to themselves, paying attention, following instructions, and respecting personal boundaries. They strung the beads proudly on the lanyards that bore their name tags. But by the end of the first day Eli had accrued noticeably fewer beads than the other campers in his group.

Is he the problem child here? Gayle wondered. Then someone else's child would ambush-hug her or throw a tantrum, and she'd remind herself that they all had their own issues. She had her issues as well, she knew, and hypervigilance was one.

———

THE COUNSELORS DIDN'T SEE ELI AS a "problem child," as Gayle feared, but it wasn't entirely in her head that he stood out—even here, surrounded by other kids with a tendency to be overfriendly—in his disregard for social boundaries and his rampant hugging. Some said that his behavioral challenges seemed more severe than usual for people with Williams.

What concerned them more, for Eli's sake, was his obsessive worry about the future. They'd noticed his tendency to get stuck in repetitive loops, fixating on upcoming events and asking about them endlessly. This, too, was common among kids with Williams syndrome, but Eli had it especially bad. "When are we gonna do crafts?" was still top on his list, followed closely by "When are you gonna light the campfire?" "When's lunch?" and "When's dinner?" also saw heavy rotation. The questions never stopped, no matter how often they were answered.

At breakfast on the second day of camp, Louie shared the staff's observations with Gayle.

"Tell me about it," she said, nodding. "I was just telling him in the car on the way up here, 'Eli, you've got to learn to live in the *now*.'" She jabbed Eli lightly with her elbow, but he was too busy inhaling a bowl of Froot Loops to respond.

Louie told her that the counselors had brainstormed a musical strategy that might help: a little jingle they'd written just for Eli. "Do you want to hear it?" he asked, turning to look at Eli.

"Yeah!" Eli said.

Clapping his hands on his thighs, Louie chanted, "*I'm ready for the here! Ready for the now! Ready for the here, for the here right now!*" Then he did it a second time, urging Eli to chime in. Eli sang along, then giggled, pleased as much with the attention as with the song. Gayle smiled, too, grateful that the counselors had gone to so much trouble even if she wasn't convinced it would effectively ground Eli in the present. When she asked him to repeat it later in the day, he sang, "*Ready for here! Ready for now! Ready to go—hooray!*" Then he added, "When's dinner?"

Right after learning the jingle, Eli had a drumming lesson with Louie. He followed Mark and the four other members of the Red Group into the same performance space where they'd had the opening day jam session. Louie sat by the windows, holding a hand drum in his lap.

"What are we doing next?" Eli asked.

"We're playing drums, Eli," Louie said.

"No, I mean, what are we doing *after* drums?"

"I'm just thinking about drums now," Louie said warmly. "It's all I can think about, man!"

Louie taught the group Eli's new song and led them in a spirited rendition. *"Are we ready for the here? Ready for the now? Ready for the here, for the here right now?"* While the rest of the group chanted, Eli noticed the counselor in charge of arts and crafts passing through the back of the room. He jumped from his seat and rushed toward her, stretching his arm out and waving as if he were hailing a cab.

"When are we gonna do our project?" he asked. She looked startled; she had no idea what project he was talking about. He apparently had big ideas of his own. Before she could answer, Louie jogged over to Eli, put an arm around him, and guided him back to the drum circle.

Louie was dressed casually for camp in a T-shirt and cargo shorts, a hemp necklace, and slip-on shoes. He had kindly eyes, expressive eyebrows, and a quick smile. He also happened to be missing the middle and ring fingers on his right hand. Eli noticed this while Louie went over the rules of the drum session. Louie had just explained what "active listening" entailed when Eli interjected: "Hey! What happened to your fingers?"

"I was born this way, and that's all I've got time to say about it right now," Louie answered, unfazed, and resumed his instructions. He moved on to a discussion of good manners, but Eli couldn't stop interrupting.

"What happened to your fingers? What happened to your fingers? What happened to your fingers?!?"

Finally, Louie stopped talking and turned to face Eli. Eli was momentarily silent. Louie looked around the room. In the same unhurried, friendly tone, he asked, "How many people here know that they are a little bit . . . a little bit different? In an awesome, supercool way?"

"Yeah," said Mark, sitting to Eli's left, with a smile that crinkled his nose.

The tall girl with Coke-bottle glasses shot her hand up.

"Ooh!" said another girl, waving her hand.

Louie surveyed the remaining three in the group.

"Your hand should be up," he told a girl whose hands were still folded in her lap.

"Your hand should be up," he told another.

"Your hand should be up," he told Eli. "Hands should be in the air! Wave 'em like you just don't care!"

By now all hands were up and waving. The six kids hooted riotously. Louie raised his voice meaningfully, like a preacher reaching the climax of his sermon.

"And that's exactly what I like to do!" he cheered, holding his hands aloft. "I was born without these two fingers, but you know what? I like to put my hands in the air and wave 'em like I just don't care. Because differences are what make people cooler. That's my opinion. A lot of people share this opinion with me. And those happen to be the cool people in the world."

Eli was listening actively when Louie resumed his instructions. After the group settled down, they took turns following Louie's lead and emulating the different rhythms he beat on the hand drum. When Eli took his turn, he lost track of the rhythm and pounded the drum wildly, channeling Animal from the Muppets. But he didn't ask about Louie's fingers again.

When Gayle heard about the session later, she wasn't surprised that Eli had asked about Louie's hand. He often fixated on physical abnormalities. Gayle was still embarrassed about the way he'd treated a Friendly's waitress, months earlier, who had severe acne. "What happened to your face?" Eli had asked the girl before Gayle could stop him. "Something bit you?"

What surprised Gayle this time was that Eli eventually stopped asking the question. Louie's answer evidently appeased him in a way that so few other answers ever had. It was often a mystery to Gayle what would mollify Eli when he got stuck on a question. The key was to intuit the true source of his anxiety. It required the same mind-reading abilities all parents used with their children, especially those too young to articulate complex feelings and desires. But Eli's thoughts and desires were so unlike Gayle's that she sometimes struggled to predict them. For example, when Eli asked what time dinner was, he didn't really care about the time: 6 p.m. meant little to him, since he didn't read clocks. He was really worried about some other element related to dinner: *Will we go out to eat? Will there be a ceiling fan? Will I meet a new waitress? Will I get dessert?*

Eli couldn't always articulate the specific object of his curiosity. In this case, Gayle thought, his question must have had less to do with the anatomical facts of Louie's hand and more to do with what it meant to be different, with where you fit in the world when you weren't like everybody else.

She couldn't be sure exactly how Eli had interpreted Louie's answer, but however he took it, it satisfied him enough to move on.

————

GAYLE WONDERED ABOUT HER OWN BEHAVIOR at camp, too. Although she focused more on Eli's anxiety, she could have used her own jingle about living in the now—or at least accepting the now for what it was. And while she knew that anxiety was a near-universal fixture of Williams syndrome, she couldn't help but think she was contributing to Eli's fear for the future with her own fears. Eli, an expert reader of moods, must have picked up on her apprehension. But she was unable to shake it.

Why couldn't she loosen up like the other parents and let Eli wander unsupervised within the boundaries of this sheltered camp-ground? One defense was that when they returned to Connecticut, he'd be expected to act differently, so she didn't want to set a precedent of free rein here and then force him to unlearn it later. She knew he'd be unable to tell the difference between a safe and an unsafe environment, between his friends here and those who would exploit him in the real world. But that was true for all the kids at camp, and their parents managed to give them a longer leash than she could tolerate for her own son.

She tried to see the benefits of following their lead and loosening up. After all, camp could be Eli's one chance to befriend other kids just like him. That connection meant everything to him. And why shouldn't he get the chance to spend time with his friends unchaperoned? Someday Gayle wouldn't be around to eat dinner with him, draw spirals for him, and applaud his singing. And someday he might prefer the company of a girl who *wasn't* his mother. Maybe even someday soon. Blushing romances abounded among the preteens at camp.

One afternoon in the Algonquin Cabin, Mark asked where Duncan was.

"Wherever the girls are, that's where Duncan is," said Amy with a sigh. "My son's a big mack daddy." A quick look out the window confirmed this: Duncan was by the pond, swinging on a tire swing with three girls who were eyeing him adoringly.

Duncan had made an impression on a number of the girls here. One of them, Ada, raced to claim the coveted spot next to him at nearly every meal. At the campfire one night, Ada practically elbowed another girl out of the way.

"Move over, honey," she cooed to Duncan, "so your wife can sit down."

Amy had warned Duncan not to pay attention to any one girl exclusively but to be nice to all of them. She hoped this would avoid a meltdown like the previous year's, when two girls at camp both thought they were Duncan's girlfriend, and then were heartbroken when they discovered each other. In this way kids with Williams weren't so different from anyone else: despite seeing everyone as a friend, they still valued exclusivity. They wanted the person they liked the most to like *them* the most.

Amy told the Algonquin Cabin mothers that she thought she had some time before Duncan's girl problems took on serious proportions, judging by his response to his school's sex ed class.

"I asked him, 'How did that go?' I was thinking, 'You're the mack daddy; did you find out anything you can use?' But he was like, 'Not good.'" She shook her head gravely, miming his response.

She'd asked what bothered him about it, and he had replied, in a horrified whisper, "We talked about *vaginas . . . They grow hair on them!*"

It had been a relief to Amy. "I thought: 'Oh, good, we're not ready for that yet!'"

Gayle laughed along with the other two cabin mothers. Mark, who had been listening from across the room, piped up, "*I am!*"

Gayle was grateful that Eli hadn't shown much interest in the girls of Whispering Trails. He was definitely not a chick magnet like his bunkmate. Apart from the usual hugging and declarations of love, he hadn't paid extra attention to specific girls, at home or at camp.

Then, later that day, he met Susie.

He noticed the willowy eleven-year-old in the crowd mingling outside the dining hall after dinner, radiant in the late golden sunlight as she giggled over something with Ada. Eli stopped in his tracks and watched her with an intensity normally reserved for ceiling fans or industrial floor scrubbers. Then he approached, as quickly as his lumbering gait allowed, and threw his arms out to hug her. Without even seeming to fully see him, she turned and ducked out of reach. She looked at Ada and rolled her eyes.

"He's weird," Susie said.

Undeterred by the brush-off, Eli positioned himself in front of her again. "Hi! What's your name?" he said. She ducked away once more. Eli wheeled around her like a planet around the sun. "I'm saying hi!" he shouted. "Say hi to me!"

Susie shook him off and sprinted toward the girls' cabin. Eli stayed frozen in place, looking stunned. The exchange had blasted cold air into what was otherwise a summertime paradise of brotherly love. Susie, it seemed, was not indiscriminately friendly, as almost everyone else here was. She had selected the friends she wanted, and Eli was not among them. Surrounded by Williams kids, where inclusion had so far been the rule, he suddenly found himself excluded again.

Gayle, too, looked stunned. She had been watching from the edge of the crowd, pretending to listen to a conversation among the grown-ups but secretly keeping an eagle eye on her son. She'd been trying to give Eli his space, to restrain her protective instincts, but now her guard went up again. After watching him effortlessly befriend everyone else he'd met here, she wondered why this encounter had ended so differently—or so *normally*. She swooped in and put her hand on his back.

"Not everyone likes to be hugged," she said gently, trying both to ease the sting and to drive home a lesson. But it wasn't a lesson she had expected to teach here. And it wasn't a lesson Eli was willing, or able, to learn in any case.

From then on, whenever Eli saw Susie, he followed her like a puppy, pleading for her attention. He learned her name. "Hi, Susie!" he'd call. "Hi! Hi! Hi!"

Often she would curl her lip into an annoyed half snarl, then stalk off. If he followed, she'd hiss, "Go away!" Gayle tried to rein in his pursuit.

"It's OK," she told him. "She just doesn't want to say hi. Leave her alone."

Although Gayle knew better than anyone how intrusive Eli could be, his request—to be acknowledged—was so meager, and Susie's rebuffs were so harsh, that eventually she couldn't help but side with her son. She felt the same urge to defend him that she would have against any bully. It was just that in this case, against all odds, the bully was another kid with Williams.

As they left the dining hall one evening, Gayle and Eli crossed paths with Susie once again. He smiled his big lopsided smile, still hoping to make instant friends. Each encounter, in his mind, was a new chance to win her over. Each time he wiped the slate clean of past snubs. But Susie only scowled and stuck out her tongue at him.

"Hey, be nice to me!" he yelped. Susie stared him down icily, then slowly shook her head.

Gayle turned to her, unable to hold her tongue. "He's just trying to say hi to you," she snapped. "You could just be nice. But whatever."

She instantly regretted her peevish tone. Now it was Susie's turn to look hurt.

"I don't want to be mean!" Susie said. "I can't help it."

Gayle softened. She wasn't sure what Susie meant, exactly, but she suddenly saw in her what she so often saw in Eli: the keen desire for approval, especially from adults. Maybe Susie was just mimicking the bratty behavior she'd seen in other, teenage girls, Gayle thought. Maybe she'd learned how to fit in in the real world, and now she couldn't unlearn it.

"It's OK," Gayle said in the gentle tone she thought of as her kindergarten teacher voice. "He just really wants to be your friend."

"But why did you say, 'You could be nice, but *whatever*'?" Susie asked.

"I just meant that you could say hi back to him. But you don't have to," Gayle said. Susie appeared to mull this over. Then, looking chastened, she trotted off. Gayle's cheeks flamed with guilt. *I can't believe I was just mean to a Williams kid!* she thought.

The next morning Susie walked by the cafeteria table where Gayle and Eli were eating breakfast. When he saw her, Eli dropped his spoon in his cereal with a splash and waved vigorously. Susie copied him, waving back with similar ardor and mirroring his oversize smile.

"Hi!" she said sweetly. "How *are* you?" As she walked by, she tossed a disdainful look back over her shoulder. Gayle was shocked. *Was that sarcasm?* she thought. *I didn't know kids with Williams even registered sarcasm.* She felt a little less guilty for having chastised her the night before.

At camp and in general, Susie was a rare exception to many of the Williams rules. While most people with Williams have a vibrant sense of humor and a fondness for puns and playful language, sarcasm and irony tend to elude them—but not Susie. She had the elfin facial features common to Williams, along with some visual-spatial problems, but overall she seemed to be of above-average intelligence for someone with the syndrome, and much worldlier. It was possible that she, like the girl in Julie Korenberg's study at the Salk Institute, was missing all but the GTF2I gene, making her less gregarious and overfriendly than others with Williams. But it was much more likely that she simply fell on the high end of the regular Williams spectrum and that, through a combination of nature, nurture, and luck, she had developed more sophisticated social skills than Eli and many others. Few people with Williams, after all, had mastered the art of saying one thing and meaning another.

Eli, for one, never doubted his new friend's sincerity. He didn't hear the sharp edge to her voice or notice the daggers she shot with her parting look. Instead he smiled blissfully, acknowledged at last.

Twelve

Learning Curve

When she signed up for camp, Gayle had hoped Eli would benefit from being around other kids just like him. She hadn't expected to learn so much from being surrounded by other moms just like her. The most salient lesson so far was that not all parents policed their kids' behavior as closely as she did. It was possible, and maybe even preferable, to give Eli more room to find his own way in the world.

She wasn't sure how well she could put this lesson into practice, though. Midway through the week, when she found herself still stuck to his side, she concluded that she'd need to start applying the same vigilance to her own behavior that she normally did to his. This meant forcing herself not to hover over him—even if he risked an unpleasant, unchaperoned run-in with Susie. She started by staying away from his camp sessions, where she had lately been the only parent tagging along.

At first Eli was outraged that she'd stayed with the other parents instead of coming with him. He refused to join the rest of his group while they sat in a circle, singing.

"Where's my mom?" he complained loudly. "I can't sit!"

"You're a big guy," said the counselor who was leading the session. "You can sit without her."

"Be a big boy!" echoed one of his fellow campers, her tone earnest and encouraging. Eli shook his head.

"We can't sing without her," Eli said gravely.

"I think we can," said the counselor, and she began the song again. When everyone else started singing, Eli got so caught up in the music that his resistance dissolved and he chimed in.

By the end of the day, he had made a full reversal and come to relish his newfound freedom and the unsupervised time with his friends. That night, after the campers had sung songs around the campfire, roasted marshmallows, brushed their teeth, and gotten into their pajamas, Eli was still so eager for more time with "his boys," as he now referred to his three bunkmates, that he implored Gayle to join the other parents for the adult campfire, a social hour that began when the kids were in bed. Baby monitors in each of the cabins gave parents the peace of mind to venture the hundred or so feet to the fire. The other Algonquin Cabin mothers had gone every night, but Gayle had never joined them. Once again they urged her to come along. This time Eli joined in their urging.

"You can go, Mom," he said encouragingly.

"Oh, I can?" she said, chuckling. "You trying to get rid of me? What would you do if I went?"

"I could go to sleep!" he promised, bouncing a little as he sat on the edge of his bed. "You could wake me up tomorrow when you come back."

She laughed again. "Oh, I don't think I'd be gone that long. It'd be nice if I found a reason to stay out all night."

But in the end she stayed in. It was one thing to leave Eli in a structured setting with a counselor; it was another to leave him in a dark cabin with no adult oversight. And she wasn't here to make friends, after all. She was here so Eli could make friends.

Long after the boys were snoring, though, Gayle lay awake in the dark, wondering if she was missing out. Every so often she heard a faint peal of laughter from the group gathered in the glow of the fire outside. How could they be so relaxed when she felt so wound up? Did parenting a kid with Williams come more easily to everyone else? She reminded herself that this was her first time here and that almost all the other parents had been here before. Maybe it did get easier.

———

AT BREAKFAST THE NEXT MORNING, GAYLE was surprised to hear that the counselors had noticed some improvement in Eli's behavior. Without Gayle's supervision, he had earned beads in nearly every session. Louie stopped by their breakfast table to congratulate Eli on his well-decorated lanyard. Gayle praised him, too, but she couldn't help wondering whether the quick turnaround meant she had contributed to his earlier inability to sit still and follow directions. Maybe she had telegraphed her own fears that he would act up, and he'd simply fulfilled her expectations. He did seem less anxious today. Maybe time away from Gayle was a vacation for him, too.

The turnaround wasn't complete, of course. As Eli shoveled cereal into his mouth, he asked Louie, "When are we gonna have lunch?"

"How about those Froot Loops, Eli?" Louie replied, ignoring the question and peering into Eli's cereal bowl. "What does the red one taste like? Is it different from the green one?"

Eli spooned a red Froot Loop in his mouth and considered it.

"Yeah," he concluded. "It tastes different."

Louie turned to Gayle. "He's doing a lot better," he said. "He's a lot less in the future. When I talk to him, it's not so much about the fireplace and the fan. It's more about what's going on now. Even if it's about cereal—that's legit."

Encouraged by his progress, Gayle sent Eli off to his daytime activities alone again. While he sang songs and made crafts, she joined the other parents in a roundtable discussion of the challenges of raising kids with Williams.

Since the campers ranged in age from six to twelve, the discussion topics varied from *Sesame Street* to sanitary pads. Some parents could speak to both topics at once, since early puberty—in children as young as eight or nine—was a common Williams symptom.

The parents shared their frustrations about doctors who didn't correctly diagnose or treat their kids, and teachers who didn't know how to teach them. They bemoaned the birthday parties their kids weren't invited to, and the invitations to their kids' own birthday parties that went unanswered. They discussed ways of dealing with the anxiety their kids had now, and mused about the ways they would treat it as it worsened in adulthood (as it tended to, combined with the depression many adults with Williams suffered). Talk turned to their children's futures: Would they live independently? Would they find meaningful work? Would their lives be fulfilling?

One woman feared that basic life skills would forever elude her son.

"He's nine now, and he still puts his shoes on the wrong feet," she said. "I have to tie his laces."

Several mothers jumped in to suggest shoes with Velcro. Gayle had made the switch long ago for Eli. The hand-eye coordination necessary for tasks like tying shoes might never fully develop, one woman explained, but it didn't mean people with Williams should need someone else to help dress them.

"Why try to force them to tie shoelaces if they don't have the dexterity?" the woman said. "You can survive without shoelaces. My grandmother has arthritis; she hasn't tied a shoelace in years."

Kathleen said she was constantly adapting her expectations for Mark and trying to get him to revise his own expectations for himself, based on his abilities.

"After all his time in hospitals for heart surgery and angioplasty, Mark decided he wanted to be a cardiologist," she said, shaking her head. "You never say, 'No, you can't be a cardiologist.' You say, 'Why do you want to do it? What appeals to you about that job?' I don't see my son as a cardiologist—that would be kind of scary. But you have to think outside the box. If he likes helping people, what's a way he can do that?"

After the family took a Disney cruise one summer, she fantasized about Mark one day finding a job on a cruise ship, doing something hospitality-related.

"He loves Disney, and I wouldn't have to worry about housing," she said. "But now he wants to be a school principal. What can I say? I think he'd do a better job than his current principal."

Several moms said they didn't expect their children ever to move away from home. They'd resigned themselves to being caregivers for life, sacrificing retirement dreams and trading empty-nest syndrome for eternal motherhood.

"I see my retired friends going on cruises and I think: 'That will never be me,'" one woman said glumly. "If I go on a cruise, my son's coming with me."

But others shared anecdotes about young adults with Williams who lived with at least a modicum of independence. One woman knew of four young men with Williams whose parents had pooled their money to buy a house where the men could live together. They hired part-time caregivers to help keep things running smoothly. Gayle jotted this down in her notepad. A little flower of hope blossomed at the prospect. But she couldn't allow herself too rosy a vision of Eli's future. Allowing that he wasn't the *lowest*-functioning kid with Williams, he certainly wasn't among the *highest*. He might never reach the point where he could live without constant help and supervision.

Someone in the group brought up court-appointed guardianship, a term Gayle knew well from her years of research into disability rights. Unless parents applied for legal guardianship when their kids turned eighteen, their adult children could be held accountable for the sometimes dire consequences of bad decision-making: entering into ill-advised but legally binding contracts, for example, or opening joint bank accounts with unscrupulous acquaintances. Having Williams syndrome didn't free them of responsibility in the eyes of the law. Guardianship gave their parents a say in contracts, credit lines, and other life choices, including health care decisions. Gayle was already planning to apply for guardianship of Eli.

The issue was not merely hypothetical. In 2015 a twenty-eight-year-old man with Williams was arrested on charges of aiding a would-be domestic terrorist, John T. Booker Jr., in his plot to detonate a thousand-pound car bomb at a Kansas military base. Booker, a twenty-year-old Kansan who'd proclaimed ambitions of joining the Islamic State terrorist group, was arrested before the plot could go forward; so was the man with Williams, Alexander Blair, who FBI officials said had known about the plan and had even given Booker $100 to rent a storage locker for the explosives.

Blair's attorneys argued that his disorder had made him especially open to Booker's friendly overtures—and vulnerable to his manipulation. "Mr. Blair, who has a genetic condition known as Williams syndrome, rarely made friends," they wrote in a court document. "He was lonely and receptive to Booker's interest in talking and being friends." But the attorneys entered a guilty plea after Blair confessed his involvement to FBI agents, saying, "Did I like it? No, I didn't. But [Booker] asked me for help, [so] I helped him."

A judge sentenced Blair to fifteen months in prison, the minimum allowed by federal guidelines, despite acknowledging that the punishment seemed excessive and that he didn't believe Blair posed any danger to the community. He said he'd been touched by the number of letters he'd received from Williams parents across the country, which partly influenced his decision to give Blair the lightest possible sentence, rather than the maximum of five years.

Although Blair still lived with his parents, they weren't his legal guardians. And while guardianship, a civil procedure, doesn't negate criminal liability, it can serve as evidence that one is unable to make informed decisions—which could conceivably help in cases like Blair's.

To Gayle, guardianship was a no-brainer. But she was surprised to hear one of the other mothers argue against it. And then doubly surprised when several more murmured their agreement.

"If you get guardianship, you're responsible for everything your kid does," the other mother said. "If he commits a crime, you can go to jail for it."

This didn't jibe with Gayle's understanding of guardianship. In fact, attorneys who handle guardianship say that no one has ever gone to jail for a crime committed by their ward: that would violate the guardian's constitutional right to due process.

But even if the other mother had gotten the facts of guardianship wrong, Gayle was stunned by how easily she seemed to shrug off responsibility for her son. Gayle objected on principle.

"If my kid committed a crime, I *would* go to jail," she blurted out. "What am I going to do, let them lock him up?"

The woman gave Gayle a look, then closed her eyes and shook her head.

"My son could be doing something right now that would change his life forever," she said. "That doesn't mean it has to ruin my life."

Gayle pressed her lips together. She couldn't imagine a path that diverged from her son's, leaving him in the rubble of his own ruined life while hers moved forward.

"He's my son," she said quietly. "Our lives are going to be connected for a long time."

———

THE QUESTION GAYLE REALLY WANTED TO ask in the roundtable discussion was: How do you handle what puberty does to our kids? But after the heated debate over guardianship, the opportunity never came up.

The people she'd asked before, other mothers of teenage boys with Williams, always laughed nervously and said something along the lines of "I just let my husband handle that." Gayle often felt like the only single mother in the special-needs community. That couldn't be true, especially if the divorce rate was as high among special-needs parents as it was sometimes reported, but she couldn't figure out where the other single moms were hiding. *Probably at home,* she thought, *exhausted from working full-time and raising kids by themselves.*

But she hoped she might find someone here who was willing to speak frankly about the subject. Puberty seemed to be rearing its awkward head more obviously with every passing day. She had noted with alarm that the last time Eli hugged the hourglass-shaped Amy, he lingered too long. Then, when Amy pulled away, he made a surreptitious adjustment to his pants. It was a quick, flicking motion—too quick for Gayle to swat his hand away, as she would have liked.

The next time Gayle found herself alone in the cabin with Kathleen, she seized the moment. Considering that eleven-year-old Mark had the thick leg hair of a thirty-year-old man, she guessed that Kathleen must have had some firsthand knowledge of puberty's effects.

"I was wondering," she began, walking over to where Kathleen was folding clothes on the edge of her bed. "Have you noticed Eli kind of touching himself lately? He'll hug someone and then touch himself, real quick. He just kind of puts his hand there."

Kathleen continued folding, her expression unchanged. "We had that problem when Mark was in fourth grade," she said, and without embarrassment told Gayle about her son's classroom erections. Mark, immune to the self-consciousness most teenagers have about their changing bodies, had made no effort to hide them. "We got several notes home from his teacher. We talked about it with him, but it just took a while to get under control. But in fifth grade we didn't get any more notes, so I think it's passed."

Gayle swallowed hard. Getting a note like that from Eli's teacher was one of her worst fears. It would probably mean that other kids in the class had noticed it and said something to the teacher. She would worry that her son had become a pariah. But Kathleen seemed to shrug it off.

"Well, I haven't gotten any notes from school," Gayle said. "But Eli's been doing these full-body hugs, you know? And then he'll just reach down there. I've tried buying him bigger, baggier clothes . . ."

"Yeah, looser clothes definitely help," Kathleen said. "We bought him different underwear, not too tight. That helped."

Gayle smiled uncomfortably. "I know he's starting to, well, *explore his body*. I've told him he just needs to take some privacy, and he's been good about it. He'll just say, 'I'm going up to my room for a while.' I've told him if he has any questions, to let me know." She grimaced and then went on. "You don't want to think about it. But you *do* have to think about it."

"I know—it's true," Kathleen said. She sighed and rearranged a pile of clothes in her open suitcase. "I have my husband talk to him about that stuff, but that's a little harder for you, I bet. He'll say he's going up to his room, and I just pretend he's up there playing video games."

"And you have to be careful not to freak out, or let him think you think it's a bad thing, or he'll feel ashamed," Gayle added.

Kathleen nodded. "And I was careful to say, 'If you need privacy, go into *your* bathroom.' If you say 'Go to *the* bathroom,' they might think it's OK to do it at school or in other people's houses."

"Exactly," Gayle said. She paused, examining her hands. "I just wanted to make sure that's a phase that'll go away."

"Oh, yeah," Kathleen said brightly. "But it took about a year. He might still hug people, but mostly he goes for the handshake or the fist bump. Although he just told one of the counselors he has a crush on her. Which is still not really appropriate, but at least it's not a hug."

Gayle nodded, smiling a tight smile. She worried that the phase might not have been as over as Kathleen thought. She thought about the way Mark had perked up at their earlier discussion of sex ed. *Just because she's not getting notes about it doesn't mean it's not happening*, she thought, and then blanched at the realization that the same could be true for Eli. At the roundtable discussion, she had heard mothers complain that their daughters were overwhelmed by the stress and physical burden of menstruation when, at eight or nine, or even at eleven or twelve, they had the maturity of kindergarteners. Eli was at the same maturity level, Gayle thought.

She wondered if the complications of puberty were more onerous for girls or for boys. Either way, pumping adolescent hormones into what was essentially a five-year-old's brain was a recipe for trouble.

———

ON THE FINAL MORNING OF CAMP, Eli sat in the cafeteria, waiting for Gayle to bring his food, when he spotted Susie at a nearby table. He waved at her, grinning his squinty smile.

"Hi, Susie!"

Not seeing Gayle, Susie did not answer. She gave Eli her trademark glare. This time Susie's mother noticed and intervened on Eli's behalf.

"Susie, he's saying hi! What do you say?"

"Hi," Susie said tersely. It was all Eli needed. Even this much reciprocity made the encounter a success in his book and marked Susie as a great friend. When Gayle later asked Eli which of his new friends he would miss the most, Susie was at the top of the list.

"You're going to miss Susie?" Gayle asked. "Why?" She tried to keep the judgment out of her voice. It crept in anyway, but Eli didn't seem to notice.

"She's my friend," Eli answered without hesitation, as if this were obvious.

"Oh, yeah? What did she say to you?"

"She said, 'Go away.'"

"So why is she your friend?"

"Because I like her!"

"So someone is your friend just because you like them?" Gayle smiled in spite of herself. "Oh, my sweet boy." It was both touching and troubling to learn that Eli would miss the person who least wanted his friendship as much as he missed the boys in his cabin, whose mutual affection was truly heartfelt.

Gayle couldn't help but suspect that an attraction Eli couldn't articulate might have helped push Susie to the top of his friends list. But it didn't discount the fact that he had forged a real connection with his bunkmates, Mark in particular. The night before camp ended, Eli and Mark had a heart-to-heart in their pj's that was one of the longest conversations Eli had ever had with someone his own age—and which didn't center on vacuum cleaners. It did, of course, touch on vacuum cleaners, but it delved more deeply into the boys' innermost thoughts and ambitions. They shared their excitement about the prospect of becoming teenagers, which they both agreed would open new, though vaguely defined, doors in their lives.

Mark's thirteenth birthday would coincide with his older brother Austin's graduation from high school, which he was dreading. So when he talked about becoming a teenager, he tended to flash forward in his imagination to his eighteenth birthday. He knew Austin would have finished college by then, and presumed he'd have moved back home. And turning eighteen, even more than turning thirteen, signaled adulthood and its limitless possibilities. Most notably it seemed to mean you could have friends over whenever you wanted.

"Eli, do you want to come over to my house sometime?" Mark asked. "When Austin's done with college?"

"Where's your house?" Eli asked.

"It's a brick house. In Wisconsin," Mark said, perched on the edge of the bed and rocking slightly with excitement about the plan. Eli sat next to him.

"What kind of fireplace do you have at your house?" Eli asked seriously.

"A real kind," Mark said, nodding affirmatively. "You can warm your hands on it if you come over."

"Cool!" Eli squeaked.

"I might be thirteen then," Mark said, confusing his timeline. "I'll be twelve in September, so you have a long way to go."

"I want to be a teenager. I'll scrub this whole floor," Eli said, waving a hand toward the carpeting.

"When I grow up, and I'm done, I want to come back here, and work here, and build a house here," Mark said.

"I like you, Mark," Eli said.

"Me too," Mark said.

"When I come over, I can see your floor?" Eli asked.

"I'll go to Meijer and get a new Wii for us to play with," Mark promised. "And a Nintendo DS."

"Can I sweep the floors?" Eli asked, indifferent to the offer of video games.

At that moment Eric and his mother entered the cabin. Mark turned to them and feverishly related his plan.

"I'm going to live here when I grow up," he said. "When I'm eighteen."

"You are?" Eric's mother asked. "What are you going to do in the winter?"

Mark thought for a moment. "Just get a TV," he said, shrugging.

"Mom!" Eli shouted, although Gayle was sitting on her bunk just a few feet away. "When am I coming back to Mark's house?"

———

ALL THE WAY HOME FROM CAMP, Eli fixated on the idea of becoming a teenager. The thrill of being part of a tribe, surrounded by his Williams peers, had left him aglow, and he was even chattier and more cheerful than usual on the trip back. He seemed to see the social inclusion of his week at camp not as an isolated experience but as a preview of his life to come. He sang improvised songs about his new friends, some of which were ballads devoted exclusively to Susie.

Although Gayle prompted him a few times to sing the song about living in the now, he quickly reverted to his habit of asking endless questions, most of which now centered on the topic of turning thirteen.

"When am I going to be thirteen, Mom?" he asked for the first time just after leaving the campground. She reminded him of his birthday: February 5.

"And then I'm going to be a man?" he asked.

"Well, maybe not immediately," she said. "Give it a little time."

Once again, none of her answers seemed to satisfy his curiosity, either about when he'd be a teenager or about what life would be like once he was. Each answer prompted another question: "I'm going to get taller?" "I can use the Tennant 5400?" "I'm going to go on dates?"

Since Gayle had some of the same questions herself, she was ill-equipped to answer. So the questions kept coming, from Michigan through Ohio, Pennsylvania, and New York. Just across the Connecticut state line, the car came to a stop in a traffic jam on the Merritt Parkway. It seemed to intensify Eli's anxiety, as if the traffic were holding him back from his progress toward adolescence.

"Mom, can I be a teenager? What time?" he asked with renewed urgency.

"You'll be a teenager on February 5 at 5:38 p.m.," Gayle said.

"And then what kind of school am I going to go to?" he asked.

"Oh, you'll still go to the same school," she said. "You won't go to high school until you're fourteen."

Eli nodded sagely, as if he'd already known this, but was just double-checking. He picked a brown crayon out of his crayon box, gripped it tightly in his fist, and swirled it across a page of his coloring book, obliterating the lines.

"I can't wait to be a teenager," he said.

Gayle looked back at him and smiled, thinking of the rosiness of his vision of adolescence. In his mind it meant boundless joy, visiting friends, scrubbing floors—all the activities he believed he'd been denied by virtue of being twelve and not thirteen.

Her own vision was cloudier. So much of normal adolescence centered on the drive for independence, but she wasn't sure what role, if any, independence would play in Eli's teenage years. It was part of the frustration many teens with Williams endured: the impulse to pull away from their parents coupled with the immaturity and vulnerability that meant their parents couldn't responsibly let them go. They depended on their parents for so much more than the typical teenager did—particularly transportation, since few sixteen-year-olds with Williams, even among the highest-functioning, could learn to drive a car—and there was a good chance that their dependence would carry over into adulthood. Gayle thought of all the things she still did for Eli: bathe him, get him dressed, help him in the bathroom. He was unlikely to be able to perform these tasks on his own by February. Would she still be helping him with them in five years? Ten, even? When *would* he be a man, and what kind of man would he be?

She was dreading the approach of adolescence: the ravages of hormones, the cruelty of other teenagers. For a moment she wished she could jump inside Eli's head and enjoy the view of thirteen through his eyes, without the sense of foreboding her own genes wouldn't let her escape.

Thirteen

The Note Home

Eli's hormones attacked almost as soon as he returned from camp. Once an equal-opportunity hugger, he was now targeting women almost exclusively and especially favoring the curvaceous. The first time he hugged a woman and walked away with an obvious erection, Gayle was mortified. Then it seemed to happen every time. He would stand there chatting happily with the woman, unaware of anything objectionable about his appearance, and Gayle would blanch and usher him away.

The secret life of teenage boys slowly revealed itself to Gayle, who had grown up without brothers and was unschooled in the particulars of male adolescence. She turned to Google to find out what half the population knows by high school: teenage boys have as many as ten to fifteen erections a day (plus another seven to ten in their sleep). She was relieved to read that her son's reactions were normal. In this area of development, at least, he was on par with his peers, despite being so immature in almost every other respect. The problem was that, lacking the social inhibitions and the sense of shame that drives most teenage boys to devise subtle methods of covering up, Eli was a stage on which puberty played out for all to see.

His body is developing, but his brain isn't, Gayle thought. When school started, she bought him longer shirts and looser pants, hoping to camouflage what he never bothered to conceal. He couldn't help it, she knew. But she worried both about his changing preference in whom to hug and how he went about doing it. He had always given bear hugs, but now he seemed to press himself more deliberately against the women he singled out, and for as long as he could get away with. He took advantage of his stature, which put him exactly at breast height on most women, to lean his head against their chests. The new technique catapulted his behavior over the line between innocent and offensive.

One of Gayle's greatest fears was that Eli would be seen as a predator, the way she'd heard others with Williams had sometimes been. One young man, while waiting with his parents at a bus stop, hugged a woman he didn't know and was nearly arrested on assault charges. The woman called the police; the man's parents called Dr. Pober. When a police officer arrived, the geneticist was able to explain the details of Williams syndrome, and the young man wasn't charged. But he could have been, Gayle thought when she heard the story. If the man's parents hadn't been there, or if the officer hadn't been patient enough to consider the extenuating circumstances, he could have ended up in a jail cell. Worse, the woman—or an irate boyfriend or husband—could have responded violently. These were the dangers waiting on the other side of the Great Divide between children who hugged everyone and adults who did.

Of course, people with Williams were much more likely to be taken advantage of than vice versa. Dr. Pober had never come across a single case in which someone with Williams forced himself on someone sexually. "That would never even occur to them," she said. "These are people who wouldn't dream of harming someone." But she could recall many cases in which people with Williams were sexually abused themselves. According to the Massachusetts Disabled Persons

Protection Commission, more than 90 percent of people with developmental disabilities—male and female—experience some form of sexual abuse at some point in their lives. And the open, uninhibited affection shown by people with Williams makes them even more vulnerable to abuse than people with other forms of developmental disability. A survey that researchers believe is vastly underrepresentative found that 10 percent of adults with Williams had reported sexual assault to the police, while another 10 percent said they'd been assaulted but hadn't filed formal charges. Dishearteningly, some people with Williams who've been abused have been discouraged from filing charges because of their disability. One boy with Williams was molested as a six-year-old by a teenage boy. While he was able to tell his parents and the police what had happened, the district attorney's office declined to take the case because they didn't think he would come across as a reliable witness in court.

While Gayle knew of no surefire way to prevent Eli from being abused, apart from never letting him out of her sight, she hoped to keep him from becoming a menace to women by instituting a strict no-hugging policy. Where she had once tried to simply limit Eli's hugging, she now enforced a zero-tolerance standard. She told him that only handshakes and high-fives were acceptable outside their immediate family. Even his cousins now fell into the no-hugging zone.

Eli didn't quite embrace the new policy. He couldn't deny knowing about it, because his mother repeated "Handshakes and high-fives only" whenever they went out—to a restaurant, say, or to practice for his special-needs soccer league. Instead, he would walk up to a woman and announce "Handshakes and high-fives!" before leaning in for the hug he craved. Most people usually hugged back, which made Gayle's job harder. As she detached him from the uninformed, she'd ask them to resist if he tried to hug again, explaining, "I'm trying to teach him it's not acceptable to hug everyone."

It could be as difficult to enforce the policy with others as it was with Eli. One woman, the mother of one of his soccer teammates, just laughed.

"But he's so adorable! I can't say no to him!" she said, ruffling Eli's hair while he beamed at the praise.

You won't think he's so adorable when you see his pants blow up like a circus tent, Gayle thought.

None of the other parents of boys with Williams syndrome seemed to have found the secret to outmaneuvering puberty, either. One mother acknowledged that she had found no way to stop her teenage son from grinding against people.

"I've told his friends just not to let him rub up on them," she said when Gayle asked how she dealt with the problem.

That's not exactly the solution I had in mind, thought Gayle disconsolately. She was still reeling from Kathleen's admission that she'd received multiple notes home from the principal about Mark's erections. *These guys have enough trouble fitting in without walking around all day with a boner,* she thought. She hoped that, with carefully chosen clothing and the no-hugging rule, Eli could minimize the potential damage to his reputation. But she knew that school was the one place where she had no control over his behavior.

———

THE E-MAIL FROM ELI'S SPECIAL-EDUCATION TEACHER popped up in Gayle's in-box on a Monday afternoon in late January, less than three weeks before Eli's thirteenth birthday. In brief but heart-stopping prose, it began: "Time-Out Report: In Tech Ed Class, Eli was rubbing against girls and touching his penis."

Gayle came as close to throwing up as she had since she first learned the term "Williams syndrome." Her fears about Eli's conspicuous sexuality seemed to have suddenly come true. *This is worse than getting a note home about an erection,* she thought. *Much worse.*

The wording of the note left much to the imagination, forcing Gayle to conjure an image of her son as she'd never want to see him. *Did he have it . . . out?* she wondered. *Wouldn't his aide have stopped him from getting that far?*

Her mind jumped to the consequences Eli might face. Would he be allowed in tech-ed class ever again? What about his other main-stream classes? She knew he couldn't be kicked out of school, since federal law forbade public schools from turning students away on the basis of a disability. (This was part of the 1975 Education for All Handicapped Children Act, renamed the Individuals with Disabilities Education Act when it was updated in 1990.) But he could be removed from the classes he attended with his nondisabled peers if his behavior distracted or endangered others.

Gayle studied the e-mail, searching for clues about what would happen next. The immediate result had been that Eli's aide led him out of the tech-ed class and back to his special-ed classroom. There, the note said, Eli "became upset again when redirected. He pushed a chair and began to swear." He went to the "time-out room," an empty room where students who misbehaved were sent to sit alone and think. He spent twelve minutes isolated in this room. Gayle knew it had seemed like a lifetime to Eli, for whom social deprivation was the worst form of torture.

Gayle called Eli's teacher, who clarified that Eli hadn't actually been grinding against girls. Instead, he'd simply stood too close to them and let his shoulder rub against theirs. It was relatively inconspicuous; the girls didn't seem to notice, but his aide did. Gayle had seen him do this before, too. He craved contact so much that when he was barred from hugging, he sought other ways to connect with people that wouldn't get him in trouble.

The touching had been fairly subtle as well; he had given himself the same kind of adjustment Gayle had seen after he'd hugged Amy at camp: a quick flick that his aide might not have noticed if Gayle hadn't forewarned her.

Gayle was at once relieved, then exasperated with the teacher for writing it up so dramatically. It was still troubling, she thought, but nowhere near as troubling as she'd initially feared. The teacher assured her that there was no question of removing Eli from his mainstream classes. But, she said, there was the question of how to keep the problem from escalating.

Gayle set up a meeting with Eli's education team—his teacher, aide, physical therapist, occupational therapist, speech/language therapist, and behaviorist—to address what they were now euphemistically calling "the tech-ed incident" and the changes it signaled. Gayle had already heard from Eli's aide that he had been standing too close to the girls in his gym class, although no one had written up a report on that. Nor had anyone yet proposed a specific plan to address the problem. Gayle hoped they could brainstorm some solutions together. But what they came up with troubled her.

First, they urged Gayle to stop dressing Eli in sweatpants. The soft, loose fabric, it turned out, was both stimulating and terrible at hiding the effects of its stimulation. Gayle cringed. She would never have put him in sweatpants in the first place if she hadn't thought the baggy material would help camouflage an erection. It always bothered her to see kids with special needs looking unkempt. She hadn't wanted to give his peers one more excuse to ostracize him, so she'd kept up with the trends in middle school fashion and made sure to keep his haircut current and his clothes stylish. Now she'd been sending Eli to school in sweatpants for weeks, unaware that her plan had backfired.

The meeting got worse from there. One of the therapists speculated that Eli might need a physical release for new sensations when they arose at school. She suggested that Eli could ask for private time and spend a few minutes alone in the bathroom if he found the urge to touch himself too distracting. There was a private bathroom he could use, she said helpfully, so he wouldn't have to worry about other boys figuring out what he was up to.

Because Gayle was one of the few mothers in the world with an adolescent son who was completely open and honest with her, she knew that Eli had explored his changing body but never with any definitive sense of purpose. That's the way she expressed it to the therapist. There was so much delicacy in the way both women talked around the topic that a casual observer might not have realized they were discussing masturbation. Then the therapist put things more directly.

"If he doesn't know how to do it," she told Gayle, "you might have to show him."

Gayle stared at her, dumbstruck. She knew the therapist wasn't joking, but she couldn't believe she was serious. *What mother could ever be expected to do that for her kid?* she thought. *I'd do anything for Eli, but that's just not even on the table.*

The woman clarified that she meant Gayle should show him an instructional video, but Gayle was still disturbed. She mined her sense of obligation to her son, probing for the feeling that she owed this to him. *Sure, I'd be uncomfortable,* she thought, *but would he? Does his need to know this outweigh my squeamishness?* She knew Eli needed extra help to navigate this stage of life and that, without male friends, a brother, or an active father figure to steer him through it, she was essentially his only guide. Still, she recoiled from the thought of being the one to instruct him on this most intimate of acts. It just seemed wrong.

She thought of her last appointment with Dr. Pober, a year earlier. The effects of puberty had been obvious enough even then that the genetic counselor who assisted Dr. Pober had recommended a few resources to help Eli understand and cope with the changes. One was a book called *What's Happening to Me?*—a guide to puberty that blended cartoon illustrations with anatomical sketches of the changing teenage body, male and female. Gayle had read parts of the book with Eli, showing him the cartoon characters and skipping the anatomical sketches. She wasn't sure he was ready to see those.

The genetic counselor had also recommended a film, *Hand Made Love: A Guide for Teaching About Male Masturbation.* It was explicit, she acknowledged, but it had been developed specifically for people with developmental disabilities. According to the video summary, it discussed "privacy, pleasure, and the realities of sharing living spaces with others."

"Watch it first," the counselor said. "See if you think it would be useful for him."

Gayle never even picked up a copy. It wasn't that she couldn't accept that her baby was growing up; it was that he was still a baby in so many ways, trapped in a body that was suddenly becoming an adult's. Gayle felt as reluctant to show her son a video about masturbation as she would have been to show the same video to a five-year-old. Then again, a five-year-old didn't run the same risk of being knocked out by some girl's boyfriend or father for a lingering hug.

The advances both Gayle and Eli had made at camp seemed to have evaporated back in the real world. Eli steamrolled through social boundaries more than ever before, which meant that, instead of giving him space, Gayle planted herself even more firmly by his side wherever they went. If she turned her back for a moment, social disaster ensued. At practice for Eli's special-needs soccer league one Friday evening, Gayle had gotten caught up in conversation with some of the other parents when she heard Eli greet a teammate's buxom mother: "Hi! I like your shirt!" She turned to see him lean in sideways for a hug and nestle his head in the woman's cleavage. Gayle dashed over, put her hands on Eli's shoulders, and guided him away while the woman giggled awkwardly.

"Eli, you have to stop manhandling people!" Gayle said in a hoarse whisper. "And there are other conversation starters besides, 'I like your shirt.'"

"I like your . . . pants?" he tried tentatively.

"You don't have to say you *like* anything," Gayle said. "Maybe try 'It's nice to see you,' or 'How are you?'"

Eli nodded. "How are you?" he said gamely.

But when they stopped at a Greek diner later that night, he couldn't keep his hands off their waitress—even after Gayle told him she would take away his favorite toy *du jour*, a plastic tiki head, if he hugged or touched anyone. He violated the no-touching policy right after breaking Gayle's rule against begging favors, first by asking the waitress to turn on the overhead fan (she obliged, even though it was a chilly winter night), then by asking for a paper menu and something to color with.

"Can you give me some coloring pencils?" he asked.

"No! Eli . . ." Gayle interrupted, but the waitress seemed not to hear her.

"I've got crayons," she told Eli. "You want crayons, honey?"

"Yes," he said, avoiding Gayle's eyes.

The waitress turned to Gayle and said, "He's a good boy."

"Yes, he is," Gayle said stiffly. She never knew what to make of strangers who said things like that. *He is a good kid, but I'm trying to teach him not to do these things,* she thought. Did they think she was being too hard on him? Or that they needed to placate her—that if she thought he was a *bad* boy, she'd beat him when they got home?

Eli, on the other hand, took the waitress's comment as sincere praise.

"I'm being so good," he said when she walked away, smiling angelically as if to preempt any claim to the contrary.

"No, you're not," Gayle said.

"I'm sorry," he said. "I will be good, I promise."

When the waitress brought their food, she set Eli's plate down first. As she did, her fingernails, painted a glittery silver color, sparkled tantalizingly close to his face. His gaze followed her fingers, and while she still held Gayle's sandwich in one hand, he reached out to shake the other one.

"You like my nails?" she asked, seeing him stare at them while he lingered over the handshake. He nodded but, seeing his mother's glowering look, said, "I'm sorry."

"Don't be sorry, sweetie!" the waitress said as he finally let go. She set down Gayle's plate and then lifted a glass coffeepot to refill Gayle's mug.

"I'm sorry," he repeated, but while she poured the coffee, he reached for her empty hand again. He stretched his other arm out, hoping she'd scratch it.

"I like tickles," he said when she didn't take the hint. "Tickle me!"

"I can't right now, honey," she said. "I've got to work, OK?"

"OK, I'm sorry," he said. The waitress whirled away to check on the next table. Gayle's face, meanwhile, had gone white with

embarrassment and anger. This was the most brazen she had ever seen
Eli in his quest for physical contact.

"I don't know what to do," she said quietly, shaking her head. "I
can't even eat right now."

"I'm sorry. I didn't mean to do that," Eli said, then added defen-
sively, "She's my friend."

"You lost a lot of privileges doing that," Gayle said.

Eli hung his head for a moment, then seemed to forget all about
his transgression and its consequences. He dug into his turkey dinner
and smiled.

"Smell it," he said happily, looking up at Gayle and pointing to his
dinner. She sighed.

"I can't believe you reached across me and asked her to tickle you.
And she had hot food in her hands, on top of it," Gayle reminded him.

"I know," Eli said.

"What if she spilled coffee on you and you got burned?"

Eli didn't answer. The waitress came by with some extra napkins.

"Thank you!" Eli said, then turned to his mother. "She's nice."

"Mm-hmm," Gayle said, chewing slowly.

Eli struggled visibly to refrain from touching the waitress for the
rest of the meal. He clapped his hands together and hid them under
the table. But the impulse was overpowering. When she returned to
clear their empty plates, Eli reached out to her again.

"It tickles," he said cheerfully.

"It tickles?" she repeated, confused.

"I like tickles," he clarified. "Tickle, tickle!"

"No," Gayle said, reaching out for his hand and pressing it flat
against the table. "Stop it! Put your hand down." She stared at him with
bulging eyes.

"I'm sorry," he said for the umpteenth time.

"It's OK, honey," the waitress said gently.

"It's OK, it's just not appropriate," Gayle said, struggling to keep
the message clear. "You're going to get in trouble one of these times."

"I don't want that," Eli said.

The waitress picked up his plate. "Do you want to color some more?" she asked soothingly. "Do you want another paper?"

"Yes," he said. She brought him another children's menu and disappeared again.

He's totally out of control, Gayle thought. *I should have dragged him out of here before we even ordered.*

A few minutes later the waitress set the bill on the table.

"Thank you," Eli said.

"You're welcome," she said. "Have a good night."

"Thank you," he said. "Bye, honey!"

He reached out once more for a handshake. She accepted his hand tentatively and gave it a quick pump.

"Have a great night," she said.

"Thanks," Gayle said. "You too."

As the waitress walked away, Eli turned to Gayle.

"She's beautiful," he said loudly.

"Aw!" said the waitress, turning back. "You're a sweetheart." She shook her head and clucked, clearly touched. Gayle, however, was not charmed. She paid the bill quickly and then ushered Eli out to the car.

Eli waited out the car ride quietly. It was clear that he remembered Gayle's warning about lost privileges but hoped she'd forgiven him by the time they arrived back home.

"Um, can I earn my tiki?" he asked politely once she'd parked the car.

"No," Gayle said quickly, shaking her head. "Uh-uh. You lost your tiki privileges. And your computer privileges."

"Can I do *something*?"

"No."

"I can't go to bed!"

"No?" she asked, following him upstairs from the garage to the living room.

"I can't!"

"Go watch TV in your room."

"I can't," he said, looking sorrowfully at the floor.

"What do you think you're going to do?"

"I think I'm . . . gonna play. With the Bristle Blocks."

"OK," Gayle said, sighing.

He wandered into the kitchen to find the blocks. There was a sudden crash: he'd bumped into the shelf that held his toys, and blocks tumbled everywhere.

"I'm sorry! I didn't mean to do that."

He sat on the floor and tried to scoop some of the blocks back into their bin. Then he gave up and began spinning the blade of a pinwheel. He asked to use the internet, but Gayle reminded him that the internet was on the computer, and he had lost his computer privileges.

"Maybe I'll earn it tomorrow?" he asked optimistically.

"You lost those privileges for the weekend," Gayle said.

"Maybe next weekend?"

Gayle wanted to focus on tonight, not tomorrow or next weekend. She still didn't think Eli was making the connection between his behavior and its consequences.

"What you did in the restaurant? That was very bad. Very, very bad."

Eli sighed heavily. He spun the pinwheel and stared at it gloomily. Gayle couldn't tell whether his distress was over the loss of computer and tiki privileges or the knowledge that he had let her down. Both seemed to weigh heavily on him. "I'm sorry about that," he said, his voice cracking. For a moment he stopped spinning the pinwheel.

It pained Gayle to see him so despondent, but she didn't know how else to keep him from overwhelming people with his affection. Even the harshest punishments she could come up with didn't seem to stop it from happening. As sad as Eli was to lose his tiki head, Gayle was sure he'd do the same thing again in a heartbeat. And she was running out of time before strangers stopped finding his hugs, or his tickling requests, so adorable.

Fourteen

Treating the Friendliness Disorder

U nderstanding the genetics of Williams syndrome hasn't yet equated to real-world treatments for the disorder. Hypothetically, however, it could lead to the development of gene therapy for the syndrome's physical symptoms, and perhaps even for its behavioral symptoms. Unlike drug regimens, gene therapy would be a onetime treatment that could permanently halt or reverse the disorder's effects—if it worked. That's a big if, and there's no guarantee that a genetic fix is possible. But some researchers are optimistic about the prospect, especially following recent breakthroughs that have brought renewed promise to the once-troubled field.

Gene therapy—introducing healthy genes to replace missing or malfunctioning ones—has been heralded as a possible cure for rare genetic disorders and a potential key to developing more efficient treatments for common maladies, from cancer and HIV to autism and schizophrenia. Its early challenges made clear, however, that it would be no simple panacea. A 1999 gene therapy trial resulted in the death of a Pennsylvania teenager being treated for a rare liver disorder, leading to a temporary suspension of similar studies in the U.S.

And early trials to repair a mutated gene in the cells of young people with severe combined immunodeficiency, or SCID—better known as "bubble boy" disease—improved their immune system function but caused five of the twenty participants to develop cancer. In the face of daunting technological challenges and an alarming number of unforeseen side effects, many researchers feared gene therapy would never amount to a plausible treatment option.

Editing genes turned out to be the easiest part, although in the early days the task amounted to the laboratory equivalent of breaking rocks. The pioneering geneticists of the 1970s cut into DNA strands using proteins called restriction enzymes. But, as the science writer Michael Specter wrote in a 2015 *New Yorker* article, "those initial tools were more hatchet than scalpel." Other methods were developed as the decades progressed, but they tended to be more imprecise, laborious, and expensive than researchers would have liked.

Then, in 2012, scientists announced that a system called CRISPR-Cas9—a self-defense device used by bacteria to chop up invading viruses—could allow researchers to carve away and replace genes with unprecedented precision, speed, and economy. The CRISPR system was a scalpel to succeed the hatchets of the past, although many researchers have compared it to a more modern tool: the find-and-replace feature of a word processing program. The pace of research quickened dramatically after this new technology was introduced; still, geneticists have been careful to point out that its safety and effectiveness as a cure for disease remain to be proven.

But while CRISPR made it simpler to edit genes, a number of challenges stand in the way of using it for gene therapy. Essentially, the system works by carrying a set of instructions into a cell; scientists can program it to cut the genome at a specific location, using the bacterial enzyme Cas9, and either disable a gene or insert a DNA patch to alter it. That's the relatively easy part; the hard part is getting the editing system to the right cells, and lots of them. One possible method would require scientists to remove a number of cells—say, blood cells—treat them with CRISPR, and then return the corrected cells to the body. But since it's impossible to remove and replace every blood cell, this method really only works well for stem cells, which can regenerate and thus, once corrected, would make more corrected versions.

The other option is to deliver the CRISPR components directly to cells within the body via an inert virus, since viruses are naturally skilled at reproducing and spreading genetic material. But the viral delivery approach has proved problematic in the past. The Pennsylvania boy who died in 1999 suffered organ failure after his immune system put up a vicious fight against the virus he'd been injected with. The SCID patients who developed cancer did so after the virus carrying a pre-CRISPR form of gene therapy landed near a so-called cell cycle gene, which codes for the production of new cells, triggering uncontrolled cell growth.

Moreover, CRISPR's predecessors often behaved unpredictably when injected into lab animals and human test subjects. Sometimes they ended up in the wrong spot or interacted with other genes in unwanted ways. And even if CRISPR does exactly what scientists want it to, its reach will be limited. Brain cells, in particular, are nearly impossible to access with our current technology, making behavioral and cognitive disorders especially challenging candidates for gene therapy. Blood and muscle cells are much easier targets.

———

ETHICAL QUESTIONS RELATED TO GENE THERAPY abound, too, and these have only increased since CRISPR enabled new research on a massive scale. Fears that the technology could lead to the creation of "designer babies" have long haunted geneticists, although they point out that they couldn't engineer an ideal person—whatever that might be—even if they wanted to; the science simply isn't there yet. Even seemingly straightforward traits, like height, depend on a complex web of gene interactions that scientists haven't yet untangled. The genetics is even more inscrutable for intellect and personality types.

More recently, scientists have debated the ethical implications of editing genes within human eggs, sperm, or embryos in their earliest stage, since those edits could be passed on to future generations, potentially causing permanent alterations to the genome and changing the very nature of the human species. In 2015 an international committee of scientists called for a moratorium on such applications after a team of scientists in China conducted the first known experiment to affect these cells.* The experiment, an attempt to repair a gene mutation responsible for a rare blood disorder, was conducted on test-tube embryos that were unviable because they had three sets of chromosomes instead of the normal two, ruling out the chance that they'd grow up to pass on their altered DNA. And as it turned out, the experiment was a case study in the limitations of using CRISPR to edit human genes. The technique failed completely in about half the embryos and made unintended cuts in the DNA of some of the others. Almost none retained lasting copies of the new genes.

"As a research tool, CRISPR could hardly be more valuable—but we are far from the day when it should be used in a clinical setting," one of the scientists who developed the technology told Specter at the *New Yorker*.

Yet, despite some disappointing setbacks, there have also been some remarkable successes and a host of new applications for gene editing since CRISPR revolutionized the field. Outside our own species, it has been used to make wheat resistant to mildew and to prolong the shelf life of tomatoes. It's been proposed as a method of altering the genes of mosquitoes to prevent them from contracting (and therefore transmitting) malaria, and modifying the DNA of mice to eradicate Lyme disease among their kind—and, by extension, ours. In 2015 scientists used CRISPR to successfully treat a form of muscular

---

* A British geneticist was given permission to use the editing tool on human embryos in 2016 as part of her research to determine which genes were active in the earliest stages of development. But she destroyed the embryos after seven days—a move that was controversial in its own right.

dystrophy in mice by injecting their muscle tissue with a virus carrying instructions to fix a mutated gene. Researchers hope that if they can show that the treatment is safe and effective in primates, human trials won't be far off.

While there have been hundreds of human gene therapy trials since 1990, none of which has yet resulted in approval by the U.S. Food and Drug Administration, that prospect appears to be getting closer. One leader in the race to bring gene therapy to market is a Philadelphia biotech firm that, in 2015, successfully restored vision to twenty-one patients suffering from a rare genetic eye disease—with no apparent immune system reactions or other serious side effects. Other contenders for FDA approval include genetic treatments for hemophilia, cystic fibrosis, and sickle-cell disease.

One of the field's biggest constraints has long been a financial one. Large pharmaceutical companies have been reluctant to invest in gene therapy for rare genetic diseases, since even successful treatments for these disorders aren't likely to turn a profit, owing to the small number of people who would use them. But the increased pace and promise of recent advances has prompted a corresponding increase in investment. In 2015, biotech companies developing gene therapies—about seventy of which were in late-stage testing—raised $10 billion globally, according to the Alliance for Regenerative Medicine. And in 2016, when European regulators approved a new gene therapy for SCID that does not cause cancer, it marked an industry milestone as the first approval granted to a major multinational drug company: GlaxoSmithKline, which also plans to seek U.S. approval for the therapy.

This newly robust interest and investment in gene therapy is a game changer for the researchers who study rare genetic disorders, including Williams. Dr. Pober, the geneticist who diagnosed Eli, believes that gene therapy trials could be possible for Williams syndrome within the next decade. So far the research related to Williams has been conducted in petri dishes, not people, but some of the results have been promising.

"This is mind-boggling for a geneticist," Pober says. "Twenty-five years ago it was 'Yup, this is what you've got. Good luck to you.' We were jealous of our colleagues who had something you could treat."

She sees particular hope in the elastin gene's involvement in Williams, since a decline in elastin production is what causes our skin to wrinkle as we age. With limited elastin, people with Williams are prone to develop wrinkles earlier than the rest of us. (They also get gray hair at a much younger age, although geneticists aren't exactly sure why, since graying hair isn't connected to elastin. Mice missing the Williams genes also turn gray earlier than their genetically intact counterparts.) And although elastin-related cardiac problems are of greater concern to Pober, she half-jokingly deems the quest for youthful skin a golden ticket to future research.

"If we design a study that could lead to a cure for wrinkles," she says, "the funding will be unlimited."

In fact, researchers at Yale recently succeeded in tricking the elastin gene into producing more elastin than normal, a step they hope could help prevent the narrowing and rigidity of the aorta and arteries in people with Williams—and lead to healthier hearts for the rest of us. George Tellides, a professor of cardiac surgery and the lead researcher on the Yale team, believes that curing the heart problems inherent to Williams could help prevent similar problems in the general population, especially among the elderly.

"In older people, wrinkles are the visible effect of the underlying loss of elastin, but it's also affecting the arteries, including the aorta," he says. "So the lessons we learn about Williams can be applied to everyone."

Because people with Williams are missing only one copy of the twinned elastin gene, they aren't devoid of elastin altogether; they just produce about half as much as they should. If the existing gene could double its protein production, the deficiency would disappear. At least, it should. But just because something works in a lab doesn't mean it'll work in a human being, Pober warns. There it becomes a matter of releasing exactly the right amount of elastin at exactly the right time during blood vessel development. That kind of fine-tuning will take time, if it can be done at all.

In the meantime, the treatment of Williams syndrome, especially its behavioral and social symptoms, remains a murkier matter. This generation must make do with the treatment options that exist in our time, none of them specifically geared to the unique symptoms of Williams. Many of the behavioral therapies used for Williams were initially developed for children with autism. Most drugs on the market for anxiety, attention-deficit/hyperactivity disorder, and low impulse control were developed for the general population, and some have very different effects on people with Williams, whose brain chemistry is just different enough that doctors are sometimes surprised by their reactions to common medications.

Dr. Pober describes the pharmacological approach to treating the symptoms of Williams as trial and error. Some medications work fine. Others have unexpected side effects. SSRIs, the most common treatments for anxiety and depression, frequently make people with Williams worse instead of better, and often exacerbate their social disinhibition. One drug Eli took for anxiety helped with those symptoms but annihilated what little self-control he had when it came to hugging strangers. Eli's psychiatrist shuffled his prescriptions several times throughout his preteen years, trying to find a cocktail—which at different times combined varying amounts of Celexa or Abilify for anxiety, plus Ritalin and Intuniv for ADHD—that would help more than it hurt.

Researchers estimate that more than half of all children with Williams have ADHD. While the class of drugs that includes Ritalin is usually effective in reducing their symptoms, it also causes different side effects than in the general population, most notably mood changes. One study found that two-thirds of children with Williams experienced sadness and malaise after taking Ritalin, as opposed to less than a quarter of Ritalin takers in the general population.

Of course, parents would prefer an approach that didn't require a prescription. All drugs have side effects, after all. And neither the parents nor the doctors of people with Williams want to risk overmedicating to the point of eclipsing their radiant personalities.

"Treating Williams is a matter of coping with the disabilities enough to let the abilities shine," Dr. Pober says. "The parents of these kids can see their potential. Unlocking it is the mystery."

————

MANY CLINICIANS SEE THE LANGUAGE SKILLS of people with Williams, especially their proclivity for storytelling, as a valuable tool to help them manage the syndrome's disabling effects. Compared to people with other forms of intellectual disability, people with Williams are much more responsive to talk therapy. The researchers Eleanor Semel and Sue R. Rosner, coauthors of *Understanding Williams Syndrome: Behavioral Patterns and Interventions*, reported that many people with Williams who suffered from phobias found it calming just to discuss a fearful situation rationally. For example, a child afraid of thunder felt soothed when an adult explained that thunder was caused by a clash of hot and cold air, and that it followed lightning but couldn't hurt anyone itself. (Talking through a fear typically only helped temporarily, however, and some people found that it made their anxiety worse instead of better.)

Interactive games—for example, having everyone in the room clap their hands along with the thunder—are also prominent in behavioral therapy for people with Williams, drawing on their love of socializing to trump the power of phobias. Stories and role-playing have proved useful as well: children afraid of going to the doctor often felt less fearful after acting out the parts of the doctor and the patient in a more familiar setting.

Since music has such a profound emotional effect on people with Williams, and because it holds their attention better than almost anything else, it has become another popular therapeutic tool. Kids with Williams learn exceptionally well when a lesson is set to music, retaining phrases more consistently even if they simply rhyme or can be said in rhythm. Music is also deeply soothing to most people with Williams, which makes it a powerful ally in battling anxiety and phobias.

Many parents have developed their own unorthodox treatments for some of the problematic behaviors common to Williams. A tendency to wander off, especially in pursuit of a stranger to greet, is one of the disorder's more alarming traits. After all else failed in preventing one child from routinely disappearing, her parents tied a small bell around her ankle to make her easier to find. Some parents, like Gayle, curb their kids' unstoppable impulse to wander after strangers by almost never letting them out of their sight.

The problem of indiscriminate hugging is a complicated one to treat, partly because several factors contribute to the urge. Neuroscientists have found evidence of anomalies in the frontal lobe—the part of the brain that controls impulsivity and helps us evaluate the consequences of our actions—which may explain why people with Williams can't stop hugging strangers even when they know they shouldn't. Additionally, some researchers point to a developmental dysfunction in the way young children with Williams form (or don't form) preferential emotional bonds. One study found that people with Williams didn't differentiate between types of relationship—say, between an uncle and the school bus driver—the way the rest of us do from a very young age. They approached and interacted with each person the same way. This is one of the heartbreaking hazards of raising a kid with Williams: your child loves you intensely and unconditionally, but he feels the same way about his bus driver.

Like many Williams parents, Gayle felt the sting of this discovery when Eli was still a baby and nearly leapt from her arms into the arms of strangers, cooing tenderly to them. Of course, he had always been effusive in his love for her, too. Even now, at an age when most kids had stopped being so affectionate toward their mothers, he overflowed with warmth and gratitude, routinely telling her, "Mom, you're the best!" But there were moments when even his warmth troubled her. It was so automatic that she sometimes thought, *Is this real? Or is he just programmed to say "I love you"?*

It sometimes seemed like Eli had little choice in whom to love—that free will didn't factor into the matter. You'd have had to go out of your way, by being intentionally cruel or abrasive, to get him *not* to love you. This could be hurtful to Gayle and the rest of Eli's family, who had earned the love that was so freely doled out to strangers. But it didn't mean that his love wasn't as real as anyone else's. All social bonding is predicated in part on the release of oxytocin, as Korenberg and other researchers have shown. We all respond to the same brain chemicals when we feel or express love. People with Williams just do so more often.

The fact that he loved nearly everyone didn't make Eli's love for Gayle any less authentic. And although she occasionally questioned this, she could tell his feelings were genuine just by looking into his eyes. The earnest emotion she saw reflected back was anything but programmed.

———

WHILE IT'S LARGELY IMPOSSIBLE TO STOP people with Williams from caring about everyone they meet, it's essential—both for safety and for social acceptance—to reinforce that different relationships entail different levels of intimacy. Many teachers use a "circles" curriculum, sometimes represented visually as a series of different-colored concentric circles and drawn on the floor to give kids the physical experience of moving between them. In the center is the "you" circle. Children are reminded that this is a private bubble and that no one else is allowed to touch them without their consent (and correspondingly, that they should respect the private bubble around other people). The circles move outward from there: the "close hug and kiss" circle, the "faraway hug" circle, the "handshake" circle, the "wave" circle, and finally the "strangers" circle. The people who fall into this circle require no acknowledgment at all, teachers explain. The curriculum insists: "Some people stay strangers forever"—a phrase that's anathema to the Williams worldview.

Gayle saw Eli's indiscriminate displays of affection as the biggest obstacle to his successful social life. She became a one-woman police force in the fight against hugging. But therapists who treat Williams say this battle is often futile. Not only do they question whether people like Eli *can* muster the self-control to stop hugging, but some therapists question whether they *should*. Physical contact is, after all, one of the primary joys of their lives. This impulse is hardwired into who they are. To hold them back from hugging would be to deny a central part of their personality.

Karen Levine, the Harvard psychologist who specializes in Williams, sees hugging as a gray area in treatment: it can be problematic, but it can also enrich the lives of people for whom social contact is paramount. Her first priority is to treat the anxiety, phobias, and fixations of the disorder because they are universal burdens: people with Williams agree that they'd be better off without them. Overfamiliarity, on the other hand, is more a question of degree, and she cautions against crossing the border between treating pathology and reprogramming a personality.

"People with Williams love people; they want to touch them. As long as they're not putting themselves in danger, or making someone else uncomfortable, I don't think there's really a right or wrong amount of hugging," Levine says. "Everyone's comfortable with a different level of physical contact. At some point, it falls to other people to either accept it or to say they don't want to be hugged."

Advocates of neurodiversity take Levine's point further, arguing that we should focus less on treating neurological conditions such as Williams or autism and more on broadening our own understanding of what constitutes normal or acceptable social behavior. The neurodiversity movement takes issue, fundamentally, with the classification of these conditions as illnesses rather than as identities. Some of its proponents oppose any effort to cure them, arguing that doing so would amount to stifling the quirks and creativity that give the world its richness. And they tend to overlap, ideologically, with the opponents of prenatal testing that could lead to the abortion of fetuses carrying similar disorders. Since Williams is too rare to be included on the standard panel of prenatal tests, and since there is no test for autism, that debate doesn't currently apply to either condition. (That could change soon, however—at least for Williams—thanks to rapidly evolving technologies such as cell-free fetal DNA testing, which analyzes tiny fragments of free-floating fetal DNA in the mother's bloodstream, and could increase the scope of prenatal screening.) Lawmakers in some states, including Indiana and North Dakota, have already proposed or passed legislation prohibiting abortion because of genetic abnormalities—which, for now, primarily affects the prospective parents of children with Down syndrome.

———

AS A WHOLE, WESTERN CULTURE IS relatively tolerant of the Williams personality. We value gregariousness and admire people who show no social fear. We celebrate icons like Oprah Winfrey—who routinely hugs strangers and asks them personal questions—for their warmth and openness. Of course, Oprah manages her warmth with more sophistication than most people with Williams possess. She can turn it off when needed. Still, she represents an ideal inherent to our culture and not to others. In a collectivist culture like Japan's, where conformity and self-control are prized above the assertiveness and self-expression of our own individualistic society, the Williams personality elicits more stigma and is seen as more dysfunctional. The same tendency to greet and touch strangers that Americans describe as endearing gets a darker gloss in Japanese culture, where it is more often described as intrusive and offensive—as another disabling symptom of the disorder, rather than its silver lining. Carol Zitzer-Comfort, who led a cross-cultural study comparing children with Williams in Japan and the U.S., noted the different tone of aphorisms about attracting attention: in the U.S. "the squeaky wheel gets the grease," while in Japan "the nail that stands out gets pounded down." Her study found that Japanese parents considered the overfamiliarity of Williams syndrome to be more disabling than did American parents. People with Williams were much more likely to be institutionalized in Japan than in the U.S.

Zitzer-Comfort's study found that while people with Williams were more social than their non-Williams peers in each culture, both groups were less social overall in Japan. In fact, American children without Williams showed the same level of social behavior as Japanese children *with* Williams, whose behavior was considered wildly inappropriate by Japanese standards. Zitzer-Comfort concluded that the disorder was at least somewhat moderated by cultural norms, even as it tended to violate those norms.

Even outgoing Americans have boundaries, after all. We prize extroversion to a point, but we tend to flinch when someone violates our personal space, no matter how charming they are. This sets us apart from close-talking, communal cultures in which platonic friends, male and female, hold hands and kiss cheeks. In Greece, for example, a survey of parents whose children had Williams syndrome found that they did not consider their kids' outgoing, affectionate behavior to be pathological, although they did list other traits as disabling, including anxiety, impulsivity, and low frustration tolerance. Greeks with Williams are hardly ever institutionalized; researchers concluded in a 2011 study that no Greek psychological services specialized in treating the disorder. The bulk of treatment for Williams came from geneticists, who focused almost exclusively on its medical symptoms.

Short of moving to Greece, though, Gayle believed the best way to give Eli a shot at social acceptance was to get him to conform to American standards of conduct—by giving strangers their space. For as much as people with Williams love everyone else equally and indiscriminately, the corollary is decidedly not true. They might show the same affection to their bus drivers as to their mothers, but even the most compassionate of bus drivers will never muster a mother's love for someone who is, at best, a casual acquaintance. No one else, anywhere in the world—Greece included—could possibly have treasured Eli's love like Gayle did.

Fifteen

Eli Turns Thirteen

T he night before his thirteenth birthday, Eli was too excited to sleep.

"What's going to happen to me when I wake up?" he asked Gayle while she helped him wash his face and brush his teeth at the bathroom sink. "Am I going to talk like a man?"

She reminded him that his voice was already as deep as a man's. He eyed her incredulously. He had learned in health class that boys' voices got deeper when they became teenagers. He believed his would drop automatically the second he turned thirteen.

He tested this theory as soon as he woke up the next morning, but his voice was the same slightly nasal baritone it had been the night before. It broke into a falsetto squeal when he opened the gift Gayle gave him at breakfast: a small plastic monster called a Scary Screecher, a red-eyed, mummy-like creature that screeched when you squeezed it. Eli had been begging for it since he saw it at Walgreens weeks earlier. Now he screeched gleefully along with his new toy. Gayle endured the noise, although she silently cursed the mummy for its seemingly eternal battery life, and denied Eli's entreaties to bring it with him to school.

For months, Gayle had been using Eli's impending birthday as an incentive to encourage good behavior. Thirteen-year-olds don't throw tantrums, she had often reminded him as the day approached. They don't whine while their mother is on the phone. They don't beg for a second dessert when they've already had ice cream. They don't hug strangers or ask to go home with them and see their vacuum cleaners.

Eager to earn the title of teenager, Eli had used all his willpower to fight his impulses. But his willpower still came up short most of the time, to Gayle's frustration. Still, Eli was starting to see himself as an adult, even if Gayle wasn't. The numerical fact of being thirteen resonated with him more deeply than the daily evidence of his immaturity.

"I can go out with the girls now," he declared proudly when he got home from school that afternoon.

"What do you mean?" Gayle asked, turning from the microwave, where she was reheating leftover macaroni and cheese for his snack.

"Boys and girls, going to the movies!" he explained.

"You mean a date?" Gayle asked. She paused. Then, choosing her words carefully, she said, "That's for older teenagers. Eighteen-year-olds." She picked the number arbitrarily, high enough to seem far in the future, low enough not to dash his hopes.

She paused again as she set the bowl of pasta down in front of him. "Why, who do you want to go on a date with?"

"With you, Mom!"

She couldn't help laughing, but composed herself enough to say seriously, "You can't go on a date with someone you're related to." She hoped he wouldn't tell the kids at school he wanted to go on a date with his mom. Then he'd *really* never get a date.

Gayle had spent more time than usual over the previous few weeks ruminating on Eli's prospects in adulthood. This was partly because of his upcoming birthday and partly because, earlier that month, she had found a lump in her breast. She'd had it biopsied and spent several worried days waiting for the results. It turned out to be a cyst, not cancer. But because one of her aunts had been diagnosed with breast cancer in her forties, the doctor told Gayle she should get tested for the gene that would predispose her to develop it herself. He drew some blood and sent it to a lab.

Now, while Eli was upstairs trying to find his shoes so they could go to Mimi's house for dinner, a nurse called from the lab. Gayle fumbled with the living room phone, nearly dropping it before she picked it up on the second ring. "Hello?" she said breathlessly.

Eli's coloring book was open on the coffee table. Gayle grabbed the blue crayon that Eli had been using on Cookie Monster and scribbled a few notes next to the picture. The nurse explained that she wasn't calling with test results. She said that the genetic test the doctor had ordered was often inconclusive, and she wanted permission to do a second, more sophisticated test. It would cost Gayle $700, even after her insurance paid its share. Gayle wrote "700" in thick blue crayon, then circled the number. She told the nurse she'd think about it.

Gayle hung up and frowned at the number. From upstairs, the trail of Eli's shoe search was made audible by his constant singing and occasional thuds as he knocked over toys and bumped into walls.

Money was tight, as always, so Gayle wasn't enthusiastic about paying $700 to learn that there was a chance she might someday get cancer. That was an abstraction; $700 was concrete. She pondered the blue number, mentally adding it to her existing medical debt. Then she looked up again, toward the sound of singing.

I have to do this, she thought. *I need to do whatever I can to make sure I'm around as long as possible for him.*

———

TAKING CARE OF HERSELF WAS PART of Gayle's plan for the future, but she expected to do it the way she'd been doing it for years: on her own. Getting remarried wasn't anywhere on her radar. She hadn't even gone on a date since her divorce. As she saw it, the right person hadn't materialized, and she didn't have the time to go looking for him. By now she'd been alone for so long that she felt entrenched in her aloneness, too set in her ways to make room for someone else.

She knew there were drawbacks to this way of thinking. When she considered the long-term implications, though, she thought less about her own potential loneliness than about what it would mean for Eli. For one thing, it meant there was zero chance that Eli would ever have a brother or sister, step- or otherwise.

She was keenly aware that Eli would likely outlive her. She'd planned for that, too, as well as she could. She had begun drafting a will years earlier, but had never been able to finish it. There wasn't much to leave behind—that wasn't the problem. Everything she had would go to Eli, of course. She'd even opened a special-needs trust for him when he was a toddler (and made one deposit of $2,000, but hadn't been able to afford another one since). What was stumping her was the question of who to name as Eli's guardian when she was gone.

With no other children and no siblings of her own, she didn't have an obvious candidate. Her youngest cousins, Jake and his sister Emily, were the most logical choices, both because they adored Eli and because they were in their twenties, so presumably they'd be around longer than Gayle. Both were named as trustees of Eli's trust fund, after Mimi.

Gayle considered Jake and Emily the closest thing she had to siblings, even though they were so much younger. She knew they'd agree if she asked them to take guardianship of Eli. But she didn't want them to enter into the obligation blindly. She wasn't sure either of them fully understood how much work guardianship would be. Once, when she mentioned her fear that Eli would end up in a group home someday, Emily scoffed at the idea.

"Oh, he'll never be in a group home," she said. "We'll take care of him."

But Gayle wondered where their lives would lead them between that moment and the day Eli might actually appear on their doorstep. She used to tell each of them, "Just make sure you marry someone who would welcome Eli. I don't want you to pick someone who'd stick him in the basement and only let him out for Thanksgiving and Christmas." It was meant as a joke, but her concerns were real. Would their careers and relationships leave enough time and space in their lives for Eli? Would their spouses balk at the responsibility of caring for him?

Would their jobs take them to the other side of the world? They were still too young to know what the blueprints of their lives would look like. They couldn't know for certain where, or whether, Eli would fit in.

Gayle's cousin Marcia was another obvious choice to care for Eli. She was older than Jake and Emily, more mature and in a more stable phase of her life. Growing up, she and Gayle had always been close—practically sisters. They'd thought their kids would grow up like siblings, too. But the differences between Eli and Marcia's daughter Kylie were too stark. Williams syndrome was always the elephant in the room. Marcia seemed never to want to talk about the disorder, even when Gayle tried to bring it up. Gayle got the sense that Marcia felt so bad for Eli, and for Gayle, that the topic overwhelmed her.

So Gayle wasn't sure how to even begin the conversation about guardianship with Marcia. And since they were roughly the same age, the odds weren't great that she'd be able to care for Eli after Gayle was gone. That left Kylie and her little sister, Morgan. Kylie, an ambitious straight-A student, said she wanted to be a lawyer when she grew up. Gayle didn't doubt that she could be. No matter what she became, she would make a great ally for Eli as an adult. Gayle wondered whether it was too soon to ask her to include Eli in her plans for the future. *Not that she'd have to move him in with her, but just to check up on him when I'm gone?* Gayle thought. *Just to make sure he's OK?*

She concluded that it was probably not appropriate to have that conversation with a thirteen-year-old. But maybe in five or so years, when Kylie was in college, she could fully appreciate the depth of Eli's vulnerability and the scope of his needs.

In moments like these, Gayle wished she had a sibling, or that Eli did. She'd always planned to have more than one child, but Eli was so high-maintenance in the early years that she had been in no rush to have another baby. Then her marriage dissolved, and with it her hope of giving Eli a brother or sister. It would have been nice to have a life-long companion for him, she thought—someone who wouldn't think of him as a burden.

Her cousins would never call him a burden, she knew. They had always been there for him. But Gayle didn't want a quick yes-or-no answer when she asked for help in the future. She wanted a frank discussion of all the challenges that caring for Eli would entail. She had been surprised once when her uncle Chris, meaning well—perhaps even tacitly volunteering—suggested, "It would probably be a good idea to leave him to someone who's retired, who has the time to watch him."

"I don't know about that," Gayle had said. "It would have to be somebody with the energy to keep up with him, to run after him when he wanders away at the store, take him to all his appointments, and do all the errands to get him what he needs."

No matter how much his relatives loved him, there was no question in Gayle's mind that Eli would be a burden to whoever took over his guardianship. *It's a big deal,* she thought. *It will change their lives.* In an ideal world she'd be able to care for him herself for as long as he lived.

In Gayle's most anxious moments, she found herself wishing Eli would die before she did. Then she felt an instant pang of guilt for even imagining such a thing: *I want him to live a long, happy life. I just want to be there for him, so he doesn't get shuffled off to some state-run group home with disgruntled caregivers. If I could live just five minutes longer than he does, I'd be happy.*

———

WHILE SHE AND ELI WERE AT Mimi's house that evening, Gayle got a phone call from her cousin Shawn, who was in his thirties and had Down syndrome. Gayle wasn't quite as close to Shawn and his parents as she was to the relatives who lived with Mimi, but Shawn had a keen memory for dates and never missed a birthday. He'd called to wish Eli a happy thirteenth.

Shawn, who was active in a local advocacy group for people with disabilities, also wanted to let Eli know about a dance at a local church just for teens and young adults with special needs, ages thirteen to twenty-one. Eli was too busy watching YouTube videos of people vacuuming to talk, so Gayle thanked Shawn for thinking of him and scratched his cell phone number on a pad of paper, next to a tiki head she had drawn earlier for Eli. She told Shawn she'd call him if Eli wanted to go to the dance. When she hung up, she eyed the phone number as warily as she had her crayon-colored "700" earlier that afternoon.

"Do you think Eli would like something like that?" Gayle's aunt Suzanne asked brightly. "Dancing? Music?" Before Gayle could respond, Suzanne answered her own question. "Oh, he'll be wanting to shake hands and hug everyone."

"He'd be all about dancing," Gayle said. "But thirteen to twenty-one? I don't know if that's appropriate for him. Maybe he'd be better with something more preteen. Movie night or something. Maybe not a dance."

As if to answer the question himself, Eli skipped back into the kitchen and stopped to admire the paper spiral that Gayle had hung from the doorframe at his insistence. He'd asked to turn the ceiling fan on earlier in the evening, to make the spiral twirl, but was denied permission on the grounds that, in February, it was too cold in the house already.

"I like this twirly," he cooed now, reaching up to spin it.

Gayle gave Suzanne a meaningful look. Eli wasn't ready for a dance. He wasn't ready for dating. Gayle knew this better than anyone, consumed as she was with the fear that he'd never be ready for a normal adolescence, or a normal adulthood—one that didn't center on vacuuming videos and depend entirely on his mother's care. Still, he seemed so happy here, surrounded by his family and the twirlies and tiki heads he adored. Gayle wondered: If this was the best it got for him, would it be good enough? He was loved, and he was happy. He didn't seem to feel deprived. Maybe he'd never change, and that would be OK. Maybe he could be a sweet little boy forever, and she could always be his protector and provider. Maybe that would be fine for both of them.

———

ONLY A WEEK OR SO LATER, Gayle and Mimi took Eli out to dinner. As soon as they walked into the restaurant he violated the no-hugging rule by running up to a waitress and throwing his arms around her. In response, Gayle drew an unusually hard line: she and Mimi turned on their heels and walked out, leading Eli back to the car and ending the meal before it began.

Eli's response was also different from his usual toddler's tantrum. He fumed in the backseat all the way home—not wailing petulantly but genuinely pissed.

"This is the worst day of my life!" he complained angrily.

Mimi lectured him about his behavior and its repercussions. Where he would normally have hung his head and apologized, this time he argued back. At the peak of his frustration with his grandmother, he muttered, "Stupid ass."

Mimi and Gayle were stunned. They had never heard him talk back that way before. His normal meltdowns were tearful and short, and they ended with heartfelt declarations of remorse. This time Eli refused to take back what he'd said. He folded his arms across his chest defiantly when Gayle chastised him for hurting Mimi's feelings.

As much as Gayle had discounted Eli's conviction that he would suddenly become a different person now that he was a teenager, she wondered if turning thirteen had in fact been the sea change he believed it was. He seemed to be transforming before her eyes from an earnest, amiable child to a smart-mouthed, headstrong adolescent. Gayle told him she was very disappointed in him. "You need to show your grandmother more respect," she said sternly. "That kind of language is totally inappropriate."

Inside, though, she felt a secret thrill of pride. This was behavior truly typical of a teenager—a developmental milestone she hadn't expected him to reach. She herself had been rude and rebellious when she was his age, albeit in very different ways. And while she couldn't encourage his behavior, she was grateful to see that Eli, too, could pull off a little impertinence. As much as most parents dreaded it, adolescent rebellion was a natural stage of maturing, and an important one. The ability to stand up for oneself was a valuable life skill, after all, especially for a boy who trusted everyone.

Sixteen

What the Future Holds

Gayle knew there were some adults with Williams who lived independently, but she knew it the same way scientists knew the giant squid existed: from anecdotal evidence, not real-life encounters. So she was thrilled, the month after Eli's thirteenth birthday, to meet a mostly independent thirty-one-year-old named Emily at a Williams gathering in Queens. Their acquaintance was brief: Emily and her father were dropping off Emily's mother, Claire, before going to lunch on their own, since the meet-up was meant for moms only. But just catching a glimpse of the self-possessed young woman gave Gayle hope for Eli's future prospects.

When the group of mothers assembled in the host's living room to chat over sandwiches and pasta salad, Gayle sat next to Claire. The lunch guests introduced themselves and discussed some of the joys and struggles of life with their children. Gayle described her endless war against hugging and the way it had escalated since Eli hit puberty. "He's very sensory. He's always wanted to touch people," she explained. "But now it's just different, because of all the hormones mixed in with it."

She detailed the disciplinary measures that had proved no match for the strength of Eli's impulses. She explained how helpless she had begun to feel and how unsure she was that Eli would ever improve.

Claire reached over and patted Gayle's arm. "All of these things that you're talking about eventually get better," she said. "It levels off. At least, with Emily it did."

Gayle stared at her incredulously.

"I think at his age, that's when they do all their learning," Claire continued. "You could stand on your head, trying to get them to do certain things, and you think they're never going to do it, and then all of a sudden, out of the clear blue sky, one day they do what you want them to do. It's almost like it was a process for them. They have to go through that process to get to the other side. But it does get easier."

Claire's tone was matter-of-fact, but her words were a salve for Gayle's anxieties. They were confirmation that Gayle wasn't a terrible mother for not being able to find just the right balance of punishment and rewards to make Eli respect social boundaries. They meant that a miracle cure for his behavior might not exist—that this might simply be a developmental stage Eli would eventually outgrow. If so, Gayle could busy herself trying to ease the hardships of this stage, but ultimately the solution was a matter of time, and all she could really do was wait for him to grow up.

————

AS THE ONLY PARENT AT THE lunch gathering whose kid was fully grown, Claire became a sort of mother hen to the group. When she talked about her daughter, Gayle and the other mothers paid rapt attention, as if she were a prophet who had been granted a vision of life after adolescence and had brought back good news. Gayle listened carefully for proof that Emily had once been just like Eli. She parsed Claire's words, searching for echoes of her own experience and for evidence that Eli might be capable of following Emily's path.

Claire and her husband had adopted Emily when she was just a few days old and seemingly healthy. Eighteen months later, after being referred to a cardiologist because Emily had a heart murmur, they learned that she had Williams syndrome. Because this was before a blood test could definitively diagnose the disorder, they were lucky that the cardiologist had just written a paper on Williams and knew what he was looking at.

Claire spoke about her daughter with obvious pride. When she talked about the adoption, she told the story of how badly she had wanted a child—she couldn't have one herself—and how grateful she was to find Emily. She believed a stroke of fate had brought them together.

"We were led to this child," she said. There was no trace of regret that the healthy baby she thought she was bringing home turned out to have a life-changing disability. Claire spoke instead of Emily's skill as a singer, of her effervescent personality, of the goals she had achieved and the obstacles she had overcome.

For the past two years, Emily had lived in an apartment about half an hour away from her parents, which she shared with a roommate who also had Williams syndrome. An aide came to help them for a few hours every day, and another spent the night there every night. The aides' salaries were subsidized by the state, but her parents paid the rent themselves.

"It's expensive," Claire said, "but she's our only child. What else is our money for? It's for her."

The move had been Emily's idea, in fact. She'd wanted to strike out on her own, away from her parents, for a long time. But only near the end of her twenties did she seem mature and capable enough to live apart from them, and even then only with supervision. In some ways she was still childlike, Claire acknowledged.

"She's turning thirty-two on Wednesday, and she can act like a perfectly normal thirty-two-year-old one day, and the next day act like a two-year-old," she said. "In the apartment, with her support staff, that's presented a challenge, because there are things she and her roommate have to do on a daily basis, and Emily doesn't always want to do them. She's been used to being an only child, living at home, and although she wants to be independent, the responsibility that comes with independence is something she fights every once in a while."

But Emily handled the basics of adulthood impressively. She bathed and dressed herself, prepared her own meals, and, most importantly, refrained from hugging strangers. On her best days, people who met her for the first time didn't realize she had a disability.

Until recently, she'd worked at a supermarket, bagging groceries, but she had lost her job in a wave of layoffs.

"Bagging groceries was great for her, because she got to talk to people," Claire said, "but it wasn't the job I would have picked for her, because I always thought she could do more. She could certainly work in an office, doing light tasks, like making photocopies. I think she would be very good in the children's room of a public library. She's a very good reader. She reads at a sixth- or seventh-grade level. So I can see her putting books away in a library. But, you know, if it comes up, she'll take anything at this point. A job is the only piece of the puzzle that's missing, really."

Gayle tried to picture Eli bagging groceries, or making photocopies, or putting away books. He was so easily distracted that it was hard to picture him doing any one task for more than five minutes. It seemed like too much to hope that, like Emily, he could venture into the world on his own one day, going off to work in the morning and coming home at night to his own apartment. It was the bare minimum that Gayle had expected her child to do, before Eli was diagnosed: leave the nest.

And while she now expected to care for him indefinitely, she had heard tales of burnout among Williams parents whose kids never left the nest. Caring for an adult with special needs could be much more difficult, and less rewarding, than caring for a child with special needs. Not only did adults with Williams have their own set of challenges, they were more likely to *be* a challenge for their parents, fighting the help they had once accepted gratefully. Strong-willed and set in their ways, like most adults, they often chafed at the limits their parents imposed.

Gayle had heard of parents who'd once planned to keep their children at home perpetually, but later changed their minds and sent them to assisted-living facilities instead. Even the most energetic parents sometimes wore out after years of uninterrupted caregiving and the exhaustion and frayed nerves it entailed. Gayle tried not to judge them too harshly. *Let's see how I feel in ten years,* she thought.

But while she was sometimes frustrated and impatient with Eli, she couldn't imagine coming to the end of her rope the way some parents had described. At gatherings and on the WSA Facebook page, they recounted constant battles with their adult kids over the minutiae of daily living—nagging them endlessly to brush their teeth, take a shower, put their dirty dishes in the sink. More than just resisting their parents' prods, they often erupted in fits of temper. One mother said that even asking her daughter to comb her hair was enough to provoke a tantrum. The mother couldn't help becoming exasperated, despite her best efforts to stay calm, and sometimes both she and her daughter ended up in hysterics.

Despite wanting to tear her own hair out sometimes, Gayle had never gotten to the point where she'd even consider sending Eli to live in an institution rather than at home. She wondered if it was inevitable that someday she would. Then again, maybe he wouldn't want to live with her forever. And maybe one day he'd be capable of leaving home and caring for himself. That possibility struck Gayle as both liberating and unsettling.

———

NOT EVERY ADULT WITH WILLIAMS ACHIEVES Emily's level of independence. Even the few who do often feel frustrated that they can't be fully autonomous. Those who live alone typically depend on others—their parents or hired aides—in at least some ways.

A woman named Dawn, roughly the same age as Emily and similarly high-functioning, lived in a state-run independent living facility in Massachusetts. She had an apartment she shared with a roommate who had special needs (but not Williams). There was support staff on-site, but for the most part the women were left to their own devices to cook, clean, and care for themselves. Dawn, whose IQ was nearly normal, worked part-time as a receptionist for a social services agency.

True to the Williams nature, she was bubbly, energetic, and kind—a fast-talking force of friendliness. She was also ambitious, and had met many of the goals she'd set for herself, including winning a medal as a roller skater in the Special Olympics. But many other ambitions eluded her. She wished she could drive a car, for example, but she knew her limited spatial awareness would keep her from ever getting a license.

"I don't know when something's in my way," she explained. "I'm not that great at walking, either. I get lost easily. If it's not a straight line, forget it."

This meant she relied on public transportation to get around, but she felt constricted by the limitations of mass transit. She had to plan ahead to go anywhere, and she might still have to ask someone to pick her up from a bus stop. She couldn't just wake up one morning and decide to drive to the beach. (This was a key component of adulthood, in her mind, and of the freedom it entailed: being able to go to the beach on a whim.)

Dawn felt similarly constrained by the fact that her parents controlled her bank account. They paid her bills and gave her an allowance, but she wished she could be in charge of her own expenses, even though she readily admitted that she was an impulsive spender and couldn't balance a checkbook. She dreamed of having her own credit card. Once she even accepted a credit card offer that came in the mail without telling her parents. It struck her as a rite of adulthood and an essential element of true independence.

"I just thought, 'I want to be able to go into a store and see something I like and just get it. And not have to ask anyone for permission,'" she said. When the first bill came, her parents discovered her deception and canceled the card.

She met regularly with a therapist to talk through her frustrations, which sometimes overwhelmed her. On an existential level, even deeper than her disappointment over not driving or having a credit card, she lamented that she was unlikely to raise a family. She'd had a boyfriend once. They met in a life skills program for young adults with Williams, but the relationship ended when his parents moved to Florida—and he, dependent on them, went too.

———

FEW PEOPLE WITH WILLIAMS SYNDROME MARRY, and when they do, Dr. Pober has described it as more a marriage of families than of partners, since the couples struggle to manage their home and their lives without assistance. Some people with Williams have had children, although most weren't aware that they had the disorder and risked passing it on. A number of people have been diagnosed with Williams only after their children were. One high-functioning woman with Williams (who had already been diagnosed) married a man who didn't have the disorder and chose to take the risk of having kids, with her family's support. She gave birth to twins, both of whom had Williams. She and her husband and children lived with her husband's parents, who helped them through the challenges of raising two kids with special needs. She didn't regret her choice, saying, "Who better to help a child with Williams than someone who has it?"

Many doctors disagree, however, and advise people with Williams against having children. Some parents of people with Williams seek to sterilize their kids, partly because of the chances of passing on the syndrome and partly because their kids, even once fully grown, aren't responsible or capable enough to raise children of their own. Parents of girls, in particular, often want to spare their daughters the burden of menstruation as well as annual pelvic exams and Pap smears, which can be trying at best and traumatic at worst for women with Williams. Some skirt the issue with long-term birth control, such as IUDs or injectable hormones like Depo-Provera. But injections have to be repeated and IUDs require maintenance, and neither is a foolproof guarantee against pregnancy. That point is often moot, since many adults with Williams are unable to make the interpersonal connections that would lead to sex or marriage. But some parents of low-functioning girls petition their doctors for hysterectomies or tubal ligations anyway, citing the risk of rape. A pregnancy would only compound the anguish in that case, they argue.

Sterilization is an extremely sensitive issue for people with developmental disabilities, however, given America's appalling record of forcing it upon them. When social Darwinism was at its height, from the beginning of the twentieth century to the 1960s, more than 60,000 Americans were involuntarily sterilized, including those with intellectual disabilities along with criminals and the mentally ill. A 1927 Supreme Court ruling embraced the practice in terms that leave a bitter taste in the mouths of most Americans today. "It is better for all the world," Justice Oliver Wendell Holmes famously wrote, "if instead of waiting to execute degenerate offspring for crime, or to let them starve for their imbecility, society can prevent those who are manifestly unfit from continuing their kind. Three generations of imbeciles is enough."

Latent in the discussion of sterilization is the question of whether people with developmental disabilities have the same inherent worth as everyone else. Up until startlingly recently, many Americans believed the answer was no—and some, as Andrew Solomon observes in his book *Far from the Tree: Parents, Children, and the Search for Identity*, still think so. It's no secret that, for much of the last century, people with disabilities faced routine abuse and neglect; less well-known is how often they were killed by their own caregivers. Solomon believes that the number is higher than we might expect, given that families tended to hide their disabled children from the outside world and that many viewed them as essentially nonhuman. Some people proclaimed publicly that filicide, in those cases, was a legitimate and even benevolent option because it put a "defective" child out of his misery and spared the rest of the family the burden of his care. Writing for the *Atlantic* in 1968, the ethicist Joseph Fletcher argued that there was "no reason to feel guilty about putting a Down's syndrome baby away, whether it's 'put away' in the sense of hidden in a sanitarium or in a more responsible lethal sense. It is sad, yes. Dreadful. But it carries no guilt. True guilt arises only from an offense against a person, and a Down's is not a person."

The shadow of this dark era still looms over the medical community. As a consequence, parents often find themselves restricted in making choices about their kids' reproductive health even when legal guardianship empowers them to make all other medical decisions. Some states do not permit the sterilization of people with intellectual disabilities at all; others require court approval for each case. In some states, hospital ethics committees are tasked with deciding whether such procedures are justified and whether patients are truly incapable of making informed decisions for themselves. These additional layers of scrutiny were meant to protect people with disabilities, although some bioethicists say that they may now work against the best interests of those very people by making it harder—and sometimes impossible— for their parents and physicians to ease their physical discomfort and prevent the devastating burden of unplanned pregnancies.

Many parents of people with Williams never consider sterilization, though, and some strongly oppose the idea. Along with those who object for religious reasons, there are some who simply find it unconscionable to deny their children the fundamental right of reproduction, especially if their kids dream of having their own families one day, as many do. It's a discussion that tends to get heated in online forums and in gatherings of the Williams community.

Opinions differ even among people with Williams. Some high-functioning people with Williams, like Dawn, feel that not having children is the right choice, even if it's also a heartbreaking loss. While a big family was what she wanted most in life, Dawn couldn't stand the thought of giving her children the health issues and learning difficulties that Williams entailed, especially when she already knew how hard it was to live with the disorder.

But that left her searching for a purpose in life, which she did with soulful introspection. She still looked forward to being married someday, but she didn't know if she'd feel fulfilled without children.

"I'm trying to find out what my mission in life is," she once wrote on her Facebook page. "Most of you know I can't have kids due to Williams syndrome. It is very painful not to be able to carry on and give my somewhere-out-there husband what he wants. I wanted to have a son who could play football and baseball, a son who could go to church, a son who could give me grandkids. I'm not married yet, but this is something I do think about. I look at myself right now and don't have a blanking clue as to what to do with myself in life. I want to get married; I know that. I am a happy aunty. I just want to be able to give more to people and myself."

She longed to share her love with someone else; she yearned to take care of another living being. Like many people with Williams, she loved animals, and often mentioned her desire to adopt a cat. But her family talked her out of it, since the responsibilities of cat care were still more than she could reliably manage. In the end, she settled for a guinea pig.

Dawn offered both a best- and worst-case example of adulthood with Williams. In addition to the warm, compassionate Williams personality, she had the intelligence and self-control to take advantage of opportunities that eluded others. But her intellect and introspection also hurt her, making her acutely aware of everything she couldn't do because of her disability.

If Emily had suffered likewise, her mother didn't share it with the group at lunch. Claire described her as well adjusted and happy—grateful to be in charge of her own life, for the most part. Emily was close to her roommate, and thereby found the social contact she craved with someone other than her parents. And although she recognized that she couldn't do everything a typical thirty-something could do, she didn't seem to resent it.

"Eventually they do accept it," Claire promised. "They do. You just have to do the best you can to give them as normal a life as possible."

Seventeen

Progress Report

Gayle's meeting with Eli's teachers near the end of his seventh-grade school year confirmed what she had already begun to recognize: teen angst was taking a heavy toll on Eli. Since the tech-ed incident, she had been getting weekly progress reports listing the number of times he hugged other students, touched himself inappropriately, refused to obey a teacher, yelled at someone, or cried. The reports showed that his teachers hadn't stopped Eli from hugging any better than Gayle had, despite a growing arsenal of disciplinary tactics—and that his intrinsically cheerful, agreeable nature was becoming increasingly overshadowed by prickliness and defiance.

While in the past Eli's teachers and aides had focused on rewarding his good behavior, lately they spent more time punishing the bad. Eli's antics now regularly landed him in the time-out room, although that didn't seem to deter him from acting up. If anything, punishment only riled him. He sometimes exploded in fits of flailing and screaming. When told he couldn't do something he wanted to do, he vented his frustration destructively, sometimes violently. Once he angrily tore a sheet of paper into pieces. Another day he knocked his desk over. On a particularly bad day, he kicked his teacher in the shin. It was the first time he'd kicked her, but she was starting to get used to him hitting and head-butting her. When he lashed out physically, he had to be restrained by a team of teachers trained in crisis intervention, who wrestled him to the ground and held him until he calmed down.

Gayle had been horrified to hear how Eli was restrained, but equally horrified to learn that he was hitting and kicking people. He'd never done that at home—at least, not since his toddler years, when he didn't have the words to express his frustration. Since he was normally so eager to please people that he'd never dream of hurting them, Gayle could only conclude that he was feeling levels of anxiety and agitation he hadn't experienced since those nonverbal years. Now it seemed the feelings were intense enough to overwhelm him before he could put them into words.

The week before Gayle's meeting had been fairly typical by Eli's recent standards. His latest progress report noted two incidents of touching other students, three episodes of crying, one destructive outburst (he threw a pencil), and one act of aggression (he pushed a special-ed classmate who was fighting with him to be first in line for lunch).

Eli's teachers suggested a new reward system for good behavior, upping the ante from tokens to social incentives. Eating lunch in the cafeteria, instead of alone in the classroom with an aide, could become a privilege to be earned, since the social aspect of lunch was such a powerful motivator. The idea of exploiting Eli's love of people to enforce his obedience bothered Gayle. But she didn't have any better ideas. Eli had become a powder keg. It was impossible to know what would set him off or how to prevent it.

Some things, of course, had always triggered meltdowns. Loud noises had upset Eli since preschool, when he would yell at younger kids for crying. And he had never responded well to being told "No." Like a lot of Williams kids, he had a low tolerance for refusal.

Furthermore, while rudeness and rejection tended to roll right off him, repeated abuse eventually wore out his patience. One girl in his special-ed class had a habit of hitting him anytime she got the chance. At first he seemed surprised whenever he opened his arms to hug her and got clocked instead. But over time he grew indignant. Eventually the sight of the girl alone was enough to make him stomp his feet and shout at her. Their teachers had to keep them separated in class to avoid an ugly scene.

But Eli's recent outbursts didn't depend on external triggers. Sometimes he just seemed to be in a bad mood, spoiling for a fight. One day he talked back so much in class that his teacher marched him down to the dean's office, where he was told that backtalk could be punished with detention. He came home that afternoon in tears, terrified. In his mind detention was a synonym for prison. Gayle, surprised as well, e-mailed the teacher, who assured her that he would never actually be sent to detention. No one from the special-ed class would.

"It was offered just as an example of disciplinary consequences," the teacher explained. In that week's progress report, she wrote that Eli had had a "very difficult day" that day. He had refused to do his schoolwork and had "yelled at his teachers for the greater part of the day," according to the report.

The fact that his teachers were keeping track of his disruptive behavior was a trigger in itself. Eli knew what it meant when he saw them writing in his chart. Their evident irritation with him heightened his own irritation. It often pushed him over the edge from cranky to infuriated.

One day Gayle was called to the school because Eli had grabbed his chart from an aide's hand and crumpled it, then head-butted the aide. When she met with Gayle, the aide suggested that Eli's behavior might be a plea for attention. Gayle disagreed, countering that his heightened anxieties, coupled with a confusing rush of adolescent hormones, were more likely to blame. The aide cocked her head, then concluded that both were factors.

"He's a complicated little guy," she said, sighing. She seemed both sympathetic and resigned to his plight. Clearly she believed that her best efforts to correct his behavior were in vain.

————

AFTER ELI'S COUNSELORS AT MUSIC CAMP urged him to develop his vocal talent, Gayle signed him up for singing lessons at a music school not far from home. She thought he would be thrilled by the opportunity, but lately his displeasure in taking instruction seemed to outweigh his pleasure in singing. He had become as noncompliant with his voice teacher as with his special-ed teachers—although less destructive, possibly because Gayle was always there to keep him in check.

His disobedience began as soon as they set foot in the building, where signs everywhere proclaimed, "This is a MUSIC SCHOOL and teachers need QUIET in the hallways." Eli pointedly ignored the warnings and spoke in his normal, booming tone—surprisingly loud for a boy with sensitive ears, but his own volume never seemed to bother him.

One evening Gayle brought Eli to his weekly lesson with the voice instructor, Erin, in a stuffy, windowless room just big enough for an upright piano, a bench, and a few metal folding chairs. Gayle sat in the corner and made a point of looking at her phone so Eli wouldn't feel like she was scrutinizing him. Erin led him through a series of scales. He hit the notes perfectly, singing with all his lung capacity.

The previous week, Erin had written down the words to a practice song so he could sing it at home. Now he belted out the song to show her he had done his homework.

"Good," Erin said. "Let's sing it once through together, and then we're going to try to sing it in a round."

Eli had other plans. "Do you remember the Cookie Monster song?" he asked. "*'C' is for cookie, that's good enough for me / 'C' is for cookie, that's good enough for me—*"

"I do," she said, cutting him off. "Does that remind you of this song?"

"No."

"Then what made you think of it?"

"Because I like Cookie Monster! NOM NOM NOM!"

Erin ignored the interruption and forged ahead, offsetting Eli's loudness with the gentle plinking of piano keys. "OK, ready? We'll sing it once through . . ."

Eli humored her for a while, but his heart wasn't in it. "Are you done?" he asked fifteen minutes into the half hour class. Erin shook her head.

"*You're not?*" he asked incredulously, as if they had been at it for hours. "What time are we gonna leave?"

"Are you being nice?" Gayle asked, looking up from her phone.

"I am. I'm being good," he said.

"Are you going to perform?" she prodded.

"I *am* perform!" he said indignantly.

Erin tried to teach him to play a few simple chords on the piano for the next song, "Oh, What a Beautiful Mornin'," positioning his fingers over the right keys and pressing his hand with her own. Eli pulled his hand away and hammered the high keys frenetically, clearly frustrated.

"Look, I'm doing *dunnuh dunnuh dunnuh dunnuh*," he said, singing the notes, and quickly added, anticipating the coming rebuke: "I'm trying my hardest!"

"Maybe we'll just focus on singing," Erin said wearily.

"Are we done?" he asked, and pounded the highest keys again. Erin wrested control of the piano and led him through the song's first verse.

"Let's do that verse again, and then I'll sing the chorus with you," she said when he finished.

"After that?"

"After that I'll play it through and you can just sing it," she said while he stared at her expectantly. Finally she gave in, well aware of the answer he was hoping for. "And after *that* we'll sing the cookie song."

"All right!" he said, smiling. He considered this a resounding triumph. Gayle, meanwhile, did not. He could sing the cookie song at home. She had hoped he'd get more out of singing instruction than lessons in manipulation. He was already skilled enough at badgering people into giving him what he wanted.

———

GAYLE ARRIVED AT ELI'S MIDDLE SCHOOL early in the morning on the last day of May to meet with his teachers, aides, and therapists, along with the school's director of special services. Under Connecticut's special-education guidelines, this group was designated as Eli's planning and placement team, which was officially required to meet with Gayle at the end of each school year to review his progress and outline his educational goals for the following year. This year, however, Gayle had already met with them a half dozen times to address Eli's behavior problems.

Gayle brought along a special-education consultant, Carrie Drake, who had attended these meetings since Eli was in kindergarten. Her services were expensive but worthwhile: she helped ensure that Eli was getting everything he was entitled to under the Individuals with Disabilities Education Act. She was better versed than Gayle in the specifics of the law, which required schools to provide specialized services such as physical, occupational, and speech therapy—or for the school district to cover the costs of these services if it didn't offer them. It also mandated that special-ed students be integrated with the rest of the student body to the fullest degree possible and have equal opportunities to participate in athletic and extracurricular activities, with modifications if necessary.

Carrie was dismayed to learn that although Eli's education plan called for him to meet regularly with a group of nondisabled students who had volunteered to help him build social skills, the group had never actually met. The volunteers also participated in student council and other clubs; their teachers thought they were overextending themselves and had urged them to cut back, starting with this extracurricular obligation.

Overall, however, Gayle was happy with the school district's staff and their efforts to accommodate Eli. They had been overwhelmingly kind and inclusive. It was clear that they cared deeply about Eli, even if he had grown less endearing since he'd started kicking them.

In the meeting, Eli's education team agreed with Carrie that he should spend more time learning and practicing social skills, particularly respecting personal space and keeping his sexual impulses under control. His behavior charts revealed alarming statistics: on two different days, aides had recorded forty incidents of "inappropriate touching of self."

Gayle was skeptical of the statistic, but she couldn't argue with the behavioral goals outlined in the team's plan for the following year, even if they were worded in a declarative voice that sounded like wishful thinking. For example, "Eli will respond to a visual cue to keep his hands on the table." *Good luck,* she thought.

She had no problem with "Eli will add novel social questions to his repertoire," since "I like your shirt" still dominated his attempts to make conversation. The plan even included a numerical objective: "Eli will add *five* new questions to his repertoire, not including 'How are you?' or compliments of clothing."

Nor did she take issue with "Eli will orient pants and shirts correctly." It was a highly pertinent goal, since, when left to his own devices, Eli put his clothes on upside down, inside out, or in any number of logic-defying ways. At home Gayle helped him get dressed, but at school he was expected to change on his own before and after gym class. His teacher described his current ability as "Unable to orient without assistance, unless by chance." Sometimes he got lucky. There were, after all, only so many ways to put on pants.

What Gayle objected to were the proportions of the educational plan, which included vastly more academic than behavioral goals. For example, in the regular-ed classes Eli attended, such as science and social studies, he was given the objective of writing down one fact for every five minutes of lecture. Goals like these struck Gayle as arbitrary and ultimately pointless for Eli. Now that he was a teenager, Gayle cared less and less about him trying to memorize geography he'd never use or scientific theorems he'd never understand.

"I just want to make sure that what we spend time on is useful and practical," she said in the meeting. "I'm not saying he can't learn. He can tell you every detail about every fan and vacuum in the universe. Of course he's capable of learning. We just have to make sure it's meaningful."

Carrie agreed, arguing that academic goals were less important than the skills that would improve Eli's quality of life in the long run. In terms of time alone, the education team's plan called for twenty-six hours of academics (math, English, reading, science, and social studies) each week, with only five hours devoted to life skills. These included: "Eli will demonstrate the ability to use the microwave for reheating or preparing simple snacks, such as popcorn" and "Eli will demonstrate the ability to fold a T-shirt."

Even some of the life skills goals listed struck Gayle as nonessential. One was telling time with an analog clock, which Gayle protested seemed irrelevant in an age of watches and cell phones, especially considering that time itself had little concrete meaning to Eli.

"I mean, he can probably learn to tell you what time it is by the numbers, but it still doesn't register with him," she explained. "He just doesn't think of time that way."

His teachers insisted that it would be a valuable skill at school, where all the classrooms had analog clocks. "At least he might be able to identify the time for specific events—lunchtime, or the end of the day," his speech therapist said. "And that would help him stay on top of his daily routine."

Gayle also balked at a proposed real-world application of Eli's math skills: going into a shop, buying something with a twenty-dollar bill, and calculating the correct change. Gayle worried that this was a financial disaster in the making.

"If he goes into a store with a twenty, I can tell you right now he's not coming back with the change," she said. "He'll get taken advantage of completely. Even if he could do the math, he'll just get distracted. They just have to say 'Hey, look at that' and he'll forget all about it."

The special-education director pointed out that the intention was partly to help him learn the skills that would make him less likely to be taken advantage of: skills like keeping his wallet secure and his money safe, and estimating his change before buying something and counting it afterward.

"I'm not sure if he's ready to even have a wallet," Gayle said. "He leaves things behind everywhere we go. He'll forget his entire backpack sometimes."

"Let's start small," the director suggested. "Maybe he just carries an ID card in the wallet for a while. Then we can practice with buying something that costs less than a dollar, and work our way up."

In the end Gayle relented. The team's goals for Eli were, ultimately, the same as hers: to help him become more independent and prepare him for his best possible future. She wasn't even sure afterward why she'd resisted the idea of giving him hands-on practice making purchases. She'd regarded it as setting him up for failure. But failure was one way to learn. It just wasn't a way Gayle was entirely comfortable with.

While she wished the school would put less emphasis on teaching social studies and more on teaching social skills, she recognized that there were other educational philosophies besides her own. She could see the value in giving Eli all the elements of a traditional school experience, rather than turning his eighth-grade year into a kind of remedial finishing school. And while her impulse was always to fight for what she believed was best for Eli, she had to concede that she didn't have all the answers, or he would already be a model of social appropriateness. She resolved to choose her battles with his teachers, just as she had begun choosing her battles with him.

Eighteen

Where the Hugging
Never Stops

Given Eli's behavioral volatility, Gayle wasn't sure whether to bring him to the Williams Syndrome Association's convention that summer. She hadn't been to one of the biennial conventions since he was little, mostly because they'd been held in distant cities. But this one would be in Boston, and she had no reason not to attend—other than the increasing difficulty of bringing Eli anywhere. Still, she knew that many of his summer camp friends would probably be there, and she didn't want to deprive him of the chance to reunite with them. She herself was eager to catch up with other Williams parents and to hear about the latest advances in Williams research from the experts who would lead panels there. So she decided to go, and enlisted her mother's help in corralling Eli.

Mimi only reluctantly agreed. She often questioned Gayle's insistence on carting Eli to picnics and parties, restaurants and sporting events. For all the effort Gayle put into it, it seemed to Mimi that every outing was a debacle. Eli either hugged everyone in sight or threw a tantrum because Gayle wouldn't let him. Gayle usually came home frustrated and exhausted.

"What do you get out of it? What does Eli?" Mimi sometimes asked. "Do either of you have a good time?"

Mimi thought it might be better to avoid situations that would rile Eli. Gayle disagreed. If he didn't go out in public, she argued, he'd never get better at handling those very situations. What scared Gayle, in fact, was that lately she had started giving in to the temptation to avoid events where she knew she'd spend her time chasing Eli down and correcting his behavior. It was easier to stay home, where Eli could entertain himself without offending anyone, and Gayle could just relax. She worried that this was a slippery slope, though, and that if she didn't make an effort to stay involved, one day they'd wake up and find themselves housebound.

So, after Gayle succeeded in recruiting Mimi, the trio traveled to Boston over the Fourth of July weekend. They joined more than 1,500 people from all over the country, roughly a third of whom had Williams. The group caused a chaotic scene in the lobby of the downtown Sheraton, where the few hotel guests who weren't there for the convention seemed awestruck by the whirlwind of gleeful greetings. When Mimi, Gayle, and Eli walked through the lobby's sliding glass doors, Mimi wondered aloud whether the hotel had issued a warning to its non-Williams patrons.

"What would they tell them?" Gayle asked. " 'Watch out for these guys: they're going to hug you and ask inappropriate questions'?"

Eli, surveying all the smiling, hugging people wearing WSA name tags, was beside himself with joy. For a moment he was stunned into inaction, unsure how to approach the social smorgasbord. People with Williams were everywhere: seated in the lobby's wingback chairs, milling around the registration tables, lining up for the elevator. A few braved the escalators, defying the limits of their depth perception with tentative steps onto the moving stairs. Some squealed with joy at recognizing friends from previous conventions. Many erupted into song.

Gayle watched Eli's eyes widen and knew she was about to lose him in the crowd, so she grasped his shoulders and guided him toward the conference room that was the assembly point for the day camp he would attend while she and Mimi sat in on panels.

The cacophony was even louder in the confined space of the conference room, where more than a hundred teenagers were gathered, wearing red T-shirts that would, in theory, make them easier to herd when they left the hotel on a field trip. The room was a blur of red forms in motion, running, jumping, dancing. Several kids—including Mark, his friend from camp—rushed over to greet Eli.

"How's it going, buddy?" Mark asked, leaning in to give Eli a hug. Gayle opened her mouth to object, then caught herself, realizing that in this case it was perfectly appropriate for Eli to hug his friend. She had been so vigilant about the no-hugging rule for so long that she had rewired her own instincts.

She felt even more sheepish after meeting the volunteers who would take charge of Eli during the day: Henry and Nicole, a brother and sister in their early twenties, whose nineteen-year-old brother had Williams syndrome. Gayle began to explain that they'd need to keep a close eye on Eli, that he would wander off and hug anyone he saw, that he was highly vulnerable—and then she stopped herself. *Of course they know he's vulnerable, that he's a hugger,* she thought. *All these kids are.* Nicole vowed not to let Eli out of her sight.

When Gayle returned to Eli, he was sitting with Mark and four other boys, talking animatedly. Seeing his mother, he preempted her good-bye by saying, "I don't want you to sit with me."

She laughed. "OK. I won't sit with you." She turned to look at him before she walked out the door, but he wasn't watching her. He was focused on his friends.

Soon the crowd of kids broke into their assigned groups for the day's outing to Fenway Park. Eli, thrilled to find himself paired with Nicole, tried to engage her in conversation.

"Where's your daddy?" he asked her in a friendly, inquisitive tone.

"He's with my mom," she said.

"Where's your sister?"

"I don't have a sister."

"That's your uncle?" he asked, pointing to Henry.

"That's my brother."

"You're so beautiful," he said.

"Thanks," she said. "You're very nice."

"You want to eat with me tonight?"

"I have to eat with my family," she said.

"Aww," he whined. "I'm going to miss you."

Just then another young woman walked by, and Eli's attention drifted.

"Where are you going?" he asked the woman, another volunteer chaperone.

"Same place you are," she said. "Fenway Park."

"I miss you," he said sadly as she walked past.

"But you just met me!"

Free from his mother's admonishments and his schoolteachers' behavior charts, Eli grew even more girl-crazy than usual. Outside the hotel, waiting for a tour bus, Eli spotted yet another pretty teenage chaperone. "How are you?" he asked.

He reminded himself aloud: "Handshakes and high-fives!" Then he hugged the girl anyway, too close and for too long. She giggled nervously and gently pushed him away.

"We're not going to hug like that, Eli," Nicole reminded him. But by now all Eli's restraint had dissolved in the humid summer air. "I love you!" he called after the girl.

Without Gayle there to rein in Eli's public displays of affection, he revealed what he was like when he lost all self-control. In the Fenway Park gift shop, while they waited for the tour to start, Eli managed to break free from Nicole and run up to a tourist in a "Cheers!" T-shirt. Eli reached out wordlessly to shake the woman's hand. She accepted it and smiled at him.

"Hello there!" she said with amused surprise. He tickled the underside of her palm with his fingers. She gave him a puzzled look. Her husband, standing nearby, put his arm around her.

Nicole pulled Eli back by her side as they started the tour. But he hardly looked at the historic ballpark; he was focused instead on the people around him. While Nicole took in the "Green Monster"—Fenway's famous left-field wall—Eli stared instead at the plump calves of a heavyset woman just ahead of him. She wore shimmery, flesh-colored tights that shone invitingly in the sunlight. Eli was transfixed. If Nicole hadn't been setting a good example by looking attentively at the tour guide, it would have been obvious to her that Eli was contemplating a sneak attack.

He crouched, looking down as if he was about to tie his shoe. Then he inched toward the woman and stretched his hand out slowly, glancing at Nicole first to see if she was watching. When he was close enough, he sprang forward and grasped the shimmering calf firmly in his hand. He squeezed.

The woman to whom the calf belonged shrieked and kicked her leg forward, turning simultaneously. Her face was pinched with anger and embarrassment. Eli straightened and looked away. Nicole whispered forcefully in his ear. The woman's scowl relaxed slightly. She was a volunteer, too, and knew enough about Williams to understand the urge to touch. Eli hung his head low enough to make a convincing show of remorse, although his cheeks were flushed and his eyes were wild. It was a look of pure bewilderment, as if he himself didn't understand what he was doing or why.

———

WHILE ELI HUGGED AND SQUEEZED HIS way through Fenway Park, Gayle and Mimi sat in over-air-conditioned conference rooms listening to Williams experts present their findings. Dr. Pober was the lead presenter for several panels, including one on health issues in adults with Williams. Gayle, curious as ever to know what the future held for Eli, attended this one.

One of the most pervasive and dangerous problems of adulthood, Dr. Pober said, was obesity. Even skinny kids with Williams seemed to have a greater-than-normal risk of becoming heavy as they aged. She projected a line graph comparing the average height and weight of people with and without Williams as they aged. For people with Williams, height plateaued well below the normal line but weight continued to rise.

"You can see that the weight here is at the fiftieth percentile or greater," she said, beaming a laser pointer at early adulthood. "But height is at the third percentile. So they're heavy for their height. This is a change over time from their body type as younger people. Most kids are skinny, but about two-thirds of the adults we studied were overweight or obese."

Then again, she added, almost two-thirds of older Americans in general were overweight or obese. So it wasn't obvious whether the weight gain itself was a factor of Williams or simply of the unhealthy American lifestyle. The distinct way people with Williams carried their weight, however, was definitively correlated with the disorder.

"Most adults have a pear-shaped distribution," she said. "It's in the hips and the butt and extends into the legs. Whether there's a genetic vulnerability to gaining weight, we don't know; but when they do gain weight, it takes this distinct shape."

It didn't help that many adults with Williams took anxiety medication and antidepressants that increased their appetites and made it harder to lose weight, she said. But carrying the extra pounds exacerbated other Williams-related health problems, such as heart trouble and sleep apnea.

"Weight is one of the most pressing issues I see in the adult population," Dr. Pober said. "Some of us gained the freshman fifteen. They have the same thing when they hit thirty and it's like, 'I'm an adult; you're not going to tell me what to do, what to eat, anymore.' It's a huge problem that has a domino effect on other medical problems."

A woman in the audience raised her hand to say that her son never seemed to feel full: he kept eating long after he should have stopped. A number of other parents nodded. One mother said she had to lock food in cupboards or it would disappear when her back was turned. Dr. Pober said that researchers were looking into whether there was something wrong with the satiety sensor in people with Williams or whether this was simply another manifestation of their poor impulse control. A different genetic disorder, Prader-Willi syndrome, causes dysfunction in the hypothalamus and other parts of the brain associated with feeling full, so people with the disorder are constantly, ravenously hungry and tend to become morbidly obese. But the correlation isn't as clear in Williams syndrome, Dr. Pober said. A healthy diet and regular exercise are usually enough to keep weight gain under control in Williams.

Gayle raised her hand to ask a question that had been bothering her ever since she saw a segment about Williams on the ABC news show *20/20* a year earlier.

"That *20/20* special said there was a lowered life expectancy for people with Williams, but that was the first I'd heard of it," Gayle said. Everyone in the room knew which show she meant, including Dr. Pober, who had appeared on it. "Is that true?"

Dr. Pober dismissed the notion. "Nobody's done any studies of the kind you'd need before you can draw those kinds of conclusions. I have Williams patients in their sixties and seventies and eighties," she said. "I *do* think that not as many Williams adults make it to their sixties and seventies as is the case in the general population, but I don't think you can say in the glib kind of way they did that there is a lower life expectancy. I think there's a younger subset that, tragically, don't make it out of infancy due to severe cardiac defects. Some older folks have passed away earlier than average. For some the cause has been vascular; for some it's been gastrointestinal. But the conclusion they came to about that wasn't backed up by science."

Gayle nodded, although she wasn't entirely comforted by the doctor's qualified no to her question. She often heard about people with Williams dying suddenly, at all ages, from cardiac complications.

She took some solace from knowing that Eli's aortic stenosis was so mild he had never needed surgery, as many with the disorder did. But his cardiologist had told her that it was a progressive condition that could change for the worse at any time, leaving her in limbo between his annual checkups.

Later in the day Gayle and Mimi attended a presentation on treating the behavioral symptoms of Williams, which was led by Christopher McDougle, a psychiatry professor at Harvard Medical School and the director of the Lurie Center for Autism at Massachusetts General Hospital. McDougle suggested some alternative medications for anxiety and depression, given that SSRIs, which increase serotonin levels in the brain, didn't work as well on people with Williams as on the mainstream population.

"SSRIs are great for a lot of typical people who have depression, panic disorder, social anxiety disorder, post-traumatic stress, OCD . . . They work for lots of things for lots of people," he explained. "Half the world is on SSRIs. But many times they make people with Williams worse: angry, irritable. They increase agitation and disinhibition, that kind of thing. That's exactly what we see with autism; if you give them an SSRI, they get worse."

Part of the problem could be that both people with autism and people with Williams have abnormal serotonin levels, or that they process the neurotransmitter differently from the rest of us. Some studies have found lower-than-normal levels of serotonin in the central nervous systems of people with autism, compared to higher-than-normal levels in Williams syndrome. But the issue is contentious; most scientists agree that it's probably not that simple.

In his talk, McDougle recommended drugs that had worked well for his autistic patients: atypical antipsychotics, particularly Risperdal and Abilify.

Gayle jotted down the names. Eli's psychiatrist had just taken him off the SSRI Celexa because it made him even more socially uninhibited than usual, as well as edgier and crankier. Gayle had wondered if the drug contributed to his misbehavior in school. However, she was reluctant to experiment with powerful psychotropic drugs. So were others in the audience, who asked about the effectiveness of homeopathic remedies and cognitive-behavioral therapy. McDougle responded politely.

"Some people say, 'I don't want to go near medicine if I don't have to.' It's always fine to try nondrug treatments first. Behavior therapy, consequences—all that's fine, and a lot of times it can be helpful," he said. "But there's a point for many people when that's just not enough. What I say to parents is: you will know when it's time. These drugs can be life-changing, because sometimes these behaviors can keep a family in their house. You can't go to a restaurant. You're housebound."

Gayle raised an eyebrow and exchanged a look with Mimi. This was her life he was describing. She underlined the names of the drugs.

———

AFTER THE PANELS HAD ENDED AND the day campers had returned from Fenway Park, Gayle and Mimi took Eli to dinner at the Prudential Center mall, a short walk through a connecting corridor from the Sheraton. Making a lap around the food court, they passed a man with Williams syndrome, in his forties or early fifties, sitting at a table by himself. Like the adults Dr. Pober had described earlier that day, he was obese and noticeably pear-shaped. His hair was dark and curly, like Eli's, but wildly disheveled. He wore a dirty T-shirt that strained to accommodate his stomach. While he sat eating pizza and drinking a large soda, people at neighboring tables, mostly teenagers without Williams, snuck glances in his direction.

When she heard laughter, Gayle wondered if it was at the man's expense. But he didn't seem to notice; all his attention was focused on the pizza.

Gayle felt a pang of excruciating pity. Eli was already chubby: would this be him in thirty years? Part of her wanted to shout at the laughing teenagers, to shield the man from derision the way she'd want to shield her son. Part of her, though, tried to put the scene in perspective. After all, he was doing what she hoped Eli would be capable of one day: taking care of himself. Clearly he had been able to navigate the mall and buy his dinner without help. He'd probably even broken a twenty and gotten the right change—or maybe he'd been shortchanged, but, either way, he'd gotten a meal. Still, Gayle couldn't get over how unkempt and vulnerable to ridicule he was. Didn't he have parents? Where were they?

She bought Eli a chicken sandwich and cut it into pieces to make it easier for him to pick up. She watched him eat, trying to see him from a stranger's perspective. He was dressed as stylishly as any teenager at the mall, wearing army-green cargo shorts and a black T-shirt with the logo of the punk club CBGB. But there could be no question that something about him was different. He squirmed in his seat, kicking his legs, which didn't quite reach the ground. His gaze flitted feverishly from person to person as he scanned the room, then looked down at the floor.

"I need to scrub this floor," he exclaimed happily, eyeing the dingy gray tiles. "It got so dirty."

He inhaled his chicken sandwich and then helped himself to half of Mimi's meal. With his mouth still full, he reached for Gayle's grilled cheese sandwich.

"Eli!" Gayle said. "You've already had your meal." He slowly pulled his hand back, his eyes locked on the sandwich.

"What's next?" he asked when he finally gulped down the last of Mimi's food. "We can have dessert?"

Since Gayle had promised him dessert if he behaved at camp— and since she hadn't heard about the calf-squeezing episode—she gave in to his request for a hot fudge sundae from Ben & Jerry's. He immediately knocked some of the whipped cream onto the table, then stuck his finger in it and licked it off.

Gayle moved to grab his hand, then sighed and shook her head. "OK, eat it however you want," she said. "Eat it off the table. Do it your way."

When he had finished his sundae, and his face, hands, and fore-arms were covered in ice cream, Gayle scrubbed him down with nap-kins. He pulled away from her. "No, Mom! I'm ready to go now!"

"I'm just trying to clean you up," she said. "This is what I want you to get more independent with."

On the way back, Eli decided that he had been so good that he deserved a trinket, too.

"I'd like a little something," he said as they walked past the maze of storefronts leading to the Sheraton. "I like Best of Boston," he said, naming the gift store they were passing, with a display of stuffed lobsters, candy lobsters, and plastic lobster-claw grabbers.

"I like that grabber," he said, pointing to one.

"I don't think so, Eli," Gayle said. "You can't get something every time we go out."

They walked on.

"Ooh," Eli said, stopping to point at a kiosk of Hello Kitty merchandise. "That's nice."

Gayle tugged him along by the hand. Eli knew there was another gift shop near the hotel, but Gayle dragged him past it without slowing down. She stopped at an ATM to get some money, and Eli's face clouded when he saw the door to the hotel just ahead and realized that all his trinket opportunities were behind him.

"I don't want to go back to the hotel!" he shouted. Gayle ignored him and slid her debit card into the machine. Eli stomped his foot and moaned. Mimi looked at him with concern.

"I really need something," he shouted again. His voice cascaded down from the skylights and echoed through the bustling corridor. A mall custodian, carrying a bag of trash past the ATM, looked at the cashier of a nearby newsstand and circled her finger around her ear in the international sign for "crazy." Clusters of people moved to the other side of the walkway, giving Eli a wide berth.

"I don't like your tone, young man," Gayle said without turning from the ATM screen. "You're not getting anything if you shout like that."

"Awww," he moaned. He kicked the floor, squeaking rubber against tile. "You're being mean."

Mimi reached a hand toward him.

"Eli, you're tired. Let's go back and rest."

"I don't want to rest," he yelled, shrugging off her hand. "I just want to get a little something!"

Mimi pointed out a pair of security guards not far away.

"Eli, those policemen are going to come talk to you if you don't quiet down," she said. But Eli ignored the threat and continued to fume.

Gayle was withdrawing her money from the machine when Eli suddenly turned to Mimi, lowered his head, and charged at her like a bull, head-butting her in the stomach. The force was enough to shove her backward, almost knocking her off her feet. She inhaled sharply, stumbling to regain her balance.

"Eli, what are you doing?" Gayle cried. She pulled him toward her. He was flailing, his head still lowered, and blind with anger. He wheeled around at Mimi and hit her again, a hard backhand to the shoulder. Her eyes filled with tears of surprise and pain. She retreated around the corner of the ATM, out of Eli's sight.

Gayle grabbed him by the shoulders and looked him in the eyes, trying to hold his gaze. "Calm down," she said in a low voice. "What's gotten into you? You do not hit Mimi. Pull yourself together."

She let go of his shoulders and put a hand on his arm as she said this, but he slapped it away, then shoved her forcefully. Gayle stared at him, shocked. He was so solidly built that even if she tried to subdue him, he could overpower her. She had never put much thought into who would win in a fight, but it occurred to her now that he might.

Just then he kicked her in the shin. He was far enough away that the kick didn't land squarely, but still she was stunned. She stood paralyzed. Eli turned to find his grandmother but didn't see her.

"Hey! Come back here," he said, jogging around the ATM to find her. She was just on the other side; he nearly collided with her. In a growl, he immediately contradicted himself. "Get away from me!" He spun on his heels, turning his back to her, and hugged his arms across his chest. "Get away from me, you bastard!"

Gayle shook herself out of her paralysis and took Eli by the arm, pulling him toward the hotel. He yelled all the way. One of the security guards watched them pass, but he only smiled and kept walking in the other direction. Mimi was relieved, because by then Eli was shouting, "Let me out of here! Don't touch me!" and she worried that, despite her earlier threat, Gayle might be the one the police actually wanted to talk to.

Eli was still howling when they entered the glass doors that separated the hotel from the mall. Gayle pulled him into an alcove and sat him next to her on a leather-cushioned bench. Anyone entering or leaving the hotel could see him, and anyone anywhere in the building could hear him. But she knew they couldn't make it across the lobby and up to the room like this. She needed to calm him down.

She could barely think straight herself, however. She couldn't remember how much money she'd gotten out of the ATM, or even whether she'd retrieved her debit card. All she could focus on was her son, now flailing at her like a windmill, scratching her bare arms. Mimi leaned over and put a tentative hand on his, but when he pumped his legs to kick her, Gayle shooed her back.

"Watch out, Mom," she said. "You'll get hurt."

Mimi stepped back.

"I think we need some alone time," Gayle said. "If you want to just wait for us in the room, I'll be up there when he's cooled down."

Mimi nodded, but she was reluctant to leave them behind. She walked away slowly, then stopped around a corner about twenty yards away. She was out of Gayle and Eli's sight, but she could hear them and see the faces of people passing by. Some looked at Gayle and Eli askance. Some were parents wearing convention name tags, who shook their heads sympathetically. Some were people with Williams, who clamped their hands over their sensitive ears and hurried past. A few others, with less sensitive ears, gave Eli a long, worried look.

In the alcove, Gayle was quickly running through her repertoire of tantrum stoppers. She had tried "I'm disappointed and embarrassed." She had tried "We're going to have to go home if you keep acting like this." She had even reused "The police are going to come if you don't cut it out." But none of it seemed to have any effect.

Meanwhile, Mimi considered going back for the lobster grabber if it was the only way to end Eli's hysterics. But she knew Gayle would object to rewarding his meltdown. Buying him the toy now would teach him that he could hold them hostage with his behavior, as the parents of toddlers everywhere could attest.

Mimi peeked around the corner and saw that Eli was still enraged. Gayle was holding him by the arm while he punched, slapped, and scratched her. Finally she let go. Eli threw himself down on the floor and rolled onto his back, stomping the marble heavily under his sneakers. His face was flushed red and wet with tears.

A new passerby appeared; a svelte, delicately featured man wearing a white polo shirt and khakis so light they were almost white. He walked straight toward Gayle and Eli. Gayle grew nervous. This was just what she needed: a stranger intervening.

"What's wrong?" the man asked. His manner was confident and disarming, his cologne citrusy, his voice inflected with a thick Spanish accent.

"Oh, he's just having kind of a rough time right now," Gayle said.

The man nodded. Eli had stopped kicking the floor and was sitting up, watching the stranger with rapt curiosity. The man knelt down to Eli's level and grasped Eli's hands firmly.

"Are you the police?" Eli asked.

"I'm an angel," the man said. "God sent me here because he said you needed a little help calming down."

Eli was suddenly quiet. Mimi could hear her heart pound.

"Now, take a deep breath, in and out," the man said softly.

Eli obliged. The man pressed Eli's hands to his heart.

"You know your mom loves you, and she feels so sad when you're upset, right?"

Eli nodded.

"Do you feel better?" the man asked.

Eli nodded again. The man stood and said good-bye. Eli was still sniffling, but by now he was sufficiently calm to walk with his mother back to the elevator, where Mimi joined them. In a daze, Gayle led them up to their room on the twenty-third floor. She was too stunned to be angry, and in any case she wasn't sure who to be angry with: Eli for punching her, or herself for letting a man claiming to be an angel lay hands on her son. She couldn't decide whether the man was delusional or just magically gifted at soothing troubled kids. Maybe both. But she was mortified that it had taken a stranger, and possibly an insane stranger, to control her son when she couldn't. After a lifetime of thinking she knew best for Eli, she felt as if she no longer had a clue how to help him.

Once inside the hotel room, Eli began to wind down from his tantrum. While Gayle examined the half-moon gouges where he had pierced her skin with his fingernails, and Mimi rubbed the tender skin on her shoulder from his backhand slap, Eli's thoughts turned to floor scrubbing. He had asked Gayle earlier to build him another cardboard-box floor scrubber. She had explained that their hotel room wasn't stocked with craft supplies, but that she thought she might be able to improvise.

"Oh, you said you can find something?" he reminded her now with contrived nonchalance. "Like, a scrubber?"

She extended the handle of her hard-shelled rolling suitcase and offered it to him. He grabbed the handle and jerked the suitcase back and forth in the quick push-pull movements of a vacuum cleaner, making vrooming noises with his mouth and trailing lines across the thick blue carpet. His intense focus on the imaginary task gave him tunnel vision. He bumped into Mimi, then collided with a wall.

"Careful, Eli," Gayle said. "You're running over everybody."

"Hey, move that bed," he barked at Mimi as he made for the rollaway bed where he slept, next to the king bed Gayle and Mimi were sharing. "I gotta clean the floor."

"Eli, I'm not moving that bed," Mimi said. "You'll have to clean around it."

"Ohhh," he whined. His brow furrowed as he continued to vacuum furiously, occasionally running over his own feet with the suitcase.

Gayle lay across the bed while Mimi sat in an armchair by the window, both of them lost in thought and exhausted. For a while the only sound in the room was Eli's vrooming and the thuds of the suitcase hitting furniture.

"What did you think of that guy who said he was an angel?" Gayle finally asked her mother. "I probably shouldn't have let him touch Eli, right? I was just—I didn't even know what was going on."

"But he calmed Eli down," Mimi offered.

"He was probably a crazy person," Gayle said. "And here I am letting him get right up in Eli's face."

She rolled onto her side and looked at Eli.

"I want to ask you something," Gayle said to him as he banged the suitcase into a corner. "What do you think about that guy in the white shirt? What do you think he was?"

"He was a big nurse," Eli said.

"A big nurse?" Gayle repeated. He could be right, she thought. The man knew exactly how to soothe a crying child: he applied pressure to Eli's hands, got down to his level, made eye contact, instructed him to breathe deeply. Maybe he *was* a nurse—or a counselor, or a teacher. Or perhaps he really was an angel. He had, after all, appeared miraculously out of nowhere and calmed Eli down when nothing else could.

Across the room, Eli suddenly seemed to realize that he was pretending to vacuum, not scrub, the floor, and that the suitcase was missing a key floor-scrubbing component.

"I need a hose for my scrubber," he declared.

"Eli, this is a hotel," Mimi said. "You can't just get a hose here. It's not like at home, where Uncle Chris gives them to you."

"No, I need a hose," he persisted. "Can you call the front desk?"

"No, we can't call the front desk," Mimi said.

"I just need a hose!" he cried.

"Eli, you have to be quiet or the people in the next room will hear you," Mimi said.

He pointed a finger at her. "Hey!" he said. "You never do anything nice for me!"

She frowned, crestfallen.

"Eli, that's a mean thing to say to Mimi," Gayle said.

He flopped onto the rollaway bed, face-first into the down pillow. He kicked his feet in the air. He had already kicked off his sneakers, and now his gray socks bunched loosely below his ankles, about to fly off.

"I can't live like this!" he complained. Gayle rolled her eyes, but Mimi interjected anxiously, "Eli, what's wrong? Is something hurting you?"

"You hurt me," he said. "You hurt my feelings."

"No, I mean, is something *hurting* you? Like your head? Or your tummy?" She turned to Gayle. "Maybe he needs an Advil or something."

"He needs a tranquilizer gun," Gayle said, then clarified: "*I* need a tranquilizer gun."

Eli lifted his face and turned to his mother, leaving a head-size impression in the down pillow. "She never lets me do anything," he said angrily, now referring to Gayle. "She's yelling at me."

"No, you're the only one yelling," Mimi said quietly. "I don't think you're being fair."

"I hate her," he said tearfully.

"Eli, I don't think you know what 'hate' means," Mimi said.

"I hate you, Mom," he said, looking Gayle in the eyes. It was the first time he'd ever uttered those words, and it felt like a punch to the gut, knocking the wind out of her. Getting kicked in the shin had been far less painful.

Seeing her stricken look, Eli buried his face in the pillow again. He continued to kick the mattress, unwilling to let the aftershocks of his tantrum die away completely, but he toned down the harshness of his language.

"I'm upset," he moaned. "I'm just tired! I don't feel good now."

"Do you want me to give you some Advil?" Gayle asked, recovering from her shock.

"I don't like Advil!" he shouted.

Gayle sighed and leaned back against the pillows.

"What I'm going to do? I'm sick!" Eli yelled.

"No, you're not sick," Mimi assured him. "You're upset."

Gayle rubbed her temples, feeling sick and upset herself. She knew that parenting a teenager was a hard, thankless job, but this was an even greater challenge. This was the surliness of a typical teen mixed with the irrational volatility of a two-year-old. She was starting to understand how other parents had reached the end of their rope. What if this was what the future held: the tantrums of Eli's toddler years, acted out by a full-grown man? She was already unable to physically restrain him. He could easily hurt himself, or her.

Just a week or two earlier, she and Mimi had joked that Eli was turning into Dr. Jekyll and Mr. Hyde: loving and happy one minute, an irascible maniac the next. As soon as his tantrums subsided, he was astonished by his own bad behavior. But while he was in Hyde form, neither he himself nor anyone else could shake him out of it.

Gayle feared that the Hyde in him was becoming more dominant, and more destructive. At times it was hard to recognize the sweet, endlessly empathetic boy with whom she had spent the last thirteen years.

While Eli lay moaning on the rollaway bed, flooded with feelings he didn't fully understand, Gayle closed her eyes, overwhelmed by the enormity and inscrutability of his needs. She was at a loss for how to ease his suffering, as well as her own. His behavior had grown so erratic that logic and reason no longer seemed like useful parenting tools. And where she had once worried only about protecting him, she now had to consider how to protect herself from him. Her love for Eli was boundless, but when it was met with insults and physical abuse, it no longer carried the same rewards it once had, when her love was only ever met with love.

Nineteen

Tough Love

The next morning Eli was his usual bubbly, cheerful self. He woke with the sunrise and sang quietly while he covered the hotel stationery in thick crayon swirls.

Gayle had not bounced back so quickly. She was a little distant, and Eli could sense it.

"I'm sorry, Mom," he said while she applied her makeup in front of the mirror.

"What are you sorry for?" she asked, curious to see if he understood the effects of his behavior from the night before.

"I'm sorry you got upset."

Gayle sighed, brushing on mascara. *He knows I'm not happy,* she thought, *but he doesn't know why.* She knew it would do no good to lecture him now, though. Mr. Hyde was gone and Dr. Jekyll was back, amiably oblivious to his partner's offenses.

For breakfast, Gayle and Mimi brought Eli to the Starbucks in the Sheraton lobby, where Gayle ordered a latte for herself and a slice of coffee cake for Eli. Scanning the café, Gayle recognized a familiar face: Susie, Eli's crush from music camp. She'd wondered whether Susie would attend the convention. Eli had wondered, too—and hoped she would. The night before they arrived he had asked Gayle, "Is Susie going to be there?"

"Who?" Gayle had said, feigning ignorance.

"Susie," he repeated cheerfully. "The one who said, 'Go away.'"

Now Susie recognized a family at the table next to the one where Mimi and Eli were sitting, and she greeted them warmly. Her expression cooled when she walked past Eli; she seemed to have recognized him, too. When he noticed her, however, he nearly jumped out of his seat, smiling and waving.

"Susie! Susie!! Remember me? Hi! Hey! Susie!"

Susie didn't break stride. Her high ponytail swished behind her like a finger wagging.

"Eli, if someone doesn't want to say hi to you, you don't keep trying. Just let her go," Mimi said, putting a hand over his. He didn't seem to hear his grandmother, though.

"Susie, remember me?" he called again at her retreating back. Finally she turned to look at him.

"Yes," she said curtly. She turned away again and disappeared around a corner.

For once, Eli did not seem satisfied with this crisp acknowledgment. His smile faded. His brow furrowed in contemplation. If she remembered him, why hadn't she greeted him right away?

Gayle could see the dark cloud moving across his face when she returned with the coffee cake. She took it as a mark of maturity, both encouraging and disheartening, that Eli finally seemed to recognize rejection. A year ago he would have simply chased after Susie, begging for her attention. Now he shifted his focus inward, brooding over the snub. Gayle was unsure how to help him cope with this new form of hurt. She picked an old technique and tried to distract him with the promise of a reward for good behavior.

"You're doing so great today," she said. "I think you're going to earn a token if you keep it up."

He swiveled in his seat to face her. Despite his newfound angst, the old technique still worked. He smiled, knowing that earning enough tokens meant Gayle would make a handle for the cardboard-box floor scrubber she had built for him at home.

"I want to earn the handle, Mom!"

———

GAYLE DROPPED ELI OFF AGAIN in the cacophonous conference room full of teenagers. They were going on another field trip, this time to see the Blue Man Group. Eli was excited because he had been told there would be drumming and dancing, although he was having a hard time understanding why the performers would be blue. He'd asked Gayle an endless string of questions about it. To clarify, she showed him a YouTube clip of the group, but he still seemed anxious, apparently concerned that he, too, would be painted blue.

"I'm going to be in the Blue Man Group?" he had asked nervously over breakfast.

"No, you're going to *see* the Blue Man Group," Mimi said.

"And what's after those blue guys?" he asked.

"Your mom will come and get you, like always. And then we'll take it from there."

Mimi, too, was more reserved than usual after the previous day's melee. She wasn't mad at Eli; she couldn't blame him for behavior that was so clearly out of his control. She felt as bad for him as she did for Gayle, since his tantrums made him as miserable as they did everyone else.

She and Gayle split up for the morning to attend different panels. Mimi attended one for grandparents of kids with Williams. When she met Gayle for lunch afterward, she was shaking her head over the saccharine spin some of her fellow grandparents put on their experiences.

"They were all smiles, saying that having a kid with Williams brought the whole family closer together," she told Gayle over a salad. "They said at first it was sad, not knowing what the future would hold, but that now it's just a joy."

"Well, I'm sure they didn't want to scare anybody, especially the families with kids who were just diagnosed," Gayle offered.

"I was this close to standing up and saying, 'Come on people, let's be honest,'" Mimi went on. "I can't tell you how many times I heard the word 'joy.' I wanted to say, 'Yes it's such a joy when a thirteen-year-old boy has a complete meltdown in the mall. That's so joyful.'"

Gayle smiled, knowing that her mother would be the last person to stand up in a room full of grandmothers and call them on it. Mimi had a heightened sense of propriety that Gayle lacked. She was usually the one talking Gayle off the ledge when Gayle threatened to give someone a piece of her mind.

"There was one touching moment," Mimi admitted. "One woman started crying. She has a five-year-old granddaughter, and a two-year-old grandson who just got diagnosed with Williams. When the parents explained about Williams to his sister, she asked, 'Will it go away when he gets older?' The parents said, 'No, he's always going to have it.' So the five-year-old said, 'Well, I'm going to be a scientist, so I can cure it.' At that point everyone started crying."

———

THE SCENE AT DAY CAMP WAS even more chaotic at the end of the day than at the beginning, since its organizers had devised an elaborate protocol to prevent the kids from leaving with the wrong people. Parents had to line up and show ID before their children would be released. The line was long, and the kids were wild.

Gayle found herself waiting behind another Connecticut woman she had known for years: Kristin, whose daughter Penny was about Eli's age. They commiserated over the bottleneck at the checkout desk and the havoc it was wreaking on their kids, who could see their parents and had to be held back from running out to join them. But they couldn't fault the organizers for being extra cautious with this group. Penny, even more than Eli, had a dangerous habit of wandering off after strangers. In a parking lot once, on a trip to the beach, Kristin had turned her head for a moment and Penny had climbed into another family's minivan after overhearing them say they were going out for ice cream.

Kristin told Gayle she'd recently enrolled Penny in a personal safety class for kids with special needs, where she was taught to seek out a trusted adult if she were ever separated from her mother or from a school group. Since Penny trusted everyone, she was given some tips on who would be the best choice: an adult in uniform, for example, or a mother with kids.

But Penny used the technique once when she wandered away from her mother in a store, and got so much attention that now she took any opportunity to try it out. If she couldn't see her mother by looking straight ahead, Kristin said, she'd seek out a "trusted adult" before looking left or right. The previous night, at a convention dance party that Gayle had skipped, Kristin was standing five feet away from her daughter in the hotel ballroom when Penny briefly lost sight of her. So Penny flagged down a hotel staff member wearing a badge. Seconds later Kristin saw a team of hotel employees mobilize to search for this poor lost little girl's mom.

"I've created a monster," she said.

Finally Gayle got close enough to the front of the line to see Eli, who was growing antsy in the throng of children still waiting to be checked out. His voice carried over the others when he started to whine.

"Aww," he moaned. "I'm ready to go. I'm hungry."

Susie suddenly appeared with her older brother and younger sister, pushing past Eli toward their parents. Without looking Eli in the face, Susie muttered under her breath as she passed, "What are *you* crying about?"

"I heard you!" Eli shouted angrily. When she kept walking, holding her little sister's hand, he added for effect: "You bastard!" Susie didn't bat an eye, but her sister gasped and turned to look at him.

Gayle didn't know what it was about Eli that provoked Susie. She hadn't seen Susie treat anyone else this way, so it seemed that Eli in particular simply pushed Susie's buttons. But now Susie was pushing his buttons, too. Gayle couldn't help but take some satisfaction in seeing him talk back to his tormentor. She signed him out of camp and led him toward the elevator, unsure whether to give him stern words or a pep talk. Before she could do either, he lowered his chin and pouted.

"Susie was mean to me," he said gruffly. "It broke my heart."

Gayle gave him a one-armed side hug, pulling him close while they walked. "You know what? You have lots of friends. You don't need to worry about her."

"I don't care about her!" he declared, nodding vigorously as if to convince himself.

"I just mean you don't need to worry about what she thinks of you."

He grew quiet, considering this. Something about it seemed to unsettle him more than it soothed: perhaps the loss of Susie as a friend he'd treasured until that day, or perhaps the way this loss hinted at a more troubling generality—that not everyone he liked would always like him back.

———

WITH 1,500 PEOPLE AT THE CONVENTION, Gayle couldn't understand why the one person they kept running into was the one who caused Eli the most anguish. When Gayle, Eli, and Mimi left their hotel room half an hour later and pushed the elevator button to go down to dinner, the door opened to reveal, once again, Susie. Gayle, plotting an escape, paused just a moment longer than normal for someone who wanted to get on an elevator. She couldn't pretend it was too full: it was empty except for Susie and her mother, who was texting, her down-turned face illuminated by the glow of her cell phone. Gayle briefly considered pretending she'd left something behind in the room, but Mimi was already stepping onto the elevator. Gayle followed, placing a protective hand on Eli's shoulder. She wedged herself between him and Susie.

Susie, wearing a sundress with jeweled sandals that showed off her pedicure, done in a rainbow of glittering metallic colors, pursed her lips meekly.

"I'm sorry," she mumbled to Gayle while carefully examining her rainbow toes.

"What's that?" Susie's mother asked without looking up from her phone. "For what?"

"Oh, don't worry about it," Gayle told Susie quickly. She assumed the apology was meant for snapping at Eli earlier, but she didn't want to have to explain to Susie's mother that Eli had called her a bastard in reply. Her mother didn't press the point.

Susie leaned forward to look at Eli on the other side of Gayle. "How are you?" she asked with forced sweetness.

"Good!" Eli said earnestly, taking the bait.

"What are you doing tonight?"

"Oh, we're going to a noodle restaurant in the mall. Wagamama," Gayle said.

"Yeah, noodles!" Eli said, beaming. "I love noodles."

He looked up at Gayle for affirmation. "Mom, I love noodles!" he said again, rubbing his hands together. "I love noodles."

"We *heard* you," Susie hissed. "I mean, not to be rude."

There was silence until the door opened on the fifth floor. Susie hurried off the elevator. Her mother trailed, head still bent over her phone. Gayle gave Mimi a long look, then glanced at Eli. This time he seemed not to have noticed the harshness of Susie's reply. He was still grinning about noodles.

But the encounter left a bad taste in Gayle's mouth. In some ways Eli seemed to be maturing, in other ways regressing. He'd stood up to Susie but hadn't stopped being a target of her ridicule. And while Susie, a year younger than Eli, seemed to have the worldliness and attitude of a teenager, Eli was still throwing tantrums over lobster grabbers and clamoring for noodles like a toddler. As they stepped off the elevator, he was clutching two crayons he had taken from the hotel room and singing the theme song from *Mickey Mouse Clubhouse*. Gayle snatched the crayons from his hand.

"Here, give those to me," she said. "You don't want to look like a baby. I'll put them in here." She shoved them into a zippered compartment of her purse.

Walking through the Sheraton's crowded lobby, however, she was reminded that Susie's apparent precocity was an exception to the Williams rule. Many of the teens here, and even many of the adults, didn't seem much more mature than Eli, and they shared some of his unusual habits and fixations.

A man in his twenties sat at a computer looking up YouTube videos of clowns, with which he was evidently as obsessed as Eli was with floor scrubbers. One link took him to a video of a ghoulishly grinning clown at a haunted house. The man looked stricken.

"Whoa, that is freaky!" he said to a friend who didn't have Williams, sitting nearby. "Wow, I've never seen a clown mask like that. I don't know about this."

"You've never seen a clown in a haunted house?" the friend asked.

"No way," said the man. "I think if I went to a clown haunted house, I'd run out before I got scared. Otherwise I could get a phobia of clowns.

"I don't want a clown phobia," he went on. "I love clowns too much. And I know people can get a phobia if they get scared."

As Gayle, Eli, and Mimi made their way toward the mall, an older man with Williams greeted them, hugged each of them, and launched immediately into his life story. Gayle politely cut him off to say they were in a hurry to get to dinner. Moving on, they passed a young woman with Williams, in her late teens or early twenties, who sat on the floor, reaching out to grab people's feet as they walked by.

At least my kid isn't the only one acting strangely, Gayle thought. It occurred to her that the parents of these young adults weren't hovering nearby, correcting their behavior. They knew their kids weren't perfect, and that they risked embarrassing themselves or offending someone else, but they allowed them to be themselves all the same. It was, of course, a risk every parent faces. Typical kids could behave in offensive or embarrassing ways, too. It didn't mean their parents could never let them out of their sight.

That thought occurred to Gayle again the next day, at the convention's closing banquet, where a chorus of nearly a hundred teens and adults with Williams performed a song they'd spent part of the convention rehearsing together. Gayle had thought about signing Eli up for the chorus, since she knew he'd jump at the chance to sing in front of a crowd. But even before his epic meltdown, she'd worried that he would be too much of a handful at rehearsal. She didn't want him hugging and harassing the other singers or becoming frustrated when asked to follow directions. She was afraid he would ruin the performance for others who were more capable.

Now, as the chorus began to sing and Eli watched them with obvious delight, she felt a pang of regret. They'd chosen a Miley Cyrus song, "The Climb," about striving against the odds to reach the top of a metaphorical mountain. The song had never really resonated with Gayle before. But in this setting, it took on a piercing poignancy. A hundred voices rang out in harmony. Some were husky, some were shrill, but they were all on key and utterly earnest when they sang, "*I can almost see it / That dream I'm dreaming / But there's a voice inside my head saying / 'You'll never reach it.'*"

Gayle's eyes glittered. She turned away while Mimi buttered Eli's dinner roll; she didn't want her mother to see her cry. Eli wasn't watching either of them. He was focused entirely on the singers as they belted out the chorus, about the inevitability of hardship and loss—and the power of hope.

Watching the group sway together in rhythm, Gayle thought, *Next time, I'll let him sing.*

Twenty

Confrontation

By gathering so many people with Williams in one place, the convention had attracted researchers of all kinds: geneticists, neuroscientists, linguists, sociologists, and psychologists, among others. An entire hotel floor became a pop-up lab for studies of cognition, musicality, and sociability in Williams. Grad students eagerly recruited subjects in the halls. Gayle signed Eli up for a study on anxiety, which struck her as timely, given that his recent irritability seemed to have come to a head at the convention.

The problem was that Eli couldn't quite understand or articulate his feelings, and he was even less able to identify what caused them. So while the researcher, a post-doc clinical psychologist named Lauren, asked him a series of questions, he instantly grew bored and began spinning restlessly in the rolling desk chair she'd put him in.

Lauren asked Eli to respond to each question with one of four responses: "Sometimes," "Often," "Always," or "Never."

"The first question is 'I worry about things,'" she began. "Do you worry?"

"Yeah . . ." Eli said, spinning clockwise in his chair and contemplating the ceiling. "Um, I really miss my home today."

"You do?" she asked with concern. Eli spun counterclockwise.

"Eli, can you look here?" she asked. "Do you worry sometimes, oft—"

"I was really worried *sometimes*," he said quickly.

"Sometimes—" Lauren began.

"Yeah," he interrupted.

"—often, or always," she continued.

"*Often*," he amended, mid-spin. "How are you?"

"I'm good," she said. "Are you scared of the dark?"

"I am scared of the dark," he repeated in monotone. If Gayle had been allowed to sit in during the study, she would have explained that he was not afraid of the dark—not always, often, or even sometimes. Eli routinely wandered around his pitch-black bedroom at night, bumping into furniture instead of turning the light on. But Lauren had guessed anyway, from his distracted manner, that his answers were unreliable.

"Do you feel afraid?" she asked.

"I feel afraid of monsters," he said, nodding.

"Monsters! That's hard. Are you *sometimes* afraid? *Often* afraid?"

"Often," he echoed.

"*Always* afraid?"

"I'm ALWAYS afraid of monsters."

"Yeah," Lauren said. "Monsters are a big deal. Eli, what else are you afraid of?"

"I'm afraid of . . . I'm gonna be . . . What I'm *afraid of* is . . ." he began, looking around the room as if searching for something to be afraid of. Then he gave up. "What time is the surprise? You're gonna tell me?" She had told him that he would get a surprise when he finished the test, and now he was impatient to be done.

"Are there other things that you're afraid of?" Lauren persisted.

"I don't like scary stuff," he offered.

"Scary stuff? What's scary?"

"There's monsters, there's skeletons," he listed. "They're spooky!"

If she had been there, Gayle would have cut in again to tell Lauren that the opposite was true: Eli loved Halloween and the monsters and skeletons it entailed. He played with toys like his Scary Screechers year-round.

"What about loud noises?" Lauren suggested.

"Loud noise is *kaboom!*" Eli said.

When Gayle came to collect Eli, Lauren confessed that she hadn't been able to get much useful information from him, but she gave Gayle a survey to fill out from her own perspective. Gayle did so after dropping Eli off at day camp, while sitting in the lobby with Mimi.

" 'Is your child afraid of the dark?' " she read aloud. Her options, like Eli's, were "Always," "Often," "Sometimes," and "Never."

"Never," she checked.

" 'What is your child afraid of?' " she read, and thought for a minute. She tapped her pen against the ring on her middle finger, a silver tarantula studded with black gems.

There were several blank lines next to the question: enough room for a list. But Eli wasn't scared of the things most kids were scared of. He had never worried about a monster under his bed or a bogeyman in the closet. He knew they were *supposed* to be scary, which was why he had named them for Lauren. But he wasn't scared of them himself. He had gone through a phase earlier that year when he became so preoccupied with Halloween props—skeletons popping up from coffins, monsters jumping out of dark corners—that he'd spent hours at a stretch looking them up on YouTube.

Gayle had wondered whether his insouciance about ghouls and goblins was simply a part of Williams. Maybe not fearing strangers translated into not fearing *anything*, she thought. But that couldn't be true, since she knew that many kids with Williams suffered from debilitating phobias. Even the young man looking up clown videos in the Sheraton lobby had been terrified when he came across one in a haunted house. Still, the absence of fear could simply reflect Eli's poor cognitive abilities. Maybe, she thought, he just didn't know enough to be scared.

She hardly let herself consider the possibility that he might take after his mother. Gayle, a lover of horror movies and a devotee of Edgar Allan Poe and Stephen King, was fascinated with the macabre and the occult. When she was a teenager, her own room could have passed for a Halloween prop warehouse. She still collected Día de los Muertos figurines and other morbid souvenirs.

She couldn't help noticing that Eli's fascination mirrored her own, but she wasn't sure what to make of the connection. She often wondered how much of his personality was predetermined by Williams syndrome. Was there any part of him that was just *him*? And was there anything in him that she had passed down, either through nature or nurture?

Geneticists offered a mathematical solution: of the roughly 20,000 genes every human carries, Williams syndrome affects only 26. So 99.9 percent of Eli's DNA remained intact, just as it had been copied from Gayle and her ex-husband. If there was a genetic basis for morbid curiosity, Gayle and Eli could both have it. A predilection for the macabre certainly wasn't prevalent either in the Williams community or the general population. Like all children, Eli was unique in the world. He wasn't merely a manifestation of a genetic deletion.

The anxiety questionnaire reminded Gayle that Eli had been lucky not to acquire the disabling fears and phobias common in people with Williams. But it also reminded her of the disorder's isolating effects, which he had not escaped.

" 'How many close friends does your child have?' " the questionnaire asked. Gayle sighed. "Zero," she wrote.

" 'How many times does your child do things with friends outside of school?' " Gayle read. "Less than one," she checked.

" 'My child complains of loneliness,' " Gayle read. She checked "Never" but wondered if her answer would soon change. Seeing Eli despondent over Susie's rudeness had made her realize that he was no longer impervious to rejection. Loneliness was certainly on the horizon; maybe it was already a factor in the angst that sometimes overwhelmed him. Just because he didn't complain about it didn't mean he didn't feel it.

"'My child exhibits strange behavior'?" Gayle read, looking up from the survey to raise her eyebrows at Mimi. "It says, 'Describe.' What am I supposed to say to that? It would take pages. I mean, he gets too close to people, he hugs them, he sings all the time. Is it strange to pretend to scrub floors? Or for a thirteen-year-old to throw tantrums?" She checked "Always" but didn't add a description. She didn't know where to begin. She was so used to his unusual habits that they'd stopped seeming strange long ago.

"'What's the best thing about your child?'" she read.

"He's a character," Mimi said. Gayle nodded. She wrote, "He's funny and engaging."

"'What's your greatest concern?'" she read. This one was easy: her go-to response hadn't changed, even if Eli had. "His future," she wrote.

———

BY THE BEGINNING OF ELI'S EIGHTH-GRADE year, Gayle's concern for his future had shifted into overdrive. In just one year he'd be in high school, where, according to his education plan, he'd begin vocational training for a possible career. Now was the time to get him more independent, to give him the best shot at autonomy as an adult.

Gayle set new standards for Eli at home, requiring him to do for himself some of the things she'd always done for him. She started small. One day he peeled himself a banana for the first time. Another day he opened his own bottle of water. She'd justified doing these things in the past because his limited dexterity meant they took him longer than they took her, and she hated to watch him struggle. Now she let him struggle.

She told him he'd have to start preparing his own cereal in the morning. This, too, she'd always done, but since Eli woke up early—usually around 5:30 or 6 a.m., when Gayle was clinging to her last hour of sleep—she decided it was time for a change. She worried that he'd dump a half gallon of milk on the floor or upend a bowl full of cereal. But day after day she came downstairs to find the milk unspilled, the floor still clean, and Eli chowing down. It was a small step, but Gayle was thrilled.

Still, she was so used to stepping in that it took as much or more effort to retrain herself than to retrain him. For the most part Eli did what she asked him to without questioning it. It was Gayle who had to fight the urge to intervene whenever he had difficulty.

One brisk fall morning, she started to help him into his coat and then dropped the sleeve she was holding.

"You need to do this yourself," she said, as much to herself as to him. "I'm going to be in trouble if you go to high school without knowing how to put your coat on." He cheerfully accepted the task, and although it took a good five minutes of flailing effort, first with the coat upside down, then right side up, he got it done.

The only thing harder for Gayle than being tough on Eli was being gentle on herself.

At the urging of a friend who worked for the Yale School of Public Health, she took part later that fall in a study of quality of life among caregivers for people with disabilities or chronic illness. She expected the questions to be strictly fact based, but when she sat down for an interview with the young woman conducting the study, she found that they were more about her feelings.

"When did you find out about your son's disorder?" the researcher asked, after Gayle had laid out the basics of Eli's condition. Gayle told her about the developmental delays, the day care mom's warning, the visit to Dr. Pober.

"How did you feel about that?" the researcher asked every time Gayle reached a stopping point in her story. Gayle shifted uncomfortably in her seat. *Shitty,* she wanted to say, but tried to offer more nuance.

The researcher asked what Gayle did to care for Eli. Gayle gave a rapid-fire list. There were the trips to the doctor, the medications, the behavior plan, and the meetings at school when the behavior plan didn't work. There were the typical parental tasks of feeding and chauffeuring, plus the additional daily duties of helping Eli with his shower, assisting with his bathroom hygiene, and getting him dressed. Then there were the ways she tried to enrich Eli's life: the singing lessons and the sports leagues, the homemade floor scrubbers and the flaming tiki heads.

"And what do you do to take care of yourself?" the researcher asked.

"Huh," Gayle said. She was silent for a long while, thinking. "Nothing, I guess."

"Do you go to the gym?" the researcher suggested. "Do yoga? Get a massage?"

"No," Gayle said. "I don't really have time to. I'd have to take Eli to my mother's."

Gayle thought some more. She was stumped, other than to say that she took medication for anxiety. That didn't seem to count.

"I don't know what I *would* do for myself," she admitted finally. "What do people do?"

She knew that the state's Department of Developmental Services ran "respite centers" where people with developmental disabilities could participate in supervised activities while their caregivers enjoyed a few hours to themselves. Gayle had heard they were nice places, although she'd never considered dropping Eli off at one. She'd never left Eli with a babysitter outside her own family.

But the child care issue was an excuse more than anything else. It simply didn't occur to Gayle to spend time away from Eli. Their lives were too tightly entwined.

Gayle had never noticed her identity slipping away. Looking back, she could see that, not so long after becoming Eli's mom, that was suddenly all she was: Eli's mom. It was partly the isolation of finding herself on the margins of parenthood, in the special-needs borderland just outside but worlds away from the seemingly sunny realm of normal families. Faced with the magnitude of Eli's needs, and the scarcity of support, Gayle had stretched herself to fill every gap in his life. She'd developed superhuman abilities she never could have imagined before Eli was born. In the process, she lost the parts of herself that functioned for anything other than caring for her son. He became not only the most important person in her life but the essence of her life. Even before her divorce, it was just Gayle and Eli, alone, together.

The Yale researcher asked Gayle whether she was dating anyone. Gayle nearly snorted; the answer was no, as it had been for years.

"As far as even meeting someone, I can't see where I would fit that in," she said. "Even if I knew where that time would come from, I still can't see taking attention away from Eli and giving it to someone else."

The way the woman knit her brows when she wrote this down made Gayle wonder whether her answer was unusual, or maybe even unhealthy.

She had never questioned the way her life revolved around Eli, but after the Yale interview she wondered whether she should. She had spent endless hours contemplating Eli's prospects for independence. Now she began to consider her own.

On the Williams syndrome Facebook page, she responded to a parent who was having trouble finding a social niche. Gayle wrote, "At this point, Eli and I are each other's best friend. As cute as that sounds, I'm realizing that it's not going to be good for either of us in the long run."

While Mimi would watch Eli almost anytime Gayle asked, Gayle never wanted to impose upon her mother unless she had a good reason, like a work trip or a doctor's appointment. Now she tried to convince herself that it was OK to ask just to take some time to herself. One night she called on Mimi's child care services so she could meet up with a childhood friend she had recently reconnected with on Facebook. Recalling the hangouts of their school days, they met at the mall, bought candy at Munson's, and sat and talked in the food court. To Gayle's surprise, she had a good time. This, she thought, was the kind of thing people did for themselves.

She made an even more uncharacteristic leap when she agreed to accompany her friend Marilyn to New Orleans for a four-day weekend, a spur-of-the-moment decision prompted by an airfare sale. It was Gayle's first vacation without Eli since the day he was born. For her, it was a form of time travel: a trip back to the life she'd had before she had him. And Eli was thrilled by the prospect of a four-day slumber party at Mimi's house, surrounded by relatives. But before she even boarded the plane, Gayle felt a pang of guilt for leaving him for so long and for spending money on herself instead of him. During her first two days in New Orleans, she checked in with Mimi by phone every few hours. Almost as soon as she managed to relax enough to enjoy herself, it was time to leave.

Back home, she took a tentative stab at dating by posting a profile on a dating website. Although her bio didn't mention having a child with special needs, she told prospective suitors about Eli after they exchanged a few e-mails. Often the conversation, and the relationship, ended there. However, a man named Brian responded with a warm note that ended, "By the way, I have a ten-year-old son with special needs. You're not alone."

Gayle was intrigued. He seemed interesting, well educated, and, judging from his photo, attractive. Gayle agreed to meet him for dinner.

But when she went to the restaurant where they'd arranged to meet, she didn't recognize the man waving at her. His profile photo, apparently, had been exceptionally flattering—and at least a decade old.

For the next two hours, Gayle sat picking at her food and listening to an endless monologue about Brian's accomplishments in the business world, the property he owned, how much money he made, even how much money his ex-wife made. His disabled son, it turned out, had only a mild sensory processing disorder. He was otherwise a prodigy, by his father's account. Brian boasted about his son's high grades and his talent as a cellist, oblivious to any sensitivity Gayle might have on the subject of academic success. He didn't ask about her son, in any case. He didn't ask much about her at all. The few questions he did ask were merely rhetorical, a springboard to his next talking point: "Have you ever been to Lake George? No? Well, I have a cabin up there . . ."

Brian texted Gayle several times over the following week. She responded politely but made it clear that she wasn't interested in a second date.

She still wasn't sure she was interested in any dates, period. Although she sometimes felt lonely, she also cherished what little quiet time she got to herself. Dating seemed like a gamble, more likely to be a hassle than a pleasure. And while she and Brian wouldn't have clicked anyway, it occurred to her that, for her or for any single parent of a special-needs child, finding the right person would require lottery-winning luck. He'd have to be a good fit both for her and for Eli—someone compassionate enough not to see her high-maintenance son as unwanted baggage, or to resent the fact that Eli would likely take up more of her time than she could devote to a relationship. She hadn't entirely given up on finding this ideal partner, but the energy it took to keep up with Eli made it impossible to put much effort into searching for someone who might not even exist.

She stopped checking the dating website.

———

FOR ELI'S FOURTEENTH BIRTHDAY, GAYLE TOOK him to see *Sesame Street Live*. He was the oldest kid there by nearly a decade, but he sang along with the music as exuberantly as the four-year-olds. Gayle even got him backstage to meet Cookie Monster. *The real Cookie Monster! In person!* It was all he could talk about for days. Despite wanting him to fit in with kids his own age, Gayle was touched to see how at home he felt on Sesame Street. She cherished the childlike parts of his personality even as she pushed him to mature.

At home Eli could often pass for a four-year-old. At school, however, his teen angst only intensified, despite the fact that his psychiatrist had switched him from Celexa, which had seemed to agitate him, to Abilify, which Dr. McDougle had recommended at the convention for anxiety-prone people with Williams. Days after swooning over Cookie Monster, Eli called his classroom aide a punk. When she sent him to the time-out room, he yelled, "This is fucking bullshit!"

He now seemed to spend more of his school day in time-out than in class. He knew that being fired was an extreme punishment for adults, so whenever the special-education staffers put him in time-out, he retaliated by telling them they were fired. Before long he had fired each and every one. But he still ended up alone in the time-out room, fuming, nearly every day.

Gayle worried that things would only get worse the following year, when he went to high school. He had been taking field trips to the new school, to meet the staff and acclimate to the environment, so it wouldn't be such a shock when he arrived in the fall. The first time he visited, he grabbed a girl's hand in the hallway and pressed it to his face. Gayle wasn't surprised to hear about the incident. *It's a whole school full of kids he hasn't met before,* she thought. *He's going to want to touch them.*

More and more, Gayle found herself withdrawing from the social world she'd tried to cultivate for Eli. She kept him home from a school dance and a class trip to an amusement park where she was sure he would embarrass himself. She even turned down an invitation to a fourteenth birthday party for his cousin Kylie. *It'll be too exhausting,* she thought. *The other kids won't want to talk to him anyway, and I'll just be running after him every time he goes to hug someone. And then he'll get pissed.* Gayle, too, had been fired a few times since the fall, although Eli always rehired her.

Her fear of becoming housebound seemed to be coming true in slow motion, and she felt powerless to stop it. After so many years spent trying to help Eli find his place in the world, she was starting to doubt whether there was anyplace, outside of his own home, where he'd be safe and accepted. By spring, when the school sent Gayle a draft of Eli's ninth-grade educational goals, she wondered whether he even belonged in public school anymore. It marked a low point in Eli's life, and a lower point in her own, when she thought he might be better off in a school just for special-needs kids, where he wouldn't stick out quite so badly.

She mentioned this to Carrie, the special-education consultant, when Carrie reviewed the school's plan for Eli.

"Maybe public high school just isn't the right fit," Gayle suggested. "Maybe it would be better to put him in a special school."

She said it sincerely, thinking Carrie might agree. But, to her surprise, Carrie reacted as though Gayle had suggested setting Eli adrift on an iceberg.

"The reason we pushed for him to be in a mainstream setting was because he's so social, and you wanted him to be around kids he could learn from and model," Carrie said sharply. "That hasn't changed."

"I know," Gayle said, sighing. "But how can he model them if he's an outcast? What if they're mean to him? If they won't let him sit next to them at lunch? I don't want to put him through that."

"Listen," Carrie said. "You're not doing him any favors by protecting him from those experiences. Even if they're not all positive, he can learn from them."

Gayle had already told Carrie about the social outings she'd avoided recently and how Eli's behavior sometimes made her want to keep him at home.

"This isn't the 1940s," Carrie said now. "You can't just hide him."

"I'm not trying to hide him!" Gayle said.

"Yes you are," Carrie said. "You have to deal with the reality of what you're saying. You're ashamed of him."

Gayle blinked back tears. She felt outraged and defensive.

"That's not true," she said, trying not to let her voice rise to a whine. "I'm embarrassed by his behavior, but not by him. I wasn't embarrassed when he was the oldest kid at *Sesame Street Live.* I didn't keep him home from that. I just don't want him to get in trouble or become a pariah because of his behavior around his peers."

Carrie's voice softened.

"I can tell you're on the verge of tears right now," she said. "But you have to let yourself feel the way you feel. If you're embarrassed, just let yourself feel embarrassed. It's OK."

Gayle's cheeks were already wet. *Am I crying because she's right?* she wondered. *Maybe it does look like I'm embarrassed by him when I'm always grabbing him and telling him to behave. But it doesn't feel that way. I just want what's best for him.*

"He could get in real trouble," Gayle insisted. "It's not OK to ogle girls and hug everyone. But he can't stop."

"Gayle, he's a good kid. He's just going through puberty. Everyone does," Carrie said. "This is nothing that people haven't seen before. You have to give him a chance. Go to parties. If he can't handle it, don't stay long. But at least let him have the chance."

Gayle was silent. *Am I keeping him out of these situations because it's hard for him or because it's hard for me?* she wondered. *Maybe I'm being selfish. I can't just be Grizzly Adams and take him to live with me on the side of a mountain.*

Carrie went on in a gentler tone: "You didn't ask for this. You didn't ask to have a child who has special needs, and you didn't ask to do it alone. But you're doing a great job. You're doing a better job raising him than a lot of kids who have two parents."

That eased the sting a little, but Gayle was still shaken by the conversation. She replayed it in her mind all day, feeling guilty for even hinting that she might be embarrassed by her son. She still wasn't convinced that this was true, either consciously or unconsciously. But she found some truth in Carrie's point about giving Eli the chance to experience life firsthand, even if it wasn't easy or pleasant. She wasn't helping him by sheltering him from the real world, whether it was out of embarrassment or protectiveness.

In the end she concluded that Carrie was right: Eli could benefit from the typical high school experience, surrounded by a mix of people very different from himself, some of them kind and some of them cruel, just like in the real world. He had the right to learn from that experience, even if the lessons of the real world were often learned the hard way. Hiding him away wasn't the answer. Eli deserved to see the world as it really was, and the world needed to see him for himself.

———

THE NEXT DAY WAS EASTER, and Eli was anxiously looking forward to a family brunch at Mimi's house. That night, while Gayle sat on the living room couch, absently leafing through a stack of mail and mulling over the troubling discussion she'd had with Carrie, Eli rocked back and forth in the blue armchair next to her, flicking strips of paper over a tea light and pretending they were flames.

"Who's going to wake me up tomorrow, Mom?" he asked with concern, as if he might sleep all day and miss the fun.

"Who do you think is going to wake you up?" she asked, looking up from the mail. "Who *always* wakes you up?"

"You, Mom!"

She laughed. "If somebody else comes into your room and wakes you up, we're going to be in big trouble."

He went back to flicking his flames while Gayle sorted the mail into piles. A few minutes later he asked again.

"Mom, can you wake me up tomorrow, on Sunday?"

"Yes," she said.

"'Cause we gotta go to Mimi's," he explained.

"Gotcha," she said.

"I hope the Easter Bunny brings me a battery-operated fan from Walmart!" he exclaimed. "And some peanut M&M's."

Gayle turned to look at him, surprised. She could never be sure in what ways he had become a teenager and in what ways he was still an overgrown toddler.

"You really think there's a big bunny?" she asked.

"Yes."

"That comes hopping down the street?"

"Yes," Eli said emphatically. "I want him to!"

Eventually, convinced that Gayle would not forget to wake him in the morning and take him to the Easter party, Eli trudged upstairs to bed.

Gayle remembered a previous Easter when he had acted up so much that she barely got to speak to anyone else. She spent the whole day racing after him, scolding him for throwing himself into the arms of family friends and generally making a nuisance of himself. She was so visibly unhappy that her mother accused her of being a wet blanket, bringing down the rest of the party. "If you're that misera-ble," Mimi had said, "Just go home." Gayle vowed not to let herself be miserable this year. *Eli is who he is,* she reminded herself. *And I'm not going to hide.*

A few minutes after disappearing into his bedroom, Eli reappeared in the living room. His ability to read Gayle's mind, or at least her mood, was uncanny: he seemed to know that something was bothering her, even though she'd tried her best to conceal it.

"Mom, I want to say hi to you," he announced, smiling beatifically.

"It's late, Eli. You're supposed to be in bed," she said.

"I can't sleep. I just want to say hi."

"You can say hi to me tomorrow," she said. "Go on up to bed."

He turned back toward the stairs and noticed a plastic milk jug on the dining table that Gayle had carved into a jack-o'-lantern for him.

"I can take this?" he asked, pointing to it.

"OK," she said. "Sure."

"Good night, my love!" he trilled, and happily scooped up the jack-o'-lantern.

Gayle watched him skip up the stairs to his bedroom, swinging his plastic jug, and felt her heart swell with the urge to protect him from the world's tough lessons. She swallowed hard as the door shut behind him.

Twenty-One

Born to Be Kind

Parents of children with Williams syndrome often struggle to teach them how to be more like the rest of us. The rest of us don't put much thought into learning to be more like them— but we might benefit from trying. Despite their disadvantages, people with Williams highlight some of humanity's best features, normally obscured by the suspicion and selfishness we have acquired over eons of evolution in competition with each other.

It's not quite fair to say that the world would be a better place if everyone had Williams, but it would unquestionably be friendlier. People with Williams don't have to learn the Golden Rule; they don't have to be taught about equality or inclusion. They're born practicing these principles. Even babies with Williams are unconditionally affectionate. They demonstrate less separation anxiety when parted from their parents, less fear around strangers, and more interest in examining faces than do other infants at the same age.

To people with Williams, every face is a friendly face and every stranger a potential friend. In fact, a groundbreaking 2010 study found that people with Williams showed no signs of racial bias, making them the first group ever to demonstrate a complete lack of prejudice, since nearly everyone past the age of three reveals an implicit preference for his or her own ethnic group. Researchers concluded that people with Williams simply didn't have the social fear that drives most of us to distinguish between in-groups and out-groups.

This kind of openness, however, is an evolutionary aberration. The fear of others who are different, and the discrimination it engenders, is deeply wired into our psyche—a vestige from our earliest genetic ancestors. Empathy, on the other hand, is a relatively recent evolutionary adaptation. It's believed to have evolved with the first mammals, enabling mothers to care for their offspring, and later allowing groups of primates to organize into societies. Until the formation of mammalian social groups, empathy was useless at best in facilitating survival and reproduction.

Some scientists believe that the first seedlings of non-maternal empathy were planted between 15 million and 20 million years ago, when a genetic mutation gave certain forest-dwelling monkeys the ability to digest unripe fruit. As the science writer David Dobbs put it, "This left some of their cousins—the ancestors of chimps, gorillas, and humans—at a sharp disadvantage. Suddenly a lot of fruit was going missing before it ripened."

To survive, these newly disadvantaged primates moved to the fringes of the forests, where there was less competition for food, partly because the border territories fell dangerously within feeding range of the savanna predators. They adapted by forming colonies for protection and, for what may have been the first time, learned to balance their individual needs with the overall good of the group. They formed bonds with other members, largely by grooming, an intimate act that flooded their brains with oxytocin. Those groups that cooperated better were more likely to survive, and thus empathy became an advantage that endured as the early hominids evolved.

Of course, there could be too much of a good thing: overabundant empathy backfired, costing an individual his chances of surviving and reproducing. Food was scarce, and the best mates were in high demand.

Standing aside for the benefit of others made it less likely that a single ape would see his genes passed down. Somewhere along the evolutionary line, a balance was struck between selflessness and selfishness, giving the most successful primates (people included) the ability to both collaborate and compete with their brethren. "Every population had its 'hawks' and 'doves,' and the doves had a tough time staying alive," writes primatologist Frans de Waal in his book *Our Inner Ape*. "In order to be successful, social animals need to be hawks *as well as* doves."

The unbridled empathy of Williams syndrome would have been both more and less disabling in the early days of humanity, when we lived in roving bands of forty to sixty members and communicated primarily through gestures, grunts, and body language. Cooperation was key in these tribes, and members, many of whom were related to one another, were unlikely to betray the trust of someone who trusted too much. The danger would have been when someone with the indiscriminate kindness of Williams encountered a new face, since members of other tribes were more likely to attack than befriend.

"Unlike other animals, the most lethal predators we faced were our own kind," explain Maia Szalavitz and Bruce D. Perry, the authors of *Born for Love: Why Empathy Is Essential—and Endangered*. "Across generations, wariness of new individuals, groups, and ideas was built into the circuits of the human brain's alarm response because those who had this wariness were more likely to survive to reproduce. It was just safer to assume danger—to expect the worst—than to count on the kindness of strangers."

This instinct served us well, at least in our early days. In modern society we might be better served by shedding some of this ancestral paranoia. But in fact we have grown less trusting, not more, in recent decades. The number of Americans who agreed with the statement "Most people can be trusted" has plummeted over the years from a high of 77 percent in 1964, according to Robert D. Putnam, the author of *Bowling Alone: The Collapse and Revival of American Community*. In 2012 a mere 24 percent of people surveyed agreed. And if we don't feel we can trust our fellow humans, we aren't likely to go out of our way to be kind to them.

Could we have evolved to be more empathetic if resources hadn't been so scarce for our primate ancestors? Probably not, says evolutionary biologist Bernard Crespi, who has studied the origins of social behavior in Williams and autism. "How plentiful resources are is not really relevant, because fitness is always relative," he explains. "Some individuals will always survive and reproduce better than others, due to the traits they express." The only species that truly put others' needs first are clonal groups, such as some aphids and certain ant colonies in which the worker caste cannot reproduce, making the success of the group paramount, Crespi says.

Among early humans, empathy and altruism helped more cooperative tribes prevail over tribes divided by selfishness and disloyalty. But within the tribes, and later within larger societies, some amount of selfishness was key to an individual's success at passing on his DNA. These days we expect people to look out for themselves, so much so that we don't quite know how to respond to true altruists. While it's no surprise that we dislike people we consider selfish, one study revealed that we also show unexpected contempt for people who are too self*less*. In the study, players in a game that involved sharing imaginary "public goods" had the option of banishing other players from future games. Unsurprisingly, most people banished free riders who took others' goods but didn't share their own. But they also consistently expelled players who gave more than they took, preferring partners who gave and took in relatively equal proportions. It was startling support for the theory that exceptional people face social rejection regardless of the ways in which they're different. The social psychologists who ran the study concluded that selfless players were being punished for setting too high a social standard, demonstrating levels of generosity that the others weren't willing to match. Their findings offer one explanation for why so many people seem uncomfortable with the outpouring of affection, compliments, and favors they receive from people with Williams syndrome: they set the bar too high. Few of us are able, or willing, to reciprocate.

But people with Williams tend not to recognize when they're being regarded with contempt or disdain, or to change the behavior that elicits this response. Despite their acute empathy, they have a blind spot when it comes to negative or threatening emotions in others. They're drawn to all people, at all times, no matter what mood those people might be in. In studies, adolescents with Williams were much more likely to judge people "approachable" when shown pictures of strangers making a variety of facial expressions—some of them menacing enough to put the rest of us on our guard. Teens without Williams were quick to notice a scowl or a furrowed brow, for example, and were keenly aware of the distinction between a happy smile and a mischievous smirk. But people with Williams didn't always notice the difference. Even obviously angry faces failed to evoke fear in people with Williams, while non-Williams teens said they'd be eager to avoid the people making those faces. Unlike race blindness, this obliviousness to expression could be as dangerous today as it was hundreds of thousands of years ago.

Neurobiologists have traced the apparent absence of social fear to abnormalities in the amygdalae of people with Williams. These almond-shaped clusters of nuclei, buried deep in the brain, help process emotions and regulate our fight-or-flight response to danger. In people with Williams, they react more dramatically than normal to images of disasters, such as fires or plane crashes, which researchers think may explain why people with Williams often develop anxiety disorders. Conversely, they respond with abnormal indifference to images of people making fearful or angry facial expressions. The amygdalae of people without Williams tend to be extremely sensitive to those expressions, since we have evolved to see them as warnings. Getting too close to a hostile person, or an aggressive ape, probably cost many of our ancestors their lives. Seeing a look of panic on someone else's face and starting to run probably saved the lives of many more.

One study found a strong correlation between this weakened amygdala response and the increased tendency of people with Williams to approach strangers, reinforcing the theory that the amygdala normally plays an important role in helping us judge the safety of social situations. It's an anatomical explanation for Gayle's observation that Eli is curious about but not afraid of angry people. When he sees someone scowl or go red with rage, he stares intently and often tries to get closer for a better view—exactly the opposite of what most of us would do.

People with Williams also have a stronger-than-normal amygdala response to happy faces, meaning that they are much more attentive to these expressions than the rest of us. Eli is transfixed by smiling faces; seeing someone burst into laughter can stop him in his tracks. It's another idiosyncrasy with little evolutionary value, since heightened awareness of joy has infinitely less bearing on survival than heightened awareness of danger. But it helps explain the intense urge of those with Williams to please other people, based on the sheer thrill of seeing them smile. And it demonstrates a marked difference from our own tendencies, which are more heavily steeped in social fear. If we notice someone laughing when we walk into a room, most of us initially wonder if the laughter is directed at us. Eli doesn't. His impulse is to approach the person and ask to be let in on the joke.

So while people with Williams often seem uncannily good at sensing other people's feelings, they aren't quite as skilled as they appear in what psychologists call "theory of mind": the ability to recognize that others have thoughts, feelings, and intentions that are different from our own—and to make inferences based on that awareness. What's missing is the ability to make the crucial cognitive leap between recognizing that someone is furious and deciding that it's a good idea to get out of his way. While a 1998 study led by Helen Tager-Flusberg concluded that people with Williams did astoundingly well in tests of theory of mind, correctly interpreting complex mental states from nonverbal cues just as well as normal controls and much better than people with similar intellectual disabilities, she later clarified these findings. In a second study, published two years later, Tager-Flusberg made the case that theory of mind comprised two distinct abilities that activated different parts of the brain. One was a perceptual component: being able to "read the mind in the eyes," or determine other people's mental states based on their facial expressions. The other was a cognitive component: using this information to make inferences about other people's beliefs or expectations, as well as to predict or explain their actions. People with Williams are adept at the former but not the latter, she found: they can read moods but not minds. For example, Tager-Flusberg presented her Williams subjects with an illustrated story about a girl who went for a walk in the park and saw a dog sitting in the grass. When the dog got up and barked, the girl ran away. Asked why the girl ran, people with Williams tended not to conclude that she was afraid of the dog but to offer factual observations like "That's a big dog." They were given another scenario featuring a boy who always brought his lunch to school. One morning, his mom made him a delicious lunch but he went to school without it. When asked why, they were less likely to guess that he had forgotten it and more likely to answer with irrelevant information, such as "His backpack is yellow."

Faced with a real-life boy who had forgotten his lunch, most people with Williams could likely sense that he was sad, but they might not be able to put their finger on exactly why. And sociologists have found that just knowing how people feel doesn't equate to social success. It's the cognitive component, being able to interpret and respond to that knowledge, that determines whether other people identify you as "agreeable." The adjective, in its sociological sense, is the single greatest predictor of strong relationships and a wide social circle. While people with Williams are usually warm, friendly, and caring, they aren't always perceived as agreeable because they lack the social cognition that makes for complete theory of mind. They might want to cheer up the sad boy in the cafeteria, but it simply wouldn't occur to them to offer him part of their sandwich. (If he asked for it, however, they'd be likely to happily hand over the whole thing.)

Of course, theory of mind isn't an all-or-nothing entity, something you either have or don't have. It is one of the slowest-developing of our faculties. Some studies have concluded that theory of mind, and the empathy it instills, aren't fully developed until our mid-twenties. Even when we have as much of it as we're going to have, we fall somewhere on a spectrum, both as individuals and in groups. Women have stronger theory of mind and display more empathy, on average, than men. But some men, and some women, fall vastly above or below the average.

While people with Williams struggle with the cognitive but not the perceptual part of theory of mind, people with autism tend to fail at both. Psychopaths, meanwhile, have the opposite problem: they have normal (sometimes even above-average) cognitive theory of mind but lack the perceptual ability to sense or respond to other people's feelings of distress. As Harvard psychiatry professor Jordan Smoller writes in his book *The Other Side of Normal: How Biology Is Providing the Clues to Unlock the Secrets of Normal and Abnormal Behavior*, "psychopathic individuals have a neurobiologic impairment in the ability to recognize and process fear and sadness in the facial expressions or the voices of other people. It's as though they're blind and deaf to the pain of those around them." Researchers have traced this impairment, at least in part, to the amygdala, which tends to be smaller than normal in people who meet the criteria for psychopathy.

Where psychopaths and people with Williams overlap, surprisingly, is in the weakened reaction of their amygdalae to other people's expressions of fear. However, in psychopathy, this blunted response also extends to sadness, to which people with Williams are highly sensitive. In addition, psychopaths can easily identify anger, while many people with Williams struggle to do so.

Most of the traits of psychopathy, including egocentrism, callousness, and cruelty, are the polar opposites of those found in Williams syndrome. People classified as psychopaths show no guilt or remorse for exploiting or hurting another person; people with Williams are deeply disturbed just to hear about such harm being done. In fact, true psychopaths appear to be incapable of feeling anxious at all, while people with Williams are acutely susceptible to anxiety. So although both suffer from impairments of the amygdala, those impairments produce vastly different effects and are likely influenced by dysfunction in other parts of the brain. In psychopathy, researchers believe this includes the orbitofrontal cortex, which plays a part in learned behavior; it conditions most of us not to repeat actions that make other people suffer. Defects in this part of the brain could help explain why psychopaths develop a malfunctioning moral compass: they never learn that it's wrong to mistreat others, while people with Williams are born knowing this.

The neurobiology of autism, on the other hand, has yet to be clearly deciphered. But some researchers have suggested a correlation between the deficiencies in empathy and the great mathematical strengths that are common to the disorder, particularly in the ability to analyze and interpret numerical sequences, which the psychologist Simon Baron-Cohen refers to as systemizing.

The fact that people with Williams are terrible systemizers is no coincidence, according to Baron-Cohen. He and other scientists believe there is a cognitive divide between the ability to think about and empathize with other people and the ability to comprehend the physical world in a mechanistic way. They argue that not only are these cognitive systems distinct from each other, occupying different regions of the brain, but each has a suppressive effect on the other, meaning that using one system inhibits our ability to use the other.

Most people have a decent command over both systems, although almost everyone is stronger in one than the other. For the most part we can alternate between the two situationally, which results in the different neural regions being "pushed up and down like a see-saw, depending on whether the task involves thinking about physical mechanisms or internal mental states," according to cognitive scientist Anthony I. Jack. Williams and autism, therefore, each represent an extreme in which one of the systems is almost entirely suppressed at all times.

Baron-Cohen makes a logical case for this, arguing that the love of order and pattern that characterizes autism requires precise black-and-white thinking that renders the social world incomprehensible. "The world of people is a world dominated by emotions, where behavior is unpredictable. How someone feels is not something that can be determined with precision," he writes in his book *The Science of Evil: On Empathy and the Origins of Cruelty*. "When we empathize, it is because we can tolerate an inexact answer about what another person may feel." People with Williams are attuned to the imprecise world of emotions but flounder in the mechanistic realms of math and logic. Both extremes pose problems for a well-rounded life, although both have distinct advantages. The extreme empathy of Williams promotes altruism, while the extreme systematization of autism has led to innovations in technology, music, science, and engineering.

Baron-Cohen acknowledges that both extremes represent an evolutionary disadvantage for individuals, even as they may benefit society. This explains why neither is our default mode: thousands of years of evolution have steered humanity as a whole toward a more stable middle ground.

———

MOST OF US AREN'T BORN WITH the same capacity for indiscriminate kindness that is innate to Williams, but many believe we should aspire to that standard. The precept "Love thy neighbor" is common to all major religions, from Hinduism to Islam to Confucianism to Judaism. The story of the Good Samaritan, illustrating the godliness of showing mercy to strangers, is among the most popular of Christian parables.

Some of the hallmarks of the Williams personality, among them empathy and a desire to help others, are the cornerstones of a holy life in Western and Eastern religions alike. In Taoist philosophy, for example, the first of the "Three Treasures," or core virtues, translates as compassion or kindness. Selfless service is one of the foundations of Sikhism and many Indian religions. And many Christians make an effort to embrace the same openness, trust, and wonder found in Williams syndrome, following Jesus's admonition, "Unless you change and become like children, you will never enter the kingdom of heaven."

Even the most modern seekers of enlightenment strive for a state of Williams-like openness. This quest partly explains the popularity of the drug MDMA, better known as ecstasy or Molly, which is classified as an "empathogen" for its ability to elicit feelings of empathy and intimacy. The drug gained prominence in the 1970s as a therapeutic tool, used especially in couples counseling as a way to foster closeness and to help partners drop their defenses and communicate freely. One of the ways the drug elicits this sense of connection to others is by increasing the amount of oxytocin in the brain, just as Williams syndrome does.

Although MDMA became illegal in the U.S. in 1985, it has re-emerged recently in therapeutic trials for social disorders. A 2012 study found that people suffering from severe post-traumatic stress disorder whose symptoms hadn't improved with other treatments found significant relief from MDMA in combination with psychotherapy. Researchers hypothesized that this relief was partly attributable to an effect that mimicked Williams syndrome, making patients' brains more responsive to happy faces and less responsive to angry or fearful faces. "MDMA may enhance the therapeutic alliance by increasing the likelihood of detecting positive expressions and finding them rewarding, while at the same time reducing the chance of excessive reactivity to fleeting or unintended expressions of anger or disapproval," the researchers reported in the *Journal of Psychopharmacology*.

In 2014, researchers launched the first FDA-approved trial to determine whether MDMA could help people with autism overcome their social anxiety. Although treatments for social anxiety already exist for the general population, they rarely work well for people with autism. But people on the autism spectrum who'd taken ecstasy recreationally reported that it had helped them connect socially in ways they hadn't been able to before. Of more than a hundred autistic people surveyed by the research team conducting the study, 72 percent said that recreational ecstasy use made them more comfortable in social settings, and 77 percent said the drug made it easier to talk to people.

Even non-autistic people who take ecstasy sometimes describe it as a spiritual experience because of the feeling of universal kinship it inspires. Like Williams syndrome, MDMA obliterates inhibitions and creates an overwhelming urge to connect with other people. Unlike Williams, however, its effects only last for a matter of hours. The drug takes users on a kind of vacation in a Williams-like state of raw vulnerability and harmony with humankind; then it wears off, returning them to the real world and their ordinary inhibitions and defenses. Glimpsed in this way, the world of Williams can be magical, even though—or more likely because—the experience is fleeting. It's a nice place to visit, but most of us wouldn't want to live there.

Twenty-Two

Science Class

Near the end of Eli's eighth-grade year, his science class reached its final unit: genetics. Each student had to turn in a research paper on a genetic disorder, except for Eli, who attended the class with an aide but whose assignments were modified to suit his abilities. The others chose from the disorders listed in their textbook. There was Down syndrome, which appealed to many students because of its familiarity. There was Turner syndrome, a condition affecting girls who lack two full X chromosomes. There was phenylketonuria, an enzyme deficiency that can lead to developmental disabilities. And there was Williams syndrome.

Although most of his classmates had gone to school with Eli since kindergarten, they were unaware that this label applied to him. All they'd known until then was that he was different; the reason for it had never come up. Now it would, and his science teacher, Kathy Holzer, e-mailed Gayle to ask her how to proceed. She promised not to mention that he had the disorder if Gayle objected, but suggested that it might help promote awareness if the students could connect the genetics lesson to a real person in their midst. She invited Gayle to come in as a guest speaker to drive the lesson home and to offer her own insights about the disorder.

Gayle was surprised to hear that the class was studying Williams syndrome. She was sure it hadn't been part of the science curriculum when she was in eighth grade. Throughout Eli's life, it seemed like no one he'd ever met, educators included, had even heard of Williams before. Now everyone in his class would know the intimate details of the disorder.

She felt torn. Normally she jumped at the chance to explain what Williams syndrome was and how it affected Eli. But eighth graders were a tough crowd. The last thing she wanted to do was give them more ammunition for taunts and teasing. She was already uncomfortable with the prospect of other students doing projects on Williams syndrome and seeing Eli as a research topic, a specimen of genetics gone wrong, rather than just their classmate. She posted her dilemma on the Williams syndrome Facebook page.

"On one hand, I feel it is great awareness, but on the other hand, not sure about the maturity of the other eighth graders," she wrote. "I am feeling a little stumped about what to do. The information about Williams syndrome is out there, so it isn't an issue of me wanting to 'hide' Eli's WS or anything like that. Would you want classmates doing a 'project' about your child?"

But the responses were mostly encouraging. Several other parents urged Gayle to seize the opportunity to educate Eli's peers and open the door to a frank discussion about how and why he was different. Terry Monkaba, the executive director of the Williams Syndrome Association, replied that her son's eighth-grade class had also covered genetics, including Williams syndrome.

"I went in that day to help explain how Williams affected Ben specifically," Terry wrote. "Ben loved it and the kids asked very thoughtful questions. It was a great experience for us."

In the end Gayle decided to go for it, although she shared two concerns with Eli's teacher: first, that Eli's condition was being described as a "disorder" and that he would pick up on the negative connotations of that word; second, that some classmates would turn the lesson into a new way to make fun of him.

"This is the first time I've encountered this situation, so I really am very open to suggestions," Kathy replied. "We do use the word 'disorder,' as it's technically correct, but I definitely understand your concern. One of our challenges at this level is getting students to understand the difference between a disease and a genetic disorder, so we address what we mean by 'disorder' early on in the unit. But generally we just call the disorders by their names—Down syndrome, Turner syndrome, Williams syndrome, etc.—so I'm not sure Eli will feel any stigma related to the terminology.

"As far as the maturity level, well, this is a tougher one. This class is one of my more *behaviorally challenging* (trying to be nice!). The crazy thing is, as disrespectful as they can be to me at times, they are AWESOME with Eli. If you have no objection, I can share with the class tomorrow that Eli has one of the syndromes I plan to teach them about and see if they can handle it responsibly. I honestly think they will be great about it, and eager to learn more, as they've known Eli for years. They've fooled me before, but this might be a great opportunity to further open some hearts and minds. But I don't want it to backfire, either."

The next day she e-mailed Gayle to say that the eighth graders had taken the news of Eli's condition with sober curiosity. Some said they'd always wondered what made him the way he was but didn't think they could ask. Kathy was convinced that they'd be gracious and attentive listeners to Gayle's presentation. She also raised the stakes by asking Gayle to speak to each of the eighth-grade science classes—Eli's plus five others—as well as to some of the teachers and staff who'd expressed an interest. Gayle agreed, and took a full day off from work to fit it all in. She, too, hoped it didn't backfire.

———

THE MORNING OF HER PRESENTATION, GAYLE chose her outfit as carefully as a teenager on the first day of school. She knew how easy it was to evoke the disdain of thirteen-year-olds, so she put some effort into making herself eye-roll-proof. She paired a gray baroque-print tank top with a black shrug over black jeans and pulled her hair into a loose ponytail. Even her nails, painted a fashionable slate gray, coordinated with the ensemble.

The first class started at 7:40 a.m. Gayle arrived early and Kathy led her to a modern library in a brand-new building adorned with rows of gleaming Macs and Ikea-style furniture. The classes would meet in a corner of the room, where round café tables were arranged in a cluster around a high-tech smart board. Gayle had come prepared with a flash drive filled with Eli's baby pictures and some more recent photos, which she plugged directly into the board to run as a slideshow while she talked. She reasoned that the photos would help humanize him, showing his classmates that he hadn't burst fully formed from a genetics lab but was once the world's cutest baby. She'd picked photos showing him with Santa as a toddler and playing sports as a preteen, to demonstrate that he shared their interests and some of their abilities.

"I'd like for the kids to know that, even with all the differences, he's just a kid who wants friends and wants to be a part of things, like them—probably even more than they do," she explained to the science teacher. They had agreed that Eli shouldn't attend the presentations himself so he wouldn't feel like he was under a microscope, and so his presence wouldn't keep the other students from speaking candidly.

The first class filed in, and two dozen sleepy-looking students attempted to find seats as far away from their teacher as possible. Gayle tried to project an air of composure, although she was starting to wonder if she'd make it through the class without choking up. It was so rare for anyone, even her closest relatives, to ask point-blank questions about the challenges of living with Williams that she feared the words would catch in her throat. Kathy's warning that there were a few wise guys in the first group made her even more apprehensive about breaking down in front of them. She took a deep breath.

When the students had settled into their chairs and stopped rummaging through their overstuffed backpacks, Kathy introduced Gayle and started the slideshow. Eli's baby pictures flashed on screen, one after the other. Each one revealed the same beaming, gap-toothed smile. The girls in the class cooed. Gayle relaxed a little.

The students had written questions for Gayle beforehand on index cards that Kathy, a scientist to the core, had collected and classified into four categories: scientific, pragmatic, emotional, and ethical.

Gayle tackled the scientific questions first, which ranged from the basic—"How did Eli get Williams syndrome?"—to the specialized: "Did he have a fluorescent in situ hybridization (FISH) test?" The student who asked the latter question admitted that she was doing her research project on Williams; she'd already guessed that the answer to this question was yes.

Several students asked about Eli's health. Gayle explained that, as with everyone who had Williams and was vulnerable to stenosis, he had to be checked every year to be sure that the blood vessel leading away from his heart wasn't narrowing. The students seemed surprised to hear about this, except for the one who was writing her report on Williams.

"It's been OK so far, luckily. But it's progressive; it could change at any time," Gayle said. "And he has stomach problems that are almost always an issue. You have to remember that sometimes he might not feel that good."

Gayle moved on to the pragmatic questions. Some focused on Eli's daily routine: Could he shower by himself? Brush his teeth? Get ready for bed?

"He does need a little help," Gayle said. "His dexterity isn't as good as yours. But he can manage for the most part."

A few of the boys in the class had asked whether Eli could play sports. Gayle winced; she had assumed they already knew how active he was in special-needs sports leagues. He had been playing soccer since he started grade school and baseball for the last few years. She explained that sports were an important part of his life. Lately he'd even expressed an interest in basketball, she said, although he'd never actually played it.

One boy raised his hand and announced that Eli had, in fact, played basketball. At the school's recent field day, he said, a group of boys had been shooting hoops when Eli saw them and asked if he could play, too. He seemed disappointed about being left out. So the boys paused their game and created a new team that Eli could join.

"He did good throwing the ball," the boy said. He seemed eager to show Gayle that he and his friends accepted Eli and tried to make him feel welcome. He added that a girl from Eli's class had helped him join the egg race later that day when she saw him on the sidelines and realized that he didn't have the coordination to carry an egg on a spoon. She took it upon herself to bend the rules, calling him over and telling the team, "When it's Eli's turn, he's gonna hold the egg in his hands."

Several other students spoke up, recalling Eli's delight at being included. One boy said he'd never seen Eli without a smile. Another complimented Eli's singing voice, telling Gayle about a particularly operatic rendition of Lady Gaga's "Poker Face," which Eli had performed in the lunchroom one day.

"How would you describe Eli in one word?" Kathy prompted the class.

"Happy," said one boy. "Enthusiastic," said another. "Never in a bad mood."

Gayle was touched.

Some of their questions were probing, but they all seemed to reflect an earnest interest in why Eli was the way he was.

One boy asked, "Why does he rock so much?"

"I'm not really sure," Gayle said. "I think it's just to keep himself busy."

"Like when he chops the desk all the time?"

"Oh, you guys remember his chopping phase! Yeah, we've moved on to other things. Lately it's been flicking paper. It's always something: tapping, rocking, singing. His body is always busy."

Another student asked: "What will he be like as an adult? Is he going to need help all the time?"

Gayle was prepared for this one. *Welcome to what keeps me up at night,* she'd thought when she first read it on the list of questions. But she found that answering it wasn't as hard as she had feared. She responded more as an educator than as a mother.

"Yes, he'll need someone living with him all the time," she said. The students were quiet now, their faces somber. *They're genuinely concerned,* Gayle realized. *They're worried about his future, too.*

"You guys are probably already thinking about learning to drive, or where you're going to go to college, but he's not going to have those things in his life," she explained. "He's going to have a very good, rewarding life, but it's just going to be different."

Because the focus of their textbook was on genetic engineering and the possibility that in the future, disorders like Williams would be eradicated, a number of students had asked the same ethical question: "If you could have made Eli different, would you have?"

Gayle answered honestly. "No one wants to have a child who's going to have difficulties. If I could change it to make his life easier, I would."

One girl, a relatively recent transfer into the school district and one of its few black students, raised her hand high.

"I wouldn't change anything about him," she said emphatically. "He's so friendly. He's the first person who ever said hi to me when I came to this school."

———

GAYLE WAS IMPRESSED BY HOW DIRECT and thoughtful the questions were. Some focused on her own experience. One student asked, "Is it hard if he does something inappropriate in public? Do you get frustrated?"

"I do," she said. "Just like your parents get frustrated with you sometimes. He doesn't always listen to me."

"Are people nice to you and Eli?" someone else asked.

"I very rarely run into someone who's directly rude to us, but I've gotten some stares," she said. "Almost everyone has been receptive of us."

Other questioners expected her to have done some soul-searching and to bare the results. For example, "How has this experience changed you as a parent?"

"I had to change my idea about what it would be to be a parent," she said. "It was an adjustment." She left it at that, without elaborating. After all, she had no idea what kind of parent she would have been to a different child. Her idea of parenting would probably have adjusted in any case. Before Eli was born, she'd never imagined the terrifying risks her child would face or the sacrifices she'd have to make. She hadn't foreseen the daily struggles and frustrations and heartbreak. But neither had the parents of any child, with or without special needs. She didn't mention that she'd had to let go of hopes for her son that parents of normal children could take for granted. She wanted to be honest with the students, but she didn't want to overwhelm them. And while she didn't want them to make fun of Eli, she didn't want them to pity him, either.

Above all, though, Gayle was amazed by the students' compassion. Several kids hung around after the end of each class to talk to her privately, telling her how much they cared about Eli and how moved they were by her presentation. One girl told her, "If I found out I had a kid with Williams, I would be really happy, because Eli is the best kid in the world."

Gayle recognized one of the girls who lingered after her presentation: Julia, who had been in Eli's class since kindergarten. When Eli was younger, Julia had been a great help to him. She'd stayed by his side at the birthday parties he'd been invited to up until third or fourth grade. At bowling parties, she helped him bowl; at a laser-tag party, she helped him shoot, although he found the experience so overstimulating, he didn't go back for a second round. Eventually he stopped going to parties, and Julia no longer played a supporting role in his social activities. But she never forgot him: in fifth grade, he came home with a Yankees cap Julia had given him. Their teacher told Gayle that Julia had gone to a game at Yankee Stadium and asked her grandmother to buy it for Eli, knowing that he was a fan. Gayle had been so moved by the gesture, and the affection behind it, that she'd written Julia a note.

"Thank you for always looking out for Eli and being such a good friend to him. Your parents should be very proud of you," she wrote. "There should be more kids like you in the world."

Now Julia approached Gayle and said, with unexpected serious-ness for a thirteen-year-old, "I know it must be hard for you, but I just think Eli is a gift."

Gayle started to tear up, but Julia looked at her stoically.

"I'm not sure if you remember me . . ." she began.

"You gave him that hat," Gayle said. "I still remember that."

"Yes!" Julia said. "I still have your thank-you card."

When the bell rang, Gayle watched Julia disappear into the throng of students pushing their way through the halls and thought about how she'd once seen her: as a rarity among the mean girls and bullying boys who must have surrounded Eli at school. Now she realized that there were others like Julia, who cared about Eli and wanted to help him.

Gayle had been convinced that she needed to protect Eli from his peers, and all the while they had been nurturing him in their own ways. She had worried that, without the sophistication required to climb the middle school social ladder, he'd be trampled underfoot by the popular crowd. But his sincere warmth, antithetical as it was to coolness, had upended the normal rules of popularity, making him a nearly universally beloved figure in his class. The power dynamics Gayle had envisioned had been inverted: instead of seeing his open-ness as a weakness to be exploited, his classmates had been drawn to him and driven to defend him from the same threats Gayle herself feared. She'd underestimated the power of his compassion to bring out the compassion in others.

Here I am thinking these are rotten kids, and they're so supportive—so kind, she thought when her long day of lecturing had ended. She'd been afraid that Eli would never make a friend. But he'd had friends all along.

Twenty-Three

Graduation

I n the darkened middle school auditorium, Gayle sat waiting for the principal to say Eli's name and clapping politely as the eighth graders at the beginning of the alphabet marched across the stage to accept their diplomas. She clutched her cell phone, poised to record a video as soon as Eli appeared. She could already feel the tears forming in her eyes and wasn't quite sure whether they were tears of joy, sorrow, or relief. She'd known she would feel emotional at Eli's eighth-grade graduation—proud, mostly—but she didn't know it would be so overwhelming.

A memory drifted back from the early days after Eli's diagnosis, when tears had formed perpetually. A friend of Gayle's, a metaphysics enthusiast, had returned from a retreat in the Himalayas and given her a book called *Journey of Souls: Case Studies of Life Between Lives*, by Michael Newton. The book describes a theory of reincarnation in which recycled souls wait in a sort of celestial depository until they can be reborn to the right parents to guide them through their next life. Although skeptical of New Agey nonsense, Gayle was nonetheless intrigued and strangely comforted by the idea. The image of Eli's soul floating in the soul bank until she came along stuck with her, although at the time she couldn't fathom why the cosmos would have entrusted a "bigmouthed bitch" like her with such a delicate soul—or such an enormous responsibility.

The last fourteen years—Eli's life so far—flashed through her mind, and she came to a realization that shocked her: she had done pretty well. Eli hadn't been abused, taken advantage of, or seriously bullied. She'd kept him safe. He was happy.

Maybe, she thought, *I was chosen because I'm a bigmouthed bitch. He can't protect himself, but I can. I'm not afraid to fight to get him what he needs. If he had gone to someone else, someone who couldn't speak her mind, who knows what would have happened to him? Someone out there knew I could handle the responsibility.*

For the first time in years, she felt a palpable sense of relief: *We've come this far. Who knows what high school will be like? But I think we can do it.*

———

IT HAD BEEN A RELIEF, TOO, to finish writing the will that had stymied her for so long. Not long before Eli's graduation, Gayle had finally worked up the nerve to ask her cousins Emily and Jake whether they'd consider being Eli's guardians. The conversation she had dreaded was, in the end, surprisingly easy. Emily even seemed indignant that it had taken Gayle so long to ask.

"Well, I'm asking you to take a big step out of your lives. It's a big burden," Gayle replied.

"But I always expected to take care of him someday," Emily said. "He's like a brother to me."

"I just don't want you to think it'll be easy."

"I don't know why you get like this," Emily said, shaking her head. "Of course it's not going to be easy. It'll have to be arranged. But, between Jake and me, we'll work it out. Don't even think about it anymore."

Of course, Gayle couldn't stop thinking about it. But Emily's assurances eased her mind greatly. And signing her name on a will that, at least in writing, guaranteed Eli a safe and happy future brought her a feeling of closure. She'd finally gotten the results of her own DNA test back; luckily, she did not have the genetic predisposition for breast cancer. Still, she knew she wouldn't live forever.

Every time Gayle replayed the conversation in her mind, her heart swelled with gratitude. Emily's words were sincere. She would look after Eli when the time came, no matter what new challenges were in store.

———

GAYLE COULD NEVER BE SURE HOW much Eli picked up on her fears, but he clearly realized that he was on the verge of an important transition: from middle school to high school, from childhood to adolescence and, eventually, to adulthood. As the focus of his schoolwork shifted from academics to life skills, he'd grown more preoccupied with the notion of independence and began distancing himself more from his mother.

On Mother's Day, at a restaurant where the family had gathered to celebrate, Eli had had a meltdown when he was forbidden to play with the electric tea light on the table. When he grabbed it anyway, Gayle told him he had lost the privilege of playing with sticky notes, his latest obsession (he liked to cut them into strips and flick them, pretending they were flames).

Eli fumed in the backseat of the car on the way home. Finding a stray sticky note stuck to his seat belt, he ripped it to shreds.

"You're ruining my life!" he yelled, then mumbled, "We can't be together anymore."

"What did you say?" asked Gayle, who genuinely hadn't heard him.

A panicked look flashed across his face, as if he suddenly feared his wish might come true. His tone became conciliatory as he revised his statement.

"I said I want to be together," he said, nodding earnestly.

"We *are* together," Gayle said. "We always will be."

"I want that."

"Just because I'm mad right now doesn't mean we'll be separated. I'll always want you with me."

"OK," he said. He let the shreds of sticky note drift from his hand and settled back into his seat.

———

ALPHABETICALLY, ELI FOLLOWED A GIRL WHO stood out among the eighth-grade class. Her hair had changed color several times during the school year. The last time Gayle had seen her it was hot pink. Today it was teal.

Before the ceremony, Eli's teacher had forewarned Gayle, so she could be ready with her camera, "When you see the teal hair, he's next."

Now the blue-green blur from the edge of her vision snapped Gayle out of her daydream. The girl with the teal hair appeared on-stage. Gayle didn't know the girl or anything about her, but in some ways she resembled who Gayle had been at her age: nonconforming, rebellious, different.

Gayle's thoughts turned to Mimi, sitting next to her in the dark. Gayle could remember a time when she and her mother had seemed like polar opposites. These days they had more in common than she ever would have imagined in her youth; for one thing, they were both highly protective of their only child. But Mimi had never tried to force Gayle into the mold of what she imagined the perfect child to be. She had tolerated the teased hair and the punk-rock attitude. She'd never stopped Gayle from being her own person.

There were still lessons to be learned from her mom, Gayle realized.

The girl with the teal hair disappeared from the stage. Then Eli appeared.

He wore a button-down shirt and tie that Gayle had picked out, along with tailored pants Mimi had bought him for the occasion. It was so different from his customary outfit—he hardly ever even tucked in his shirt—that when he looked in the mirror before the ceremony, he was startled by his own reflection.

"I look like a businessman!" he said. He had lost weight over the past year, partly thanks to a change in medications and partly to Gayle's efforts to improve his diet and make him more active. His thinner face was more angular, more adult. In his formal wear, he looked handsome and self-possessed.

As soon as he stepped onto the stage, the crowd burst into applause. It was more than the polite smattering of claps they'd given everyone else: this was a roar. Then they were on their feet. Gayle heard Eli's name shouted from everywhere around her. She was so stunned that she forgot to cheer for him herself. He couldn't have heard her over the din anyway.

But he heard the crowd. His smile widened. He threw both hands in the air, the way he'd seen Pavarotti do for standing ovations, except that he kept walking toward the principal, hands raised all the way. He dropped them to accept his diploma, then yelped and threw his arms up again as he walked down from the stage. The applause took a while to subside. When it did, Gayle realized she had been so overcome by the moment that she had forgotten to record it.

High School

The lunch tables had been cleared away. The cafeteria was empty except for the school janitor, Mike, and a piece of industrial cleaning equipment Eli had coveted for years: the Tennant 5400. Eli hustled past Mike and said a hasty hello, but never took his eyes off the floor scrubber. It was already on and waiting for him in the middle of the room.

Given a choice of vocational training as part of his ninth-grade curriculum, Eli had begged for the chance to do janitorial work. Mike said he'd be happy for the help. So every Friday for the past few months, Eli had gotten to scrub the floor after lunch.

Now, on a Friday afternoon in November, he ran his fingers over the Tennant 5400's dials and knobs. He savored the hum of the machine for a moment. Then he wrapped his hands around the handles, the way he'd always pretended to do while watching YouTube videos of the scrubber in action, and pushed forward.

It was harder in real life than it had looked in the videos. He flung his upper body forward, bending nearly in half with the effort of pushing, even though the motor did much of the work. This was more strenuous than any exercise he had done in gym class, and required much more concentration. His brow creased from the exertion, but he was smiling. He maneuvered in roughly straight lines; Mike put a hand on the scrubber to help him turn when he got to the end of a row.

"It sounds good, right, Mike?" Eli shouted over the roar of the motor.

The Tennant 5400 had recently been repaired after its motor started acting up, which Eli had recognized instantly because the noise it made was not quite right. Now it was back at the right timbre and pitch, to Eli's relief. Mike wasn't sure how long the fix would last, though. It was an old piece of equipment, likely to wear out before too much longer.

"You got a new battery?" Eli asked.

"No, but I'm sure we'll need a new one soon. This one's about four years old."

Eli's attention span had grown since middle school. He was less easily distracted from the task at hand. His greatest impediment now was his strength, which gave out after he'd cleaned about two-thirds of the cafeteria floor. He dragged his feet, sneakers squeaking on the wet linoleum; his smile became a grimace. Finally he stepped out of the way and Mike took over. But his stamina was improving. Every Friday he got a little farther.

"When can I clean the kitchen?" he asked hopefully. Mike had promised him that once he was able to clean the entire cafeteria, he could move on to the kitchen. It was a tighter space, and required navigating around islands, but Eli was dying to scrub it because it had real floor tiles, not just linoleum.

"Maybe by the end of the year," Mike said. "You're really getting good at this."

———

GAYLE WISHED SHE COULD SAY SHE'D noticed a gradual change in Eli's behavior, perhaps corresponding to the various strategies she and his therapists had tried over the years: the token system and the social stories, the time-outs and the revoked privileges, the praise and the tough love. But it seemed to have happened almost overnight: the tantrums subsided, the hugging diminished, and Eli emerged as a more mature, reserved version of his former self. Whatever had prompted the change, it seemed to have come from within him. Just as all of Gayle's efforts to teach him to walk and talk had amounted to nothing until one day he was suddenly ready, this newfound restraint seemed to be a developmental stage that he had reached on his own, in his own time. It's not that her strategies hadn't helped. It's just that they percolated until he knew what to do with them. And one day they clicked.

It might not have been a coincidence that the click coincided with Eli's first year of high school. Maybe, just as Eli had believed he would magically transform into a teenager overnight, sprouting a mustache the moment he turned thirteen, he saw high school as a place where no one threw tantrums, or gawked at ceiling fans, or hugged everyone in sight. Maybe he believed this so firmly that he'd simply willed himself to mature.

Or maybe it was the medicine. Eli's psychiatrist had once again tweaked his combination of anxiety and ADHD drugs over the summer, which could partly explain his improved impulse control.

Either way, Eli had become calmer and more composed. His conversational skills had improved. He listened to what other people said and offered topical responses, rather than hijacking the conversation to spew facts about fans and floor scrubbers. Most importantly, he greeted his classmates with a handshake or a high-five, or even just a "Hello."

Part of the credit for his transformation went to his new teacher, Alicia Losada, who headed the life skills class in which Eli spent most of his school day. A seasoned special-education teacher with three decades in the classroom, she kept Eli on track with discipline backed by genuine warmth and caring. As his middle school teachers could attest, he had always responded badly to correction from people who were frustrated or annoyed with him. He preferred to win them over, of course, but if he sensed that he couldn't, he might head-butt them instead. With Ms. Losada, he was highly motivated to please, to reward her faith in him by behaving as she wanted him to.

She set high standards for him, as she did for all her students. She considered behavioral issues her top concern as a teacher of special-needs kids. In ten years, she reasoned, the average person who met Eli or one of his classmates would have no idea whether he could read a chapter book, but they'd judge him instantly if he intruded on their personal space. Like Gayle, Ms. Losada was a pragmatist who recognized that, in an ideal world, everyone her students encountered would tolerate their differences and treat them with compassion. But since that was unlikely to happen in real life, she strove to help them to fit in with the world as it existed.

Still, she wasn't as worried about Eli's behavior as Gayle had been. His occasional displays of affection didn't bother her, since every high school student displayed affection sometimes. Because Eli's hugging had been a problem in the past, she still had to talk to him whenever he did it, and to make a note of it in his records, which she shared with Gayle. If not for that, she wouldn't have given it a second thought. She once confided in Gayle that Eli's middle school reports, especially the one documenting forty counts of "inappropriate touching" in a single day, had given her pause—but only because she was so surprised by how little trouble he'd caused when he began his freshman year.

It was almost Thanksgiving now, but she'd had to confront Eli about his behavior only once, and that had been in the first week of school. A number of high schoolers volunteered in a peer-mentoring program called Best Buddies, which partnered them with special-needs students. One volunteer, a blond girl Eli adored, was in the life skills class one day when Eli ambush-hugged her, wrapping his arms around her from behind. One of the older boys in the class, a high-functioning senior who had taken Eli under his wing, told him, "Eli, you can't do that. It's not appropriate."

Eli, embarrassed, lashed out at the older boy. He chased him around the room, yelling, "Don't tell me what to do!" Ms. Losada pulled Eli aside and ushered him into a small room behind the cubbies where the students stored their coats and bags. She didn't call it a time-out room, describing it simply as a quiet place where students could collect themselves.

"Eli," she said, "you know we don't hug people without their permission. That's one of the rules here."

"You don't tell me what to do!" he yelled, his face red and tears streaming down his cheeks. "Get out of here! You're fired!"

"I'm not going anywhere," she said calmly. "You can't fire me. I'm here for you because I care about you. And I want to see you do well."

He turned away from her, crossed his arms, and sulked for another few minutes. Then he wiped his tears on his sleeve.

"I'm sorry," he said. Not long after, he told her that he loved her. Now he said so daily.

———

ELI'S PARTNER IN THE BEST BUDDIES program was a bright, charismatic junior named Scott. Around Halloween, a nearby school had hosted a fund-raising walk for the Best Buddies program, and Gayle and Eli joined Scott, Ms. Losada, and some of Eli's classmates there. The school's parking lot had been transformed into a fairground, with an orange bounce house and booths for face painting and pumpkin decorating. After greeting Ms. Losada and a gaggle of students, Gayle noticed the registration tent.

"Oh, I have to go register us," she said, mostly to Eli, who she assumed would accompany her.

"You can go," Ms. Losada said, her voice a teacherly reminder that part of making Eli more independent required Gayle to *allow* him more independence. "He'll be fine here."

Feeling chastened, Gayle headed for the tent alone. She had been trying to give Eli more space, but it still didn't come naturally. This was another of the daily tests in stepping back that she had not quite passed.

When she returned from registration, Scott and the pack of girls who formed his entourage had coalesced around Eli: a textbook example of the social opportunities that emerge when your mother isn't hovering close by. Eli beamed at the attention. Gayle, eager to prove to herself and Ms. Losada that she had learned her lesson, maintained a respectful distance—not quite out of earshot, but far enough away that Eli could easily ignore her. A year ago she would have rushed to his side, most likely to peel him off of whomever he was hugging. But now he seemed comfortable, not overstimulated, and capable of interacting with a group of peers on his own. He wasn't manically greeting or hugging everyone. He was just chatting about school with a girl named Meghan.

When a Selena Gomez song came on, Scott pointed toward the speakers and said playfully, "Eli, that's my girlfriend singing."

Eli turned to look where Scott was pointing and waved to a girl standing near the speakers. She waved back tentatively.

"No," Scott said. "I meant Selena Gomez is my girlfriend."

Eli turned again to face the girl by the speakers. "Hi, Selena Gomez!" he yelled. The girl cocked her head; Scott and the others laughed. Eli smiled, pleased to have made a joke, even if unintentionally.

When the walk started, Eli jogged a little to keep up with Scott and the girls, but then turned and looked at Gayle with Ms. Losada a few paces behind. He slowed to hang back with them.

"Go ahead! Walk with your friends!" Gayle said, shooing him away.

"But what about you, Mom?"

"I'm going to walk back here. You go ahead."

He turned and skipped forward. "Hey, guys!" he shouted. "Wait up! Wait for me!"

He maneuvered next to the girl he'd been talking to earlier. Snippets of their conversation drifted back toward Gayle.

"So, Meghan, how old are you?" he asked.

"I'm fourteen," she said.

"Me too! I'm fourteen!" he said excitedly. When she didn't reply, he tried another line of questioning.

"Meghan, what are you doing tonight?" he asked.

"I'll be at home," she said.

"Doing what?"

"Hanging out with my parents."

"Not going to a party?"

"Nope."

"I was invited to a party, but I have to work," interjected Scott, who had a part-time job at Dairy Queen. "So I can't go to the party."

"Can I come to the party?" Eli asked.

"Well, it's not my party. It's my friend's party," Scott said.

"So I'm not invited?" Eli asked.

Scott laughed. Eli stared at him with an expectant half smile.

"Oh, you don't know him, Eli," Scott said tactfully.

Still just shy of five feet tall, Eli stood chest-high to Scott and nearly a head shorter than Meghan. Eli's doctor had already warned Gayle that Eli was nearly done growing; the dark facial hair she helped him shave twice a week signaled the end of an early puberty.

"He might get another inch if he's lucky, but that's about it," the doctor had said.

From behind them, Gayle could see a patch of gray hair forming near the crown of Eli's head. It looked almost white compared with the rest of his thick, dark hair—a reminder that people with Williams go gray much earlier than normal. It was hard enough for Gayle to think of Eli as a teenager, and the sight of his graying hair unsettled her. He seemed so much younger than his classmates, but somehow also aged beyond his years.

———

GAYLE WAS EVEN MORE EXCITED AND nervous than Eli was when Scott asked him to lunch at Ruby Tuesday one weekend a few weeks after the Best Buddies walk. They had already gone to the movies together. Gayle had dropped Eli off at the theater with a ticket for *Cloudy with a Chance of Meatballs 2* and ten dollars for snacks. When she picked him up, his face was smeared with chocolate. She pulled a napkin from her purse and wiped him clean while Scott told her they had both enjoyed the movie and had no trouble other than that Eli had gotten so excited, he occasionally squealed with delight. Eli glowed for the rest of the day, boasting to anyone who would listen: "I hung out with my friend today. He's a really cool guy."

Gayle wasn't sure if the feeling was mutual or whether Scott would feel that he had fulfilled his obligation to Eli, and that would be that. So she was thrilled when he called to ask about lunch. It meant he was getting something out of their time together besides fodder for the community service section of his college application.

Still, going to a restaurant required more advanced social skills than sitting through a movie, and she couldn't picture Eli making it through a meal without disaster of some variety. She knew he would want to visit the salad bar; she usually got his salad for him. Images of dropped plates and strewn toppings flashed through her head. In addition to the mechanics of mealtime, there were also the subtleties of small talk to contend with.

"What are you going to talk to Scott about?" she asked as the lunch date approached.

"School," Eli said. "And exams."

"Not about floor scrubbers?"

"No, Mom!" he said in a tone that conveyed, "*Duh.*"

When Scott met them outside the restaurant, Gayle tried to act casual but couldn't stop giving instructions and warnings.

"He's going to need help with the salad bar," she told Scott.

"OK, got it," he said, smiling politely.

"And sometimes he eats too fast," she said. "You have to kind of watch him so he doesn't choke."

"Got it."

"And he might not be able to cut his food. You might have to help him with that."

"Got it."

Gayle finally broke off, although there was more she wanted to add. Scott and Eli retreated into the restaurant, while she went to a nearby Panera Bread and ate lunch alone. When she thought back on her list of instructions, she wanted to kick herself: *Scott probably doesn't find Eli annoying at all. It's his crazy mother who's the problem.*

She picked at her own salad, trying to sort out her feelings. On the one hand, she felt immensely proud. She wouldn't have thought it possible, even a year earlier, for Eli to be out on his own, doing something social with a friend. Even if Scott might not have befriended him outside the Best Buddies program, the fact that Eli could interact with him meaningfully, without smothering him with hugs and compliments, was an accomplishment beyond Gayle's past expectations. She was filled with new hope for Eli's future and the prospect that he might be capable of more than she had ever thought possible.

On the other hand, she felt a twinge of sadness and loss, as if she were mourning the boy who couldn't go anywhere without his mother. It was the bittersweet feeling that comes to all parents with the realization that their baby is no longer a baby. But for Gayle it marked a transition she hadn't been sure she'd ever see.

Now the signs were hard to miss. Sometimes Eli could be as surly as a typical teenager, fighting her intense involvement in his life. When he came home from school one afternoon, she asked him what he had eaten for lunch.

"I don't know," he muttered.

"You don't know?" she asked. "It was three hours ago."

He didn't answer.

"You don't know or you don't want to tell me?"

"Yeah," he said.

"Why not?"

"Because it's none of your business, Mom!" he said indignantly.

Watching him walk into Ruby Tuesday with his buddy, she'd been struck by how sure of himself he seemed. Now she wondered if she had grown too attached to the earlier, defenseless version of her son. Had she become too dependent on him, even as she feared that he depended too much on her? And, if so, had she held him back from the things he could have done if she hadn't been standing in the way, trying to shield him from the world?

Eli's transition to life skills training in high school had saddened her some, even though she'd pushed for it. She had heard that kids with Williams syndrome tended to plateau academically around middle school. And she appreciated that Eli's quality of life would improve most by learning those skills of daily living the rest of us take for granted: being able to bathe himself, feed himself, clothe himself, and get around without the constant assistance of his mother. Still, the idea of Eli studying a bus schedule and learning how to shop for groceries depressed her. Partly she lamented that this would be the focus of his high school experience, and partly that he needed these skills because she wouldn't always be around to provide for him.

So far, high school had been harder for her than for Eli, who had embraced its challenges as steps on the path to adulthood. He loved being able to eat lunch in the cafeteria without an aide hovering close by. He loved cooking in his life skills class, loved doing laundry. He especially loved his weekly turn with the floor scrubber. When one of his doctors asked, during a checkup, how high school was going, Eli answered, "It's my new life. It's my dream come true."

————

WHEN SHE VISITED THE WSA FACEBOOK page, which she still did daily, Gayle saw parents of kindergartners who weren't talking yet asking, "Should we try Hooked on Phonics?" Parents of elementary schoolers asked, "Which math program works best for our kids?" It was as if they believed there was a single secret technique that would unlock their children's potential. *They'll talk when they're ready to talk,* Gayle thought when she read their posts. *They'll learn when they're ready to learn. You can't stop them from having a developmental disability.*

But she didn't judge the parents for trying. It wasn't so long ago that she herself had been searching for the magic bullet. *I thought I was going to outsmart Williams syndrome, too,* she recalled. *Now I'm grateful if Eli can put his shirt on right side out.*

Eli didn't seem to have a clear grasp yet of what his future held, exactly. Seeing his schoolmates get their learner's permits, he had asked Gayle when he would be able to drive. She didn't want to dash his hopes, so she simply said, "Driving might make you nervous right now. Let's wait awhile." He hadn't asked again. He wasn't as interested in driving as he was in floor scrubbing, anyway.

Apart from a new set of skills and aspirations, Eli had also acquired a new vocabulary in high school. When he described something as "sexy" for the first time, Gayle asked him what the word meant. He couldn't—or wouldn't—answer.

"Do you know what 'sex' means?" she asked. Still no answer.

"Well, where do babies come from?" she tried.

"A stern and an egg!" he shouted triumphantly.

"It's a *sperm* and an egg," she explained. "Not that you really need to work that into conversation."

But the topic of babies started to come up more often than Gayle would have expected.

"I can't wait to be a dad," Eli said one day, apropos of nothing.

"Why's that?" Gayle asked.

"Because I want to take care of a baby, and hold him, and tell him I love him."

Gayle blinked, feeling the familiar wetness in her eyes. If love were all it took to raise a child, Eli would be the best father in history. He'd probably still be better than many who stumbled into fatherhood. But Gayle knew this would not be a part of his future, or shouldn't be, at least. She reminded him that not every man becomes a father.

"You can love a baby without being a dad," she said gently. "If Emily has a baby one day, you can still hold him and tell him you love him. And he can call you 'Uncle.'"

Gayle wasn't sure if it was Eli's health class, or maybe a TV show, that had planted the seed, but he suddenly seemed fixated on babies and birth. He asked Gayle to tell the story of his own birth over and over.

"I went to the hospital, and I was in labor," she began.

"You couldn't wait to meet me, right?" he interjected.

"I couldn't wait to meet you," she said. "Then you came out, and you had all this hair, and your cheeks were so chubby, and you were so cute."

"And I had Williams syndrome!" he said happily.

"Well, I didn't know that yet," she said. She didn't tell him that finding out was the most difficult discovery she'd ever made, and one she was still coming to terms with. She didn't want to complicate his cheerful narrative. To him, Williams syndrome was merely a detail in the story of who he was, and how he came to be.

Acknowledgments

Getting to know the Williams syndrome community, especially Gayle and Eli, has been a life-changing experience for me. Apart from being tremendously fun to spend time with, Gayle and Eli have given me an invaluable education in friendship, courage, and kindness. They, along with Mimi and the rest of their family, welcomed me into their lives and treated me with genuine warmth and generosity. I learned more from them than I ever hoped to, and I feel privileged to consider them true friends.

I couldn't have written this book without the aid of Terry Monkaba, Barbara Pober, and the Williams Syndrome Association. They, and others in the Williams community, have been an endless source of help and support throughout the six years that I spent researching and writing the book. A number of families invited me to their homes, shared their stories with me, and patiently answered my questions. I am grateful to them and to the clinicians and researchers who walked me through the science behind Williams syndrome, including Julie Korenberg, Ursula Bellugi, Helen Tager-Flusberg, Karen Levine, Carolyn Mervis, Bernard Crespi, and Maria Mody. Attorneys Meredith Greene and Mary Denise Cahill helped me navigate the complexities of disability law.

Heartfelt thanks to my amazing agent, Brettne Bloom, for working tirelessly to bring this story into the world. I'm grateful as well for the excellent editorial guidance I received from both Karyn Marcus and Millicent Bennett. I was lucky to work with an awesome team at Simon & Schuster, including Sydney Morris, Megan Hogan, and Lisa Rivlin, along with copyeditor extraordinaire David Chesanow.

This project began as my MFA thesis at the University of New Hampshire's creative writing program, and it wouldn't have gotten off the ground without the mentorship of Sue Hertz and Meredith Hall, as well as the unflagging support of my fellow writers, including Larry Clow, Alicia de los Reyes, Alan Schulte, and Ambre Earp Lahar. I'm lucky to have been influenced by some stellar editors and teachers over the years: Deb Davis, Susan Rieger, Joseph Shaw, Michael Wagar, Gordon MacCracken, Fred Gaskins, Felicia Mason, Will Sutton, Tony Freemantle, Tara Young, and Mark Washburn.

To my unpaid editor, advocate, and life coach David Kaplan, I owe a debt of gratitude, plus that Porsche I promised him. I'm indebted as well to the readers who gave incisive feedback on the early (and middle, and late) drafts of this book: Andrew Sessa, Mollie Goldstein, Christine Cullen, Claudia Kolker, Carrie Feibel, Weiwei Zhong, Jacob Sargent, Seth Freedland, Alicia P.Q. Wittmeyer, Molly MacLaren, Patrick Lynch, Cynthia Cho, Dan Taylor, and my parents, Carole and Chuck Boster.

The Norman Mailer Center and the Hambidge Center for the Creative Arts gave me the gift of time and space to write parts of this book in the company of other artists and writers. My sincere thanks go to them and to the talented people who inspired me there, especially Mimi Swartz, Kurt Pitzer, and Greg Curtis.

Moral support and other forms of assistance came from Eric Kayne, Katie Slater, Jessie Gill, Guin Basnight, Jena Moreno, Sarah Viren, Bella Latson, Brad and Michelle Latson, Julia and Tommy Brooks, and Larry the cat, even if his help included walking on my keyboard whenever I tried to type.

Finally, thanks and love to David Brooks for his patience and support, and for enriching my life in every way.

How to Get Involved

The Williams Syndrome Association provides resources and support for the roughly 30,000 Americans with Williams syndrome and their families. It also sponsors research, promotes awareness, and organizes medical conferences and family events as well as camps and enrichment programs for people with Williams. For more information, or to donate to the WSA's scholarship funds, research grants, and other programs, visit williams-syndrome.org.

Best Buddies is an international nonprofit organization dedicated to helping people with intellectual and developmental disabilities form meaningful friendships, find employment, live independently, improve communication skills, and feel valued by society. To volunteer, visit bestbuddies.org.

To donate to a fund that benefits Gayle and Eli directly, go to www.youcaring.com/gayleandeli.

Bibliography

Andari, Elissar, et al. "Promoting Social Behavior with Oxytocin in High-Functioning Autism Spectrum Disorders." *Proceedings of the National Academy of Sciences* 107, no. 9 (March 2010): 4389–94.

Angier, Natalie. "Family of Errant Genes Is Found to Be Related to Variety of Skeletal Ills." *New York Times*, Nov. 1, 1994.

Asada, Kosuke, and Shoji Itakura. "Social Phenotypes of Autism Spectrum Disorders and Williams Syndrome: Similarities and Differences." *Frontiers in Psychology* 3 (July 30, 2012): 247.

Bailey, Melissa. "Gene Therapy Treats Duchenne Muscular Dystrophy in Mice." *STAT*, Dec. 31, 2015.

Baron-Cohen, Simon. *The Science of Evil: On Empathy and the Origins of Cruelty.* New York: Basic Books, 2011.

Bellugi, Ursula, and Marie St. George. *Journey from Cognition to Brain to Gene: Perspectives from Williams Syndrome.* Cambridge, MA: MIT Press, 2001.

Bellugi, Ursula, Paul P. Wang, and Terry L. Jernigan. "Williams Syndrome: An Unusual Neuropsychological Profile." *Atypical Cognitive Deficits in Developmental Disorders: Implications for Brain Function.* Ed. Sarah

H. Broman and Jordan Grafman. Hillsdale, NJ: Lawrence Erlbaum Associates, 1994, 23–56.

Berdon, Walter E., Patricia M. Clarkson, and Rita L. Teele. "Williams-Beuren Syndrome: Historical Aspects." *Pediatric Radiology* 41 (2011): 262–66.

Blair, R. James. "Empathic dysfunction in psychopathic individuals." *Empathy in Mental Illness*. Ed. Tom Farrow and Peter Woodruff. Cambridge, UK: Cambridge University Press, 2007, 3–16.

———. "Neurobiological basis of psychopathy." *British Journal of Psychiatry* 182, no. 1 (Jan. 2003): 5–7.

Bloom, Paul. *Just Babies: The Origins of Good and Evil*. New York: Crown, 2013.

Boodman, Eric. "New Therapy Offers Gene Fix for 'Bubble Boy' Disease." *STAT*, April 20, 2016.

Chong, Jessica X., et al. "The Genetic Basis of Mendelian Phenotypes: Discoveries, Challenges, and Opportunities." *American Journal of Human Genetics* 97, no. 2 (Aug. 2015): 199–215.

Christian, Susan. "Perfect Pitch: Gloria Lenhoff Is a 'Musical Savant' Who Sings and Plays Beautifully but Can't Understand Mathematics." *Los Angeles Times*, Dec. 23, 1990.

Crespi, Bernard, Kyle Summers, and Steve Dorus. "Genomic Sister-Disorders of Neurodevelopment: An Evolutionary Approach." *Evolutionary Applications* 2, no. 1 (Feb. 2009): 81–100.

Dai, Li, C. Sue Carter, Jian Ying, Ursula Bellugi, Hossein Pournajafi-Nazarloo, and Julie R. Korenberg. "Oxytocin and Vasopressin Are Dysregulated in Williams Syndrome, a Genetic Disorder Affecting Social Behavior." *PLoS ONE* 7, no. 6 (2012).

Dai, Li, et al. "Is It Williams Syndrome? GTF2IRD1 Implicated in Visual-Spatial Construction and GTF2I in Sociability Revealed by High Resolution Arrays." *American Journal of Medical Genetics* 149A, no. 3 (2009): 302–14.

Davidson, Cathy N. *Now You See It: How Technology and Brain Science Will Transform Schools and Business for the 21st Century.* New York: Penguin, 2012.

de Waal, Frans. *Our Inner Ape: A Leading Primatologist Explains Why We Are Who We Are.* New York: Riverhead, 2005.

Dickens, Charles. *Barnaby Rudge.* London: Chapman & Hall, 1841 (reprinted by Penguin Classics, 1986).

Dobbs, David. "The Gregarious Brain." *New York Times Magazine,* July 8, 2007.

Dodd, Helen F., and Melanie A. Porter. "Psychopathology in Williams Syndrome: The Effect of Individual Differences Across the Life Span." *Journal of Mental Health Research in Intellectual Disabilities* 2, no. 2 (2009): 89–109.

Doherty-Sneddon, Gwyneth. "Eyes: A New Window on Mental Disorders." *Scientific American,* Sept. 16, 2008.

Eblovi, Darren, and Christopher Clardy. "Charles Dickens and Barnaby Rudge: The First Description of Williams Syndrome?" *Pediatric Annals* 45, no. 2 (Feb. 2016): 67–69.

Edelmann, Lisa, et al. "An Atypical Deletion of the Williams-Beuren Syndrome Interval Implicates Genes Associated with Defective Visuospatial Processing and Autism." *Journal of Medical Genetics* 44, no. 2 (Feb. 2007): 136–43.

El-Fishawy, Paul, and Matthew W. State. "The Genetics of Autism: Key Issues, Recent Findings, and Clinical Implications." *Psychiatric Clinics of North America* 33, no. 1 (2010): 83–105.

Fishman, Inna, et al. "Contrasting Patterns of Language-Associated Brain Activity in Autism and Williams Syndrome." *Social Cognitive and Affective Neuroscience* 6, no. 5 (Aug. 27, 2010): 630–38.

Frostad, Per, and Sip Jan Pijl. "Does Being Friendly Help in Making Friends?" *European Journal of Special Needs Education* 22, no. 1 (Feb. 2007): 15–30.

Gantman, Alexander, et al. "Social Skills Training for Young Adults with High-Functioning Autism Spectrum Disorders: A Randomized Controlled Pilot Study." *Journal of Autism and Developmental Disorders* 42, no. 6 (June 2012): 1094–1103.

Ghosh, Pallab. "Gene Therapy Drug Approval Granted to GSK." *BBC News*, May 27, 2016.

Gillberg, Christopher, and Mary Coleman. *The Biology of the Autistic Syndromes.* London: Mac Keith Press, 2000.

Gottfredson, Linda S. "The General Intelligence Factor." *Scientific American Presents* 9, no. 4 (Winter 1998): 24–29.

Green, Tamar, et al. "Phenotypic Psychiatric Characterization of Children with Williams Syndrome and Response of Those with ADHD to Methylphenidate Treatment." *American Journal of Medical Genetics Part B: Neuropsychiatric Genetics* 159B, no. 1 (Jan. 2012): 13–20.

Guastella, Adam J., et al. "Intranasal Oxytocin Improves Emotion Recognition for Youth with Autism Spectrum Disorders." *Biological Psychiatry* 67, no. 7 (April 2010): 692–94.

Haas, Brian W., et al. "Genetic Influences on Sociability: Heightened Amygdala Reactivity and Event-Related Responses to Positive Social Stimuli in Williams Syndrome." *Journal of Neuroscience* 29, no. 4 (Jan. 28, 2009): 1132–39.

Hanna, John. "Topeka Man Plans to Plead Guilty in Fort Riley Bomb Case." *AP: The Big Story,* May 5, 2016.

Hatton, Chris, Eric Emerson, Hilary Graham, Jan Blacher, and Gwynnyth Llewellyn. "Changes in Family Composition and Marital Status in Families with a Young Child with Cognitive Delay." *Journal of Applied Research in Intellectual Disabilities* 23, no. 1 (Jan. 2010): 14–26.

Hollander, Eric, et al. "Oxytocin Increases Retention of Social Cognition in Autism." *Biological Psychiatry* 61, no. 4 (Feb. 2007): 498–503.

Huron, David. "Is Music an Evolutionary Adaptation?" *The Biological Foundations of Music.* Ed. Robert J. Zatorre and Isabelle Peretz. New York: New York Academy of Sciences, 2001, 43–61.

Hutson, Matthew. "You're Just Like Me! Why We Choose Partners Who Share Our Traits." *Atlantic*, Jan.–Feb. 2015: 25.

Jabbi, Mbemba, et al. "The Williams Syndrome Chromosome 7q11.23 Hemideletion Confers Hypersocial, Anxious Personality Coupled with Altered Insula Structure and Function." *Proceedings of the National Academy of Sciences* 109, no. 14 (March 2012): 860–66.

Jack, Anthony I. "A Scientific Case for Conceptual Dualism: The Problem of Consciousness and the Opposing Domains Hypothesis." *Oxford Studies in Experimental Philosophy*, Vol. 1. Ed. Joshua Knobe, Tania Lombrozo, and Shaun Nichols. Oxford, UK: Oxford University Press, 2014.

Järvinen-Pasley, Anna, et al. "Defining the Social Phenotype in Williams Syndrome: A Model for Linking Gene, the Brain, and Behavior." *Development and Psychopathology* 20, no. 1 (Feb. 2008): 1–35.

Jiang, Yuexin, Daniel I. Bolnick, and Mark Kirkpatrick. "Assortative Mating in Animals." *American Naturalist* 181, no. 6 (June 2013): 125–38.

Kaylin, Jennifer. "Yale Scientists and a Patient's Family Join Forces to Find a Cure." *Yale Medicine*, Winter 2013.

Kettlewell, Julianna. "'Fidelity Gene' Found in Voles." *BBC News Online*, June 16, 2004.

King, Michael. *Wrestling with the Angel: A Life of Janet Frame.* Washington, D.C.: Counterpoint, 2000.

Kozubek, Jim. "How to Cure a Bubble Boy." *Atlantic,* Aug. 6, 2013.

Lenhoff, Howard M. "A Real-World Source for the 'Little People': A Comparison of Fairies to Individuals with Williams Syndrome." *Nursery Realms: Children in the Worlds of Science Fiction, Fantasy, and Horror.* Ed. Gary Westfahl and George Slusser. Athens, GA: University of Georgia Press, 1999.

———, et al. "Williams Syndrome and the Brain." *Scientific American* 277, no. 6 (December 1997): 68–73.

———, et al. "John C.P. Williams of Williams-Beuren Syndrome." *Pediatric Radiology* 41, no. 2 (Feb. 2011): 267–69.

Lenhoff, Howard M., Olegario Perales, and Gregory Hickok. "Absolute Pitch in Williams Syndrome." *Music Perception* 18, no. 4 (2001): 491.

Levitin, Daniel J. "Musical Behavior in a Neurogenetic Developmental Disorder: Evidence from Williams Syndrome." *Annals of the New York Academy of Sciences* 1060 (Dec. 2005): 325–34.

———, et al. "Characterizing the Musical Phenotype in Individuals with Williams Syndrome." *Child Neuropsychology* 10, no. 4 (Dec. 2004): 223–47.

Leyfer, Ovsanna, Janet Woodruff-Borden, and Carolyn B. Mervis. "Anxiety Disorders in Children with Williams Syndrome, Their Mothers, and Their Siblings: Implications for the Etiology of Anxiety Disorders." *Journal of Neurodevelopmental Disorders* 1, no. 1 (March 2009): 4–14.

Lipscomb, Suzannah. "All the King's Fools." *History Today* 61, no. 8 (Aug. 2011).

Mandelberg, Josh, et al. "Long-Term Treatment Outcomes for Parent-Assisted Social Skills Training for Adolescents With Autism Spectrum

Disorders: The UCLA PEERS Program." *Journal of Mental Health Research in Intellectual Disabilities* 7, no. 1 (2014): 45–73.

Mervis, Carolyn B., and Shelley L. Velleman. "Children with Williams Syndrome: Language, Cognitive, and Behavioral Characteristics and their Implications for Intervention." *Perspectives on Language Learning and Education* 18, no. 3 (Oct. 2011): 98–107.

Nettle, Daniel, and Bethany Liddle. "Agreeableness Is Related to Social-Cognitive, but Not Social-Perceptual, Theory of Mind." *European Journal of Personality* 22 (2008): 323–35.

Ng, Rowena, Philip Lai, Daniel J. Levitin and Ursula Bellugi. "Musicality Correlates with Sociability and Emotionality in Williams Syndrome." *Journal of Mental Health Research in Intellectual Disabilities* 6, no. 4 (2013): 268–79.

Osborne, Lucy R. "Animal Models of Williams Syndrome." *American Journal of Medical Genetics* 154C, no. 2 (May 15, 2010): 209–219.

Papaeliou, C., et al. "Behavioural Profile and Maternal Stress in Greek Young Children with Williams Syndrome." *Child: Care, Health and Development* 38, no. 6 (2012): 844–53.

Park, Alice. "Life, the Remix: A New Technique That Lets Scientists Edit DNA with Ease Is Transforming Science—and Raising Difficult Questions." *Time*, July 4, 2016.

Parks, Craig D., and Asako B. Stone. "The Desire to Expel Unselfish Members from the Group." *Journal of Personality and Social Psychology* 99, no. 2 (Aug. 2010): 303–10.

Pham, Hoangmai H., and Barron H. Lerner. "In the Patient's Best Interest? Revisiting Sexual Autonomy and Sterilization of the Developmentally Disabled." *Western Journal of Medicine* 175, no. 4 (Oct. 2001): 280–83.

Pober, Barbara. "Medical Progress: Williams-Beuren Syndrome." *New England Journal of Medicine* 362 (2010): 239–52.

Pollack, Andrew. "Eye Treatment Closes In on Being First Gene Therapy Approved in U.S." *New York Times*, Oct. 5, 2015.

Putnam, Robert D. *Bowling Alone: The Collapse and Revival of American Community*. New York: Touchstone Books, 2001.

Regalado, Antonio. "Gene Therapy's First Out-and-Out Cure Is Here." *MIT Technology Review*, May 6, 2016.

Riby, D. M., and P. J. Hancock. "Viewing It Differently: Social Scene Perception in Williams Syndrome and Autism." *Neuropsychologia* 46, no. 11 (Sept. 2008): 2855–60.

Robinson, Marnia. "Oxytocin, Fidelity, and Sex." *Psychology Today*, Nov. 25, 2012.

Sacks, Oliver. *Musicophilia: Tales of Music and the Brain*. New York: Knopf, 2007.

Sakurai, Takeshi, et al. "Haploinsufficiency of GTF2I, a Gene Deleted in Williams Syndrome, Leads to Increases in Social Interactions." *Autism Research* 4, no. 1 (Feb. 2011): 28–39.

Santos, Andreia, Andreas Meyer-Lindenberg, and Christine Deruelle. "Absence of Racial, but Not Gender, Stereotyping in Williams Syndrome Children." *Current Biology* 20, no. 7 (April 2010): 307–308.

Scudellari, Megan. "Gene Therapy Might Be the Best, and Perhaps Only, Chance at Curing Brain Diseases." *Newsweek*, April 28, 2016.

Semel, Eleanor, and Sue R. Rosner. *Understanding Williams Syndrome: Behavioral Patterns and Interventions*. New York, NY: Routledge, 2009.

Sforza, Teri, Howard Lenhoff, and Sylvia Lenhoff. *The Strangest Song: One Father's Quest to Help His Daughter Find Her Voice*. Amherst, NY: Prometheus, 2006.

Shapiro, Bruce K., and Pasquale J. Accardo. *Neurogenetic Syndromes: Behavioral Issues and Their Treatment.* Baltimore: Paul H. Brookes, 2010.

Skwerer, Daniela Plesa, and Helen Tager-Flusberg. "Williams Syndrome: Overview and Recent Advances in Research." *The SAGE Handbook of Developmental Disorders.* Ed. Patricia A. Howlin, Tony Charman, and Mohammad Ghaziuddin. SAGE Publications, 2011.

Smoller, Jordan. *The Other Side of Normal.* New York: William Morrow, 2012.

Solomon, Andrew. *Far from the Tree: Parents, Children, and the Search for Identity.* New York: Scribner, 2012.

Specter, Michael. "The Gene Hackers." *New Yorker,* Nov. 16, 2015.

Spiegel, Alix. "A Life Without Fear." *Morning Edition,* National Public Radio, April 26, 2010.

Szalavitz, Maia, and Bruce D. Perry. *Born for Love: Why Empathy Is Essential—and Endangered.* New York: William Morrow, 2010.

Tager-Flusberg, Helen, Jenea Boshart, and Simon Baron-Cohen. "Reading the Windows to the Soul: Evidence of Domain-Specific Sparing in Williams Syndrome." *Journal of Cognitive Neuroscience* 10, no. 5 (Sept. 1998): 631–39.

———, and Kate Sullivan. "A Componential View of Theory of Mind: Evidence from Williams Syndrome." *Cognition* 76, no. 1 (July 2000): 59–90.

Tordjman, Sylvie, et al. "Presence of Autism, Hyperserotonemia, and Severe Expressive Language Impairment in Williams-Beuren Syndrome." *Molecular Autism* 4, no. 29 (2013).

———. "Autistic Disorder in Patients with Williams-Beuren Syndrome: A Reconsideration of the Williams-Beuren Syndrome Phenotype." *PLoS ONE* 7, no. 3 (2012).

Turkheimer, Eric, Erik Pettersson, and Erin E. Horn. "A Phenotypic Null Hypothesis for the Genetics of Personality." *Annual Review of Psychology* 65 (2014): 515–40.

Wade, Nicholas. "Genetic Cause Found for Some Cases of Human Obesity." *New York Times,* June 24, 1997.

Walker-Hirsch, Leslie, and Marklyn P. Champagne. "The Circles Concept: Social Competence in Special Education." *Educational Leadership* 49, no. 1 (Sept. 1991): 65–67.

Williams, J.C.P., B.G. Barratt-Boyes, and J.B. Lowe. "Supravalvular Aortic Stenosis." *Circulation* 24 (Dec. 1961): 1311–18.

Wingerter, Justin. "Topekan Alexander Blair Sentenced to 15 Months in Prison for $100 Loan to John Booker Jr." *Topeka Capital-Journal,* Oct. 18, 2016.

Young, Edwin James. "Genomic Rearrangements in Human and Mouse and Their Contribution to the Williams-Beuren Syndrome Phenotype." PhD Thesis, University of Toronto, 2010.

Zimmer, Carl. "The Girl Who Turned to Bone." *Atlantic,* June 2013.

Zitzer-Comfort, Carol, Teresa Doyle, Nobuo Masataka, Julie R. Korenberg, and Ursula Bellugi. "Nature and Nurture: Williams Syndrome Across Cultures." *Developmental Science* 10, no. 6 (Sept. 2007): 755–62.

Zitzer-Comfort, Carol, Judith Reilly, Julie R. Korenberg, and Ursula Bellugi. "We Are Social—Therefore We Are: The Interplay of Mind, Culture, and Genetics in Williams Syndrome." *Formative Experiences: The Interaction of Caregiving, Culture, and Developmental Psychobiology.* Ed. Carol M. Worthman et al. New York: Cambridge University Press, 2010, 136–66.

About the Author

Jennifer Latson is a former *Houston Chronicle* reporter whose work has appeared in *Yankee Magazine, Rice Magazine,* and the *Boston Globe,* as well as on *The Hairpin* and Time.com. She has a BA in English from Yale and an MFA in creative nonfiction writing from the University of New Hampshire. In 2013, she was a recipient of the Norman Mailer Fellowship for nonfiction. Although she grew up in Connecticut and still considers herself a stoic New Englander at heart, she now lives in Houston with her partner, David, and their eighteen-pound cat, Larry. This is her first book.